Formatting Legal Documents With Microsoft Office Word 2007

Tips and Tricks for Working With Pleadings, Contracts, and Other Complex Documents

Jan Berinstein, Ph.D.

Formatting Legal Documents With Microsoft Office Word 2007
Tips and Tricks for Working With Pleadings, Contracts, and Other Complex Documents

ISBN 061-5-58713-5

Originally published in slightly different form.

Warnings and Disclaimers

Trademarks

Screen Shots

Printed and bound in the United States of America.

First printing: April, 2009.

Second printing: January, 2012.

For my mother, who taught me the virtues of curiosity and persistence.
And for my father, who always knew I had it in me.

Acknowledgments

This book owes its very existence to my software training clients and students. I started writing handouts in order to give them tangible instructional materials to use both during our hands-on training sessions and afterwards. Even though we don't always follow the handouts step by step in class, people seem to find them at once helpful and comforting, and many have told me they appreciate having a profusion of "cheat sheets" to use as a reference.

My trainees' thoughtful, probing, and at times anxious questions have motivated me to delve ever more deeply into the software and to strive to explain its more perplexing aspects in a clear, straightforward manner. Further, their ingenious solutions to common problems have inspired me and have shown me new ways of working with software I use—and teach—every day. In short, they have made me a better trainer / teacher / author. Several of those clients and students, as well as colleagues, offered valuable feedback (anonymously) on various drafts of the book. I am grateful for their comments.

I am also grateful to Eva Eilenberg, who helped me work out some of the thorny issues involving legal-style numbering and shared other valuable insights, and to Robin Jacobson, who took time from her hectic schedule to review an early draft of the manuscript, help me with the arduous job of proofing that draft, and test a couple of my tutorials. Robin also cheered me on when I particularly needed cheering.

In addition, my mother, Norma Baron, and my sister, Paula Berinstein, provided loads of encouragement and other sustenance throughout the lengthy process. Paula also generously gave me the benefit of her extensive writing experience in the form of practical publishing advice. My father, Nathan Berinstein, didn't live to see me undertake this project, but I'm certain he would have been delighted for and proud of me for completing it—although, computer-phobe that he was, he would have protested that he didn't really understand it.

My friends also supplied much-needed, and much-appreciated, support. Linda Hopkins, especially, was there for me in many different ways, tendering huzzahs as well as constructive suggestions and inspiration. Both Linda and Eva also tipped me off to the need to exercise particular care when dealing with cross-references, which can break if you accidentally delete or move the hidden "target" codes. I also wish to thank Marilyn Thomas for her enthusiasm about the project and her faith in me. She unexpectedly served as a beta tester of a portion of the book under rather stressful circumstances: On short notice, she was asked to work in a law office that, unbeknownst to her, recently switched to Word 2007. To her great relief as well as my own, the "cheat sheets" I furnished helped to make her introduction to the program relatively painless.

Finally, a word of appreciation for Barry, whose impish sense of humor, kibbitzing, unwavering belief in me, and loving interventions made the work—and everything else—less onerous.

Deeply felt thanks to each of you for the significant contributions you've made to this book, and to my life.

About the Author

Jan Berinstein runs her own software-training company, CompuSavvy Computer Training & Consulting, which provides hands-on classes and on-site training, primarily for law firms, government agencies, and corporate legal departments throughout California. She also has worked as a legal word processor since 1986. In addition, for nearly 15 years, she was an instructor for UCLA Extension, where she designed and taught computer courses for legal secretaries and paralegals, as well as "computers for seniors" workshops. She has led similar classes at the University of West Los Angeles and Learning Tree University, and has taught "Internet Legal Research" seminars in Los Angeles, San Francisco, and San Jose for the Center for Professional Education / Center for Legal Education.

Ms. Berinstein has given presentations about various computer-related topics at LegalTech Los Angeles, before the Beverly Hills Bar Association, and for several legal secretaries' groups.

A native of Los Angeles, Ms. Berinstein holds a Bachelor's degree in political science from UCLA, as well as an M.A. and a Ph.D. in government from Cornell University. After working for several years as a freelance writer and editor, she enrolled in UCLA Extension's journalism program and obtained her certification in print journalism in 1993. More recently, she served as a contributing author on Laura Acklen's Absolute Beginner's Guide to WordPerfect 12 (Que Publishing, 2005) and a technical editor on Ms. Acklen's Absolute Beginner's Guide to WordPerfect X3 (Que Publishing, 2006). Ms. Berinstein, who uses both MS Word and WordPerfect to format legal documents (and for other purposes) on a daily basis, is also the webmistress and administrator of the WordPerfect Universe web site, a user-to-user support group (www.wpuniverse.com).

Ms. Berinstein's training company web site can be found at www.compusavvy.com.

CONTENTS

PAGE

CONTENTS (Cont'd.)

PAGE

CONTENTS (Cont'd.)

PAGE

CONTENTS (Cont'd.)

PAGE

CONTENTS (Cont'd.)

PAGE

CONTENTS (Cont'd.)

PAGE

Introduction

This book is not—and is not intended to be—a "complete" reference for Microsoft Word 2007. Indeed, there are plenty of other tomes that span nearly the full range of topics, from the most basic features of the program to highly advanced, specialized tasks such as blogging, creating web pages, and working with Extensible Markup Language (XML) coding. Those books certainly have their place, but for the most part they don't address the specific needs of the legal profession: to generate and format documents that meet strict formatting rules imposed by courts or other judicial bodies.

By contrast, this book takes a relatively narrow focus. It is designed mainly to help law firms, government agencies, and corporate legal departments use Word 2007 to prepare the specialized legal documents they work with on a daily basis: pleadings, contracts, wills and trusts, and even multi-page letters. Because of this more limited emphasis, the book covers only certain features of the program—some of them fairly simple and others rather advanced—needed for legal document formatting. I have chosen those features based on my extensive experience (more than two dozen years) as a legal word processor, as well as on feedback from my clients (mostly legal secretaries, lawyers, and paralegals) over the two decades that I've worked as a software trainer specializing in the legal field. Obviously, my decisions about which features to include and which to exclude, while far from arbitrary, reflect my own subjective judgment.

Throughout the book, I also offer assorted tips for improving efficiency in general, along with troubleshooting suggestions.

The instructions I provide for formatting pleadings are designed to comport with the California Rules of Court, since California is the jurisdiction with which I am most familiar. However, with minor modifications, the guidelines should work for other jurisdictions as well. In most cases, all that's necessary is a few simple tweaks to margin settings and/or line spacing.

The book assumes fundamental computer literacy on the part of the readers. As a result, I don't go into much detail about basic tasks such as moving around the screen, copying and pasting, and applying font attributes such as bolding and italics. I make exceptions to that general rule where (1) a commonly used feature has lesser-known aspects that can be useful (such as Paste Special, which allows you to paste copied text from another program or from the Internet without any formatting) or (2) the steps to perform a simple function in Word 2007 differ significantly from those in earlier versions of Word.

One more caution: The book decidedly is ***not*** an introductory text for aspiring legal word processors. (That's one reason I haven't included any samples of legal documents.) Rather, it is meant to assist people who already work in law firms, corporate legal departments, and government agencies to get the best possible results—and meet deadlines without experiencing undue stress—when they prepare the pleadings, contracts, estate plans, letters of intent, and other papers that constitute the bulk of their daily work.

Genesis of the Book; What's Included

In large part, the book is based on handouts I have previously written for on-site trainings and lab classes. Most of those handouts deal with specific features (or the way in which a particular feature is used to format legal documents—for example, how to set up a California Rules of Court Rule 2.110-compliant footer). I have written quite a bit of original material for the book, ranging from brief introductory and transitional passages to entire new sections.

I've also added to and clarified several of the handouts. For instance, I've expanded the material on resources to include information about locating key files (in order to back them up on a regular basis), as well as lists of useful web sites. And I've included a discussion about converting from WordPerfect to Word, saving Word files to PDF, and enabling clients and others who don't have Word 2007 to read documents created in its native (.docx) format.

What's Not Included

I'm not a macro guru, so I haven't covered macro writing in great detail. It's relatively easy to create macros that accomplish basic tasks—essentially it's a matter of recording keystrokes—but anything more complex, such as building customized dialog boxes, requires fluency in Visual Basic for Applications (VBA). That is beyond my abilities, and it's also beyond what most of my training clients want (or need) to learn. Instead, I've provided a gentle introduction to macros, illustrating the process with a simple example (creating a macro to print the current page, then adding a keyboard shortcut and toolbar button to run the macro).

Many people use the term "macros" rather loosely to refer to the insertion of boilerplate text such as signature blocks and standard paragraphs in contracts. These items can be created by using the Building Blocks / Quick Parts feature (formerly known as AutoText), something I also cover in the book.

Another feature I have de-emphasized to some degree is styles. I'm aware that a number of trainers and IT people swear by styles, and I agree that the uniform use of styles for headings, body text, and other formatting makes sense in large firms where consistency in the appearance of documents is at once highly desirable and somewhat difficult to accomplish. I believe, as well, that it's important for all Word users to have enough fluency with styles to be able to apply them where necessary, troubleshoot them, and remove them where they're problematic.

However, for some users styles are neither necessary nor desirable. They add a layer of complexity that can make working with Word intimidating and frustrating, which in turn can cause legal staff to resist learning the program. That is particularly true for people who are migrating to Word from WordPerfect—a program that allows for the creation and use of styles but downplays them. Also, in an environment where people often face strict deadlines, taking time to ensure that styles have been applied methodically throughout a given document can mean an unacceptable delay in the work flow. Thus, I have made a conscious—if seemingly heretical—choice to cover only the essentials of working with styles in this book, recognizing that firms that depend heavily on styles can find comprehensive instructions elsewhere.

Screenshots

I have used screenshots as visual aids where I thought they would make it easier to follow the step-by-step instructions. Again, note that images on your screen might not look exactly the same as those in the book as a result of customization (at your end or mine), disparities in printer drivers (which can affect the appearance of text on the screen), and/or differences between the various editions of the program.

Organization of the Book

The book moves from the general to the specific. It begins with what I consider the key to success in using Word to format complex documents: understanding the program's "logic." This somewhat theoretical section briefly compares the essential underpinnings of Word and WordPerfect, but it is intended for ***all*** users, even those who have never worked with WordPerfect. The discussion about how Word works "under the hood"—and in particular, its singular emphasis on paragraph and section formatting—will give you insights and diagnostic tools you need to troubleshoot problems that otherwise might be maddeningly obscure.

After exploring those core issues, I take a brief look at some of the most significant changes (additions, deletions, and modifications) to this version of Word, including but not limited to the drastically different interface.

Next, I offer a number of tips on how to make the program more user-friendly—and, in particular, how to get it to work the way you want it to. Some simple customizations, such as adding buttons to the Quick Access Toolbar, can dramatically improve your efficiency (because it gives you ready access to the features you use most often). Also, Word has lots of built-in keyboard shortcuts that can save you oodles of time and wasteful mouse clicks, and it's easy to set up additional shortcuts of your own.

One aspect of making Word 2007 more user-friendly involves tweaking it so that it works more or less like prior versions of the program. I provide instructions for modifying the default font face and size and the default line spacing—which differ from earlier versions—and explain how to set your own defaults by modifying the default Style Set and Theme, as well as the Normal paragraph style, heading styles, and various other elements of the program.

The next part of the book concentrates on selected features legal staffers use every day but often find puzzling—among them how to adjust page margins, how to insert and format a date code, how to work with tabs, how to set up "Quick Parts" (boilerplate text that you can insert in a document with a couple of keystrokes), how to indent (including methods for indenting via the Ruler), and how to work with that all-important but somewhat enigmatic feature, headers and footers.

Because automatic numbering (of paragraph headings, cross-references, and the like) is so essential in the legal field, and because it can be complex, I've put instructions for the various types of numbering (as well as for bulleted lists) in a separate section.

Following the more general sections of the book, I concentrate on legal document formatting. I go into considerable detail about setting up and modifying case captions, inserting pleading footers, marking text for inclusion in a Table of Contents (TOC), marking citations for inclusion in a Table of Authorities (TOA), and generating a TOC and a TOA. I also discuss the common problem of aligning text with pleading line numbers in Word and provide some workarounds.

Toward the end of the book, I proffer some general troubleshooting tips (in addition to the troubleshooting tips I incorporate into instructions about the use of specific features). Because so many firms are moving from WordPerfect to Word, or work with both programs, I touch upon some of the typical issues involved in converting between the two, with some cautions against the ill-advised practice of "round-tripping." And I briefly address concerns about metadata—"private" or confidential information embedded in your documents that can be revealed to others inadvertently unless you take active steps to remove it. (Word 2007 contains a new tool for removing metadata, the Document Inspector.)

Finally, I list certain helpful resources, including links to web sites you might find useful as you explore the software.

Conventions Used in the Book

When describing keyboard shortcuts, I follow the convention of mentioning a sequence of keys to be used in combination, such as Ctrl Alt 1, without any linking character such as a plus sign between the keys. The context should make it clear that the keys are intended to be used together.

I have attempted to make it easier to follow step-by-step instructions by using boldface to emphasize items that should be clicked or pressed, such as a particular tab of the Ribbon, a group within a tab, a dialog box or task pane, a button or icon, or a keyboard shortcut.

In places, I use boldface and capital letters to make the following advisories stand out:

TIP or **QUICK TIP**: A helpful hint for using a feature more efficiently or, sometimes, for working around a problem.

WORKAROUND: Just that. A method of bypassing something that you find problematic, whether an actual bug in the program or whether it's "Working As Designed" (a term of art that you'll occasionally see abbreviated—though not in this book—as "WAD").

NOTE: Something to keep in mind—typically advice that might or might not apply to your situation, but is worth taking into account when you are working with a feature.

CAUTION: A warning about a potential glitch or unexpected/unintended result.

SIDEBAR: A brief section that is peripherally related to the previous section or chapter.

Second Printing

Because of unexpected changes in the policies governing the distribution of my books, I am reprinting/republishing this book as of early 2012. I have made only minor textual revisions since the first printing/publication in April/May of 2009. If time permits, I will publish a true second edition of the book at some point.

My Style

The book, like my training, is highly task-oriented. My foremost goal is to help you get your work done—as efficiently, smoothly, and quickly as possible.

I make an effort to use realistic examples (based on my real-life experience as a legal word processor). Mixed in with the realism, I sometimes employ offbeat humor to keep my students/trainees alert during long sessions. It's just a technique; I've tried to use it sparingly so that it doesn't get in the way of the substantive points I'm trying to make.

Typically, my instructions about using a particular feature also include "background" or contextual information about that feature. My intention in providing that additional commentary is to make it easier to understand ***when*** to use the feature as well as ***how*** to use it. Often the contextual explanation also helps users recognize the limits of a feature or to help them work around its quirky behavior.

You might notice a certain amount of redundancy: A few tips appear in several places. That's mostly due to the fact that I wrote the handouts as individual tutorials, intended to stand on their own. Because it seems to me that the tips are important enough to bear repeating, I haven't attempted to eliminate the duplicates.

Finally, there is almost always more than one way to accomplish a particular task in Word. I'm not presumptuous enough to think that my way of doing things is the "right" way. If you have a favorite method of doing something that works well for you, by all means use it. The whole point, after all, is to make the software do your bidding and get something done. We might take different approaches at times, but what matters is attaining a desirable end result with minimal frustration. And that's what I'm trying to achieve with this book.

* * * * *

I hope the book proves useful to you. I welcome your constructive suggestions for ways to improve and enhance it (you can write c/o the e-mail address listed below), and I will incorporate the best ideas in future editions.

Jan Berinstein, Ph.D.
CompuSavvy
Computer Training & Consulting
Northridge, California
compusavvy2@earthlink.net
Winter, 2012

Word's "Logic"
(and How It Compares With WordPerfect's)

<u>WordPerfect vs. Word—Some Fundamental Differences in "Logic"</u>

The following chart makes it easy to compare the essential differences between WordPerfect's "logic" and that of Word. Understanding how the two programs work "under the hood" gives you more control over document formatting in at least two significant ways: (1) it makes the behavior of the software less mysterious / easier to predict; and (2) it provides clues about how to troubleshoot problematic formatting.

TIP: The information in this chart, together with the explanations that follow about paragraph and section formatting, is the key to mastering Word.

<u>WordPerfect's Logic</u>	**<u>Word's Logic</u>**
Based on ***text-stream formatting***:	Based on ***paragraph formatting***:
You insert a code at the cursor position, and everything that follows—i.e., in the stream of text—is governed by that code (until you insert a new code that supersedes the first one).	The paragraph is the basic formatting unit in Word. (***Section formatting*** is used for features like page orientation, margins, and headers/footers; ***character formatting*** is used for attributes like bold and italics that can be applied to individual characters).
Examples: Font face / size Text alignment (left, center, right) Line spacing	Examples: Justification (left, center, right) Indentation
Implications:	Implications:
Easy to format small bits of text—e.g., you can indent or center <u>part</u> of a line	Harder to format individual pieces of text, because Word sees everything as a paragraph
Formatting codes are visible with Reveal Codes (and many codes can be expanded)	Formatting codes are contained in the paragraph symbol (¶); they're not directly visible[1]
Formatting you apply to a specific paragraph usually ***does not*** carry over to the next paragraph	Formatting you apply to an entire paragraph ***carries over to the next paragraph*** when you press the Enter key

[1] This aspect of paragraph formatting in Word is critical to understand because it means, among other things, that you can modify the formatting of one paragraph by copying and pasting the pilcrow from the end of another paragraph—an extremely handy "fix-it" tool.

<u>WordPerfect's Logic</u>

Uses "***select, then do***" to some extent, but generally more stream-based than Word

Extensive use of function keys, both alone and in combination with Alt, Ctrl, and/or Shift key

Reveal Codes simplifies troubleshooting because 90% of problems with the document can be diagnosed and fixed by using Reveal Codes. (It's very easy to delete offending codes, move codes around, and/or double-click codes, thereby opening dialog boxes so you can change configuration settings.)

"***Plain vanilla***" unless you apply formatting (but is becoming more like Word—using more automatic formatting features)

<u>Word's Logic</u>

Much formatting requires "***select, then do***" (example: changing fonts in the document)

Extensive use of Ctrl key + letter

Word has no single feature comparable to Reveal Codes, but there are at least four different ways you can get information about document formatting:

1. **Reveal Formatting** (Select text, then press **Shift F1** ***or*** launch the **Style pane** and press **Style Inspector** / **Reveal Formatting**)—somewhat useful

2. **Paragraph dialog** (available from the Home tab and also from the Page Layout tab)—very useful!

3. **Page Setup dialog** (available from the Page Layout tab)—also quite useful

4. **Show/Hide Non-Printing Characters**—helpful in a variety of circumstances

Automatic formatting (which can be great if it's what you want, but can be annoying if it isn't)

The Key to How Word Works: Paragraph Formatting

KEY CONCEPT 1: Word, unlike WordPerfect, interprets all text as part of a paragraph[1].

KEY CONCEPT 2: When you type a document from scratch, paragraph formatting normally carries over from one paragraph to the next. The formatting instructions (codes) are contained within the paragraph symbol (¶) at the end of the paragraph, which is copied to the next paragraph when you press the Enter key.

Obviously, paragraph formatting is an important concept in Word. What exactly *is* paragraph formatting?

Basically, the term refers to any attribute of paragraphs that you can change through the **Paragraph dialog box (Home tab, Paragraph group**, click the dialog-launcher arrow at the bottom right to display the dialog, ***or*** **Page Layout tab, Paragraph** group, click the arrow to display the dialog, ***or*** click **Alt O, P**). In other words, it includes **alignment** (justification), **indentation** (which means not only the left and right margins of the paragraph, but also the first line thereof), **spacing before and after the paragraph, line spacing**, and **tabs**.

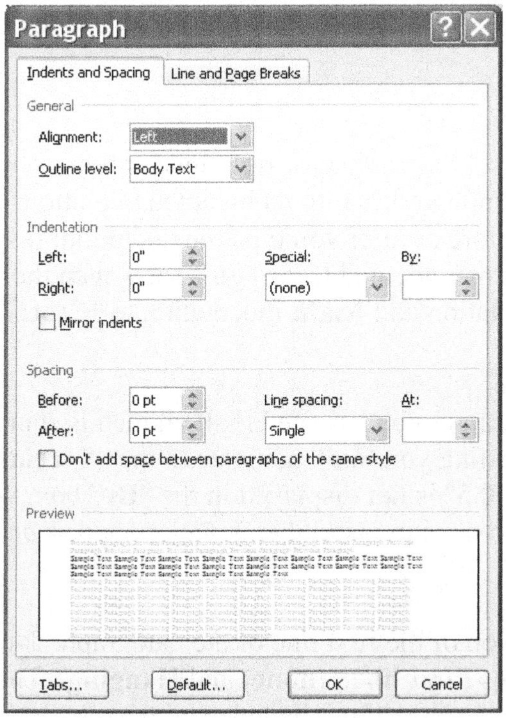

Indents and Spacing tab

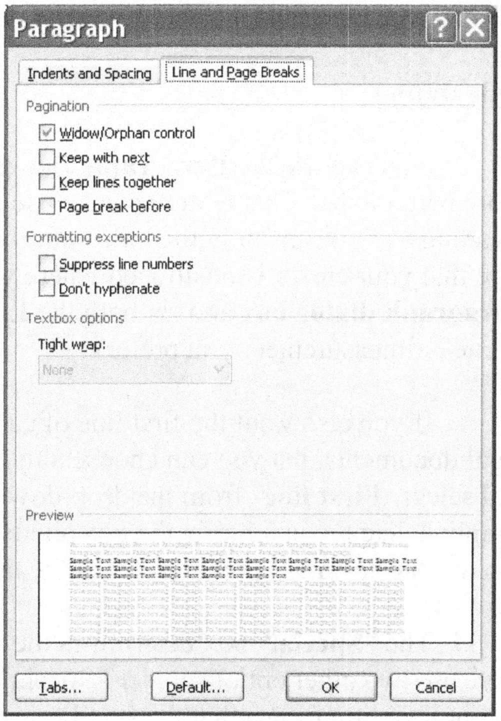

Line and Page Breaks tab

[1] In Word, the paragraph is the basic unit to which you apply most types of formatting. In WordPerfect, formatting such as alignment and indents can be applied separately to smaller units (text strings or streams).

It also includes **outline numbering** (where applicable). In addition, paragraph formatting encompasses **line breaks** and **page breaks** (whether you allow lines or paragraphs to break across pages).

The dialog box pictured on the previous page shows my default or "normal" paragraph settings in Word 2007. (I've modified the settings because the defaults that came with the program—1.15 line spacing and 10 points after each paragraph—didn't suit my needs.)

If you use either the configuration options in the Paragraph dialog box or the equivalent keyboard shortcuts to change the formatting of a few paragraphs (e.g., the line spacing) and then want to resume "normal" formatting, you can either (1) restore the default settings through the **Paragraph dialog box** ***or*** (2) press the **Enter key** to start a new paragraph and then press **Ctrl Q** to remove all "manually applied" paragraph formatting and restore the default settings.

NOTE: Ctrl Q will remove paragraph formatting in most instances. There is one important exception to this rule, however. If you (or someone else) used a ***STYLE*** to format a paragraph (or series of paragraphs), Ctrl Q won't work because ***it won't remove the style*** that is affecting the paragraph formatting. Instead, with the cursor within the paragraph you want to change back to the default settings, press **Ctrl Shift N**. That key combination is the keyboard shortcut for the **Normal paragraph style**; use it to replace any existing paragraph style with the Normal (default) style.

Indentation

You can use the **Paragraph dialog box** to set the left and/or right indentation of one or more paragraphs. This feature can be useful for (among other things) indented quotations in pleadings. You can apply the indentation either before or after you type the quotation; just make sure that your cursor is positioned where you want the indented text to go. Then open the **Paragraph dialog box** and set both the **Left** indentation and **Right** indentation to 1" (or whatever measurement you prefer).

If you also want the first line of each paragraph to be indented (half an inch is standard in legal documents, but you can choose almost any setting you like), navigate to the "**Special**" box and select "**First line**" from the drop-down list. If 0.5" is not displayed in the "**By**" box, you can simply delete the number in the box and type .5 (no need to insert the quotation marks) ***or*** you can use the **spinners (arrows)** to set the number.

The "**Special**" box determines the indentation of the first line of the paragraph. Note that there are two other options under "**Special**" besides **First line**: **(none)** and **Hanging**. The "(none)" option means that the first line of the paragraph will not be indented beyond the indent you've set for the paragraph as a whole; the "Hanging" option means that every line of the paragraph ***except the first*** will be by indented an additional amount beyond the Left indent you've set for the entire paragraph. The default setting in Word is half an inch, but you can change this setting to suit your needs.

Understanding Paragraph Spacing ("Spacing Before" and "Spacing After")

"**Spacing Before**" and "**Spacing After**" refer to the amount of space—usually measured in points—Word will insert automatically before and after a paragraph. If you want Word to insert one blank line between paragraphs, you can set the "Spacing After" to 12 points, the equivalent of a standard single-spaced line. (Remember that "points" refers to the ***height*** of the characters.) Or you can set both the "Spacing Before" and the "Spacing After" to 6 points (half a line).

Spacing Before and Spacing After are commonly used with styles to achieve uniform spacing between paragraphs in a document. **CAUTION**: People who use this feature have to get into the habit of not pressing the Enter key twice after typing a paragraph.

NOTE: In Word 2007, there is an additional item in the Paragraph dialog labeled "**Don't add space between paragraphs of the same style.**" This option is disabled by default for the Normal paragraph style, which means you can increase the "Before" and/or "After" paragraph spacing for this style and your changes will go into effect as expected. However, if the option is enabled, Word ***will ignore*** the "Before" and/or "After" settings. (Even with the box checked, you'll be able to add space between paragraphs manually—i.e., by pressing the Enter key.)

Note that Microsoft ***applies this setting differently to different built-in styles***.[2] By default, it ***enables*** the setting for bulleted and numbered lists (especially those that are created by applying a List Bullet or List Number style)—depriving you of the ability to determine the amount of white space between items in those lists via Before or After Spacing.

If you find that you can't add white space by changing the settings in the Before and/or After Spacing boxes, note whether "Don't add space between paragraphs of the same style" is checked. Close the Paragraph dialog, then make sure to select the list (or other text to which you wish to add more white space), reopen the Paragraph dialog, ***uncheck*** the option, and click **OK**.

In the event that you wish to make "Don't add space between paragraphs of the same style" the default for the Normal paragraph style, ***check*** the checkbox for the option, click the "**Default**" button at the bottom of the dialog, and then when prompted about having the change affect all new documents based on the NORMAL template, click "**Yes**."

Understanding How Word Handles Line Spacing

In Word, the **Line Spacing drop-down** provides some unusual configuration options, including "**Exactly**," "**At Least**," and "**Multiple**."

"Exactly" allows you to set custom line spacing that remains fixed, whereas "At Least" gives you the option of specifying a minimum line spacing and letting Word adjust the spacing if and as necessary to accommodate graphics (or other characters) that wouldn't otherwise fit.

---

[2] **NOTE**: Any style you create that is based on a built-in style will inherit the settings of the underlying style.

(This option probably is used widely in desktop publishing but, for obvious reasons, isn't suitable for pleadings or any similar type of document that is subject to strict formatting rules.)

The "Multiple" option is for setting line spacing at an interval other than single, double, or 1.5. For example, if you wanted triple spacing, you would use the "Multiple" option and type "3" in the "At" box.

"Exactly" can be important when you are working on pleadings. The process of generating pleading paper usually results in line numbering that does not use true double-spacing. True double-spacing is approximately 240% of the size of your chosen font; with a 12-point font—standard for most pleadings in California—true double-spacing is roughly the equivalent of 28.8 points. But for technical reasons, the line numbers on pleading paper often are spaced ***22.75 points*** apart (or some other fraction). In order to get the text of the pleading to align properly with the line numbers, you have to make sure the line spacing of the text matches that of the line numbers (which you can determine by going into the document's header, clicking somewhere within the line numbering, and then launching the Paragraph dialog by clicking the **dialog launcher** in the **Paragraph group** on the **Home tab** or by pressing **Alt O**, **P**). If it doesn't, you'll have to select the text and change the setting via the "Exactly" option.

Understanding Line and Page Breaks in Word

Always keep in mind that this feature is found in the **Paragraph** dialog box. That means that each option under "**Line and Page Breaks**" applies to ***an entire paragraph***.

Thus, "**Keep lines together**" means keep the entire paragraph—all of its lines—on one page. In other words, don't split a paragraph across pages. When this option is checked (enabled), if the entire paragraph won't fit at the bottom of one page, Word bumps the paragraph to the next page.

Note that this feature is different from Widow/Orphan Control. With "**Widow/Orphan Control**" checked (enabled), Word does allow paragraphs to split across pages, but won't allow ***a single line of a paragraph*** to dangle by itself at the top or bottom of a page.

"**Keep with next**" also differs from "Keep lines together." Whereas "Keep lines together" refers to the lines of a single paragraph, "Keep with next" refers to more than one paragraph. That is, when "Keep with next" is checked (enabled), Word will attempt to keep the paragraph that contains this setting with the following paragraph, and if the following paragraph is on the next page, Word will bump the current paragraph to the next page, as well.

One common use of this feature is to keep a heading on the same page as the body text that follows the heading (but **NOTE**: you usually have to apply the "Keep with next" setting to ***both the heading and the blank line below the heading***, because Word considers the blank line a separate paragraph that requires its own formatting. If you apply the setting only to the heading, it will keep the heading together with the blank line but it won't keep the blank line together with the text immediately below).

CAUTION: This feature sometimes causes text to move around within your document for no apparent reason! If text won't stay where you type it, put the cursor into one of the meandering paragraphs, open the **Paragraph dialog**, and look to see whether "Keep with next" is checked. If it is, uncheck it. You might have to select the entire document, or several paragraphs, and then uncheck that option.

"**Page break before**" means exactly what it sounds like. When this option is checked, Word will insert a page break before the paragraph that contains that setting. This result also can be achieved by pressing **Ctrl Enter** (the keyboard shortcut for page break).

Other Paragraph Formatting Options

There are three additional paragraph formatting options -- **Outline level**, **Suppress line numbers**, and **Don't hyphenate**. Of the three, you probably will find the "Outline level" option the most useful.

In Word 2002, Microsoft introduced the ability to mark any text (i.e., text ***not already formatted with a heading style***) for inclusion in the Table of Contents simply by applying a particular outline level to that text. This method is much easier than marking text the old way — using the Mark Table of Contents Entry dialog box. With the cursor positioned within some text you wish to mark for inclusion in the TOC, open the Paragraph dialog and select the appropriate level in the "Outline level" drop-down. When you generate the TOC, the text should appear automatically (with the correct indentation). If you select the wrong level, simply start over, select a different level from the drop-down, and regenerate or update the TOC.

In point of fact, I never use Suppress line numbers or Don't hyphenate. As for the former, it's difficult to imagine a situation where you would want to suppress line numbering in a legal document. As for the latter, hyphenation options in Word are set from the **Page Layout tab**, **Hyphenation drop-down**, **Hyphenation Options**. By default, hyphenation is turned off. If you enable automatic hyphenation, you can use the **Paragraph dialog** to exclude certain paragraphs from automatic hyphenation.

New to Word 2007

In Word 2007, there is a **"Default" button** at the bottom of the Indents and Spacing tab of the Paragraph dialog. This new feature allows you to change the default paragraph settings for the existing document ***and all future documents*** with a couple of clicks.[3]

Simply go through the dialog and modify any settings you wish. Then, before closing the dialog, click the "**Default**" **button**. A message box will open, prompting you to confirm that you wish to change the underlying template so that the default paragraph style in future

[3] **CAUTION**: In previous versions of Word, you could set defaults for the Normal paragraph style and they would remain in place unless and until you deliberately changed them. In Word 2007, the Normal paragraph style ***can be overwritten by Style Sets***, template-like objects that use XML coding to determine most of the basic formatting of your documents.

documents will reflect the changes you are making now. If you want to do so, click "**Yes**." Otherwise, click "No" or "Cancel." ("No" closes both the message box and the Paragraph dialog; "Cancel" closes only the message box, leaving the Paragraph dialog open on your screen.)

Also new in this version of Word is the **"Mirror Indents"** command on the **Indents and Spacing tab**. Essentially that allows you to set either a left or right indent for a paragraph that goes into effect on even pages only and is indented (usually by the same amount) from the other margin on odd pages only. For example, you might set a 2" **left indent** that goes into effect on even pages and then becomes a 2" **right indent** on odd pages. Note that when you use this feature (by checking the "Mirror Indents" box), the labels in the Indentation section of the dialog change from "Left" and "Right" to "Inside" and "Outside."

Paragraph Formatting vs. Section Formatting

Unlike in WordPerfect, formatting in Word is applied mainly to ***paragraphs*** or to ***sections*** of a document. The types of formatting you can apply to paragraphs (usually via the **Paragraph dialog box**) are listed in the left-hand column of the chart below. For more detailed information, see the discussion of paragraph formatting in the preceding section.

Page layout actually is applied section by section in a document in Word. When you need to ***change*** page layout, you must insert a ***section break (next page)*** in order to apply different formatting. The break goes ***on the page before*** any formatting change.[1] (If you don't want to change the page layout anywhere in your document, you don't need a section break. You simply apply the formatting to the entire document or to one or more paragraphs.) The types of page formatting that are applied section by section—and for which a section break is needed if you wish to make a change—are listed in the right-hand column of the chart.

Paragraph Formatting	**Section Formatting (Page Layout)**
Alignment (Justification)	Margins (page margins)
Indentation—Left and Right	Headers and footers (especially multiple headers and footers)
Indentation—First Line, subsequent lines (hanging indent)	Page orientation—portrait vs. landscape
Spacing before / Spacing after	Columns (i.e., mixed with regular text on the same page)
Line spacing	Page numbering
Tabs	Footnotes
Widow and orphan	Page borders
Keep with next (paragraph)	
Keep together (i.e., keep entire paragraph together on one page)	
Page break before	

---

[1] In Word 2007, you add a section break by clicking the **Page Layout tab**, **Breaks** (**Alt P**, **B**).

Practical Implications

What does the chart on page 9 mean in practical terms?

It means that if you want to change the page margins somewhere in your document (as opposed to the margins of one or two isolated paragraphs), you need to insert a section break on the page before the page where the change is to go into effect.

It means that if you need to format one page of a document so that it has a "landscape" (sideways) orientation, you have to insert a section break on the last "portrait"-oriented page before the landscape-formatted material (and, if you're changing back to portrait orientation afterwards, you need a second section break on the page before the formatting reverts to portrait).

It means that if you are writing a book or other material where footnotes in the various chapters or sections need to start over with the number 1, you need to insert a section break on the page before the renumbering is to start.

It means that if you are working on a pleading that includes a Table of Contents and a Table of Authorities and you need the page numbering to restart—and/or you need to switch from Arabic numerals to roman numerals and back again—you must insert section breaks ahead of the page(s) where the value and/or style of the page numbering will be different.

And it means that if you want to use more than one header or footer in your document, you need to insert a section break on the page before any page where a new/different header or footer is to begin (or, if appropriate, use the Different First Page option, which automatically sets up a first-page header or footer that is distinct from any header or footer that follows).

Keep these general rules in mind when you are working with page formatting, and eventually they will become second nature.

Help! Word Doesn't Have Reveal Codes!

Part of what can make the transition from WordPerfect to Word formidable is the fact that Word doesn't have any single feature comparable to WordPerfect's Reveal Codes, which means troubleshooting can be tricky at times. Word does, however, have several other features that can help you troubleshoot problems.

Reveal Formatting

One of these is **Reveal Formatting**. Reveal Formatting gives you some information about paragraph formatting in your document, such as indentation and alignment, and about character formatting, such as the font and whether the text is bolded or italicized.

To use Reveal Formatting, press **Shift F1** and then click some text (or select some text and then press Shift F1).[1] NOTE: This feature has been significantly "jazzed up" in recent versions of Word. It now appears in a Task Pane that opens at the right-hand side of the screen (see below).

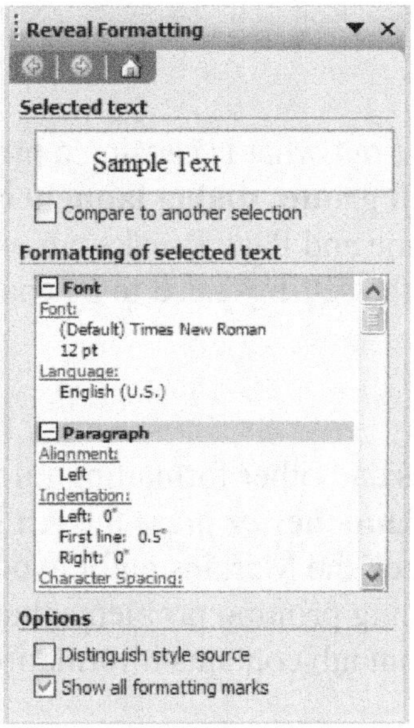

The Reveal Formatting Task Pane also can be used to compare the formatting of selected text with other text in the document, or to determine whether a style has been applied. In addition, if you position the mouse pointer over the "**Selected text**" box, an arrow appears that allows you to select all text with formatting similar to the text you've selected, apply the formatting of the surrounding text, or clear the formatting altogether.

---

[1]In some old versions of Word, you can click the Help Button (question mark in the upper right corner of the standard toolbar) and then click the text.

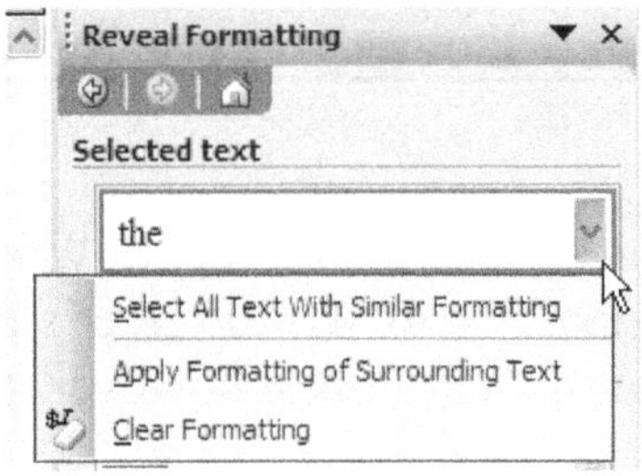

<u>The Style Inspector</u>

In Word 2007, there is a new feature called the **Style Inspector** that allows you to see—and clear (remove)—certain paragraph formatting that has been applied via a style or directly (manually). Position your cursor in the paragraph you want to "inspect," click the **Styles dialog launcher** (**Home tab**, **Styles group**) and click the **Style Inspector button** at the bottom of the **Styles pane**.

The Style Inspector actually doesn't provide as much information as Reveal Formatting, but it does allow you to clear either paragraph formatting or style formatting, or both, with the click of a couple of buttons. For more information, see the Sidebar on page 122.

<u>The Paragraph Dialog</u>

Another way to try to figure out what is causing a problem is to open the **Paragraph dialog box** (**Home tab**, **Paragraph group**, **dialog launcher** ***or*** press **Alt O**, **P**). Check both the Indents and Spacing tab and the Line and Page Breaks tab (called Text Flow in some earlier versions of Word) to see if any of the settings need to be changed.

<u>The Page Setup Dialog</u>

Also, check margin settings and other formatting information by opening the **Page Setup dialog** (**Page Layout tab**, **dialog launcher** ***or*** press the **Alt key**, then **P**, **S**, **P** ***or*** press **Alt, P, M, A**). In particular, make sure to check the Margins and Layout tabs. (The Paper tab is less important unless you are experiencing printing problems that could be affected by the paper format or paper source.) The Layout tab contains information about headers and footers.

> **TIP:** Be sure to look at the "**Apply to:**" box on both tabs, since occasionally you will find that formatting that should have been applied to the whole document has been applied to just one section.

<u>Show Non-Printing Characters</u>

When you are having problems, it can be helpful to display **non-printing characters**, such as paragraph symbols, tab marks, and spaces. Remember that the paragraph symbols contain the formatting codes—affecting justification, indentation, line spacing, before and after spacing, line and page breaks, and automatic numbering—***for the immediately preceding paragraph***.

Sometimes you can fix a problem by deleting a paragraph symbol, or by copying a symbol from a correctly formatted paragraph to the end of a paragraph that isn't formatted the way you want it to be. To display the paragraph symbol in order to delete or copy it, click the **paragraph icon (Home tab, Paragraph group)** or press **Ctrl Shift * (asterisk).** Click again to hide the non-printing characters (it's a toggle).

Select, Then Do

There are a couple of other things to keep in mind that can help you with troubleshooting. Remember that Word is based on the concept, "Select, Then Do." Occasionally you will try to apply paragraph formatting, such as a first-line indent, and it won't "take." If that happens, ***select*** the paragraph you want to apply the formatting to, and ***then*** perform the steps to apply the formatting.

Remove (or Apply) Paragraph Formatting

Other times, paragraph formatting carries over to the next paragraph when you don't want it to. This characteristic of Word is something that WordPerfect users have a little trouble getting used to. To prevent paragraph formatting from carrying over to the next paragraph, you can do one of several things, including the following:

(a) Press Enter to start the next paragraph, and then press **Ctrl Q** to remove the formatting that carried over from the previous paragraph; ***or***

(b) Start the next paragraph, select the paragraph, and apply the formatting you want; ***or***

(c) Start the next paragraph, then insert the cursor into a paragraph that contains the formatting you want to apply. Click the **Format Painter** icon in the **Clipboard Group** on the **Home tab**, then click the new paragraph; ***or***

(d) Start the next paragraph, then select the paragraph symbol at the end of a paragraph that contains the formatting you want to apply, copy the paragraph symbol (Ctrl C) and paste it at the end of the new paragraph (Ctrl V); ***or***

(e) Create a paragraph style (open the **Styles Pane** and click the **New Style button**) that specifies ***different*** formatting (i.e., a different style) for the following paragraph. See the section on Styles, starting on page 113, for more detailed instructions.

When All Else Fails…Try "Undo"

Also, don't forget that you can undo actions (up to the last 300 actions, in fact!) with the **Undo icon** on the **Quick Access Toolbar** (or **Ctrl Z**). Occasionally something as simple as using the Undo command will fix your problem.

Migrating From an Earlier Version of Word

The Most Significant Differences Between Word 2007 and Prior Versions

If you're moving to Word 2007 from a previous version of Word, you'll notice a number of differences—some of them quite dramatic, and others more trivial. The most obvious changes include the following:

- A completely new interface, the main feature of which is a "Ribbon" (sort of a chunky toolbar) containing several "tabs," rather than traditional menus and toolbars. Customizing the Ribbon is possible, but difficult and far from straightforward (it involves XML coding). The good news is that most of the keyboard shortcuts you used to open dialog boxes in earlier versions still work in Word 2007, and there are other steps you can take to make the program more user-friendly, as described in the next section of the book.

    - **Ribbon, Tabs, and Groups**

        - There are several permanent "tabs" on the Ribbon: Home, Insert, Page Layout, References, Mailings, Review, and View.

            - Some additional context-sensitive tabs appear when you perform specific tasks (e.g., when you're working with tables or with headers and footers).

            - Word comes with a couple of optional tabs (the Developer tab and the Add-Ins tab) that can be added permanently to the Ribbon, as well.

        - Each "tab" consists of "groups" of related commands (with command buttons).

        - Some groups, such as the Font group and the Paragraph group on the Home tab, have a dialog box launcher (an arrow) in the lower right-hand corner. Clicking the arrow opens the dialog box.

        - Note that the Ribbon can be "minimized" to save screen space (by right-clicking somewhere within the Ribbon, then clicking "Minimize the Ribbon" ***or*** by double-clicking any tab). When you minimize the Ribbon, everything disappears except the tab labels (names). Double-clicking any tab label opens the Ribbon again, with the tab you double-clicked at the forefront. Alternatively, simply right-click within the tab labels and click to uncheck "Minimize the Ribbon."

    - **The Office Button** (upper left-hand corner of the screen)

        - This button or "orb" functions somewhat like the File menu in previous versions, but has a few additional features.

        - The Office button is also where you'll find the "Word Options" button (i.e., options for configuring the program). That crucial button is at the very bottom of the Office menu.

- **The Quick Access Toolbar** (sometimes referred to as the "QAT")—the main functional toolbar remaining in this version
    - Convenient for most commonly used commands (highly customizable).
    - Can be placed below the Ribbon so that it expands into a full-sized toolbar.
    - Because the QAT is stationary, it's a good place to add items that you want to keep visible at all times, regardless of which tab is active. If, for example, you want to keep track of the font size and the styles at various places in your document, you can add a font size box and a style box to the QAT.
- A **View Mini-Toolbar** and **Zoom Controls** are now prominently featured on the Status Bar in the bottom right corner of the screen

- The **default font** (Calibri) and **font size** (11 points), as well as the **default line spacing** (1.15) and **spacing between paragraphs** (10 points after). (You can change these defaults via the Font dialog and the Paragraph dialog, but certain caveats apply.)

- Built-in "**Style Sets**" determine a number of default settings in your document that in previous versions of Word were configured mainly via the Normal paragraph style. (You can create your own Style Set or even replace the default Style Set, although that isn't a complete solution.)

- Built-in "**Themes**" determine the default font face and color for text as well as for built-in heading styles. (You can create your own "Themes" using your preferred fonts for text and headings and then set one of them as the default for use with a particular template.)[1]

- The **default file format** (**.docx** rather than .doc), which uses Extensible Markup Language (XML) coding. The new .docx format is ***not compatible with older versions of Word***, which use the .doc format. You ***can*** open documents created in older versions directly into Word 2007 (they will open in Compatibility Mode—as .doc files—but some of the new features won't be available when you're working in that mode).

  However, in order to open native Word 2007 (.docx) files into older versions of Word, you and your contacts will need to install a converter (also called a ***compatibility pack***)—unless you specifically re-save the files in the older (.doc) format. This converter is available for download from Microsoft: http://support.microsoft.com/kb/924074.

- Word 2007 provides several "**Galleries**" that consist of built-in styles or formats—for headings, headers and footers, a Table of Contents, and other commonly used document elements. You can select one of the built-in styles or, if you prefer, simply create your own.

---

[1] For a full discussion of these issues and instructions for changing the defaults, see the next section, starting on page 23.

- AutoText has been replaced by "**Building Blocks**" (also known as "**Quick Parts**" and located on the **Insert tab**, **Text group**, **Quick Parts**). You might find that some of the "canned" entries provided in earlier versions of Word, such as Page X of Y, are not as easy to use or are not formatted to your liking, so you might decide to re-create them from scratch.[2] Note, however, that if you are migrating from a prior version of Word, you can import your existing AutoText entries into Word 2007 (see the instructions starting on page 97).

- **AutoCorrect** is now found under the **Office button**, **Word Options**, **Proofing**, **AutoCorrect options**.

- **AutoComplete** has been dropped from Word 2007. To expand a Quick Part / Building Block, you need to type the abbreviation for that entry and press F3. (In some cases, you can get away with typing the first few letters of the abbreviation and pressing F3, but the partial abbreviation must be unique—it can't be a complete word or the beginning of a different Building Block / Quick Part.)

- Because of a new feature called **Live Preview**, you can see what your document would look like before you actually apply a particular style or font attribute. To preview a style, simply position your mouse pointer over a style name in the **Quick Styles gallery**; to preview a font attribute, select some text and then click one of the drop-downs in the **Font group** on the **Home tab**.

- There is a **Word Counter** on the Status Bar that keeps track of the number of words in your document (including footnotes) as you type. When you click it, a pop-up displays the number of pages, lines, characters, and paragraphs as well as words.

- **Text selection** is blue-gray, rather than black.

One of the first questions people who have migrated to Word 2007 from an earlier version usually ask is, "Where did it go?"—referring to a feature they used on a daily basis. Indeed, many familiar commands have been moved, and the tabs in Word 2007 don't correspond to menus in prior versions.

For help in tracking down those essential features, take a look at "Locations of Word 2003 commands in Word 2007," which is available at http://office.microsoft.com/en-us/word/HA100625841033.aspx. The article, which gives an overview of the Word 2007 interface, also contains a link to an extensive Excel spreadsheet that shows where various commands have moved in Word 2007.

Also, I've sprinkled a few tips for finding everyday features (labeled "Where Did It Go?") throughout the book.

---

[2] I have provided step-by-step instructions for setting up a Page X of Y Quick Part in the section on Quick Parts on page 96.

<u>WHERE DID IT GO?—Section Breaks</u>

Section breaks, located on the Insert menu in the most recent prior versions of Word, have been moved in Word 2007 to the **Page Layout tab**, at the top right-hand corner of the **Page Setup group**.

Page breaks, however, can be found on the **Insert tab**, under **Pages**.

Getting Word to Work the Way You Want

Making Word 2007 Work Like Older Versions of MS Word

With Word 2007, Microsoft changed the default formatting in the following three ways:

1. It changed the default font for regular (body) text to **Calibri** (and changed the default font for heading styles to **Cambria**[1]);

2. It changed the default line spacing to **1.15**; and

3. It changed the default "spacing after" paragraphs to **10 points**.

Microsoft says it increased the line spacing and "spacing after" paragraphs in order to improve readability (so far, I haven't seen the company's explanation for changing the default font). However, these modifications pose problems for those of us in the legal field, especially people who work on litigation documents for submission to the courts, because we have to abide by strict formatting rules. Hence, one of the first things you'll probably want to do after installing Word 2007 is to ***restore the default formatting you used in prior versions***.

In the past, restoring the default formatting was a relatively simple matter of changing the **Normal paragraph style** and the **default font** and saving those changes in the **NORMAL template**—the template that is the basis for all new documents on each user's machine. The Normal paragraph style is what traditionally determined the characteristics of such key elements as the default font face, font size, font color, line spacing, paragraph justification, first-line indent (if any), left and right indentation (if any), before and/or after spacing (if any), and tab settings.

However, the "architecture" underlying Word 2007 is fundamentally different from that of previous versions. The default settings actually derive from a "**Style Set**" that is applied behind the scenes ***to the document as a whole*** ("**Document Defaults**"). Complicating the picture even more, Word 2007 also applies "**Themes**" that can change the font attributes for headings and body text—in effect, overriding your customized defaults. Style Sets work in conjunction with Themes, and these two obscure but critically important features must be addressed if you are to gain control over your document formatting.

Of course, if you just need to get up and running in a hurry, you can simply change the paragraph and font settings, but ***those changes won't necessarily persist***, even if you make them the defaults. The most lasting, and perhaps the easiest, method of replacing the built-in settings with your own preferences is to edit the default Style Set. That will ensure that new documents you create on your computer reflect your chosen font attributes, line spacing, indents, before and after spacing, tab settings, and so forth.[2]

---

[1] You might find, as well, that the default font color for headings is blue rather than black.

[2] For more details on the way that Word 2007 determines so-called "Document Defaults," see http://blogs.msdn.com/microsoft_office_word/archive/2008/10/28/behind-the-curtain-styles-doc-defaults-style-sets-and-themes.aspx. I have borrowed the term "Document Defaults" from this blog article because it strikes me as particularly clear and succinct.

In this section, I will explain how to modify the default Style Set, as well as how to create a New Style Set and a new set of Theme Fonts; change the default font; alter the Normal paragraph style; and edit certain other styles, including heading styles.[3]

The Role of "Style Sets" and "Themes" in Determining Default Settings

You probably don't realize it, but right out of the box, Word 2007 applies a Style Set and a Theme to your documents. That initial Style Set, working together with its companion Theme, is what sets most of the default paragraph and font formatting in your documents. You can take back control of that formatting, but first you have to understand what is going on under the hood.

The program comes with a number of different Style Sets and Themes. You can switch Style Sets and/or Themes (they can be mixed and matched) whenever you want to change the appearance of a document without actually using another template. In theory, that sounds appealing. However, put into practice in a law office, corporate legal department, or government agency, it can lead to frustration because it's hard to trace the cause of sudden formatting changes, especially if you're accustomed to how defaults worked in earlier versions of Word.

In Word 2007, the so-called Document Defaults are based on an XML-coded **Style Set** that determines the font size, line spacing, "after" spacing, and certain other formatting. In particular, it is the "**Word 2007**" Style Set, operating unobtrusively in the background, that imposes the 11-point font size, the 1.15 line spacing, and the 10 points "after" spacing that are in effect in every new document.[4] A **Theme** called "**Office**," also operating in the background when you first start using Word 2007, is what produces the Calibri font face for regular (body) text and Cambria for built-in heading styles and tints the heading fonts blue.

In general, Style Sets establish a document's ***paragraph formatting***: the indents (including first-line indent), the line spacing, the before and/or after spacing, and tab settings. Style Sets also can dictate ***font attributes*** such as font size, boldface, italics, and the like. Typically, however, it is a companion Theme that determines the ***font face and color*** of regular (body) text and headings.

---

[3] I strongly advise you to make a backup copy of your NORMAL template (normal.dotm), which is where many of your customizations are stored, right after you complete the modifications described in this section. Otherwise, you might have to start over from scratch in the event that Word crashes, because when it does it usually creates a new—generic—normal.dotm. If you have a backup normal.dotm, it is easy to restore your customizations after a crash. With Word closed, launch Windows Explorer or My Computer (or a similar file management utility) and locate the backup. ***Make a copy of it*** and then rename either the original backup or the copy "normal.dotm" (without the quotation marks). When you reopen Word, all of the customizations that were stored in your NORMAL template prior to the crash should be available, and you'll still have a backup copy.

[4] This Style Set resides in a file called Default.dotx. You can edit this file directly, but you'll probably need to create a new set of Theme Fonts and make it the default, as well. Read on for an explanation, as well as for instructions on editing the file.

Themes, which can be thought of as a layer placed on top of an underlying Style Set, consist of three main elements:

(1) a set of **font faces** for regular (body) text and headings;

(2) a **color scheme** similar to those found in PowerPoint presentations (matching various colors with various design elements, namely text, background, and "accents"); and

(3) styles for "**effects**" like graphic lines and fill.

For our purposes, the only aspect of Themes you really need to understand is how Themes affect font faces, though basic knowledge about relationship between Themes and font color will help you prevent unexpected color changes.

Each Theme has its own distinct fonts for body text and headings, as explained in more detail later in this section. When a particular Theme is in effect, its font attributes (font face and color) are applied by default to regular (body) text and heading styles.[5] Thus, if the Office Theme is active, body text will appear in the Calibri font and headings will appear in Cambria. Heading fonts will be blue. It doesn't matter which Style Set you're using. If you superimpose the Office Theme on any of various built-in Style Sets, the font faces and colors for body text and headings change accordingly.

As noted above, you can switch Themes or—more importantly for our purposes—you can switch ***Theme Fonts*** (without changing the Theme colors or effects). Better yet, ***you can change which Theme or set of Theme Fonts is the default for all new documents***.

None of the built-in Themes or sets of Theme Fonts is well-suited for legal documents (at least, not according to the state and local formatting rules here in California), but it's possible to create your own customized Theme Fonts for body text and headings and then make them the default. Doing so will ensure that your preferred font settings take precedence. Instructions follow on page 30.

Working With Style Sets

You can't get rid of Style Sets (or Themes) entirely (even if you work in Compatibility Mode), but you can customize Style Sets in a couple of different ways. You can create your own

---

[5] **CAUTION**: The conventional wisdom is that Themes work only in native Word 2007 (.docx) files and are disabled when you are working in a .doc file (i.e., a file saved in Compatibility Mode). That isn't entirely accurate. It's true that the Themes buttons are grayed out when you open or save a file in .doc format. However, even if you do not normally use .docx files—for example, if you have changed your default file format to .doc—you can in fact apply a Theme to ***a blank document*** and the Theme settings ***will persist even after you save the file as a .doc***.

Style Set and make it the default, or you can edit the default Style Set directly.[6] I provide instructions herein for both options, starting with the more drastic one.

The "Nuclear" Option: Editing the Default Style Set

The most effective way to change the Document Defaults is to edit the default Style Set. As discussed above, that Style Set, which is stored in a file called "Default.dotx" but actually appears in the Style Set menu as "Word 2007," is responsible for the basic paragraph formatting of your documents. That is to say, it controls all of the aspects of formatting that can be set from within the Paragraph dialog: alignment (justification), indentation, first-line indent, before and after spacing, line spacing, tabs, and so on. By editing the Default.dotx file, you can modify a number of those settings in one fell swoop.

At first blush, that might not seem necessary: Word 2007 actually comes with a number of different Style Sets, any of which you can make the default. (To see the built-in Style Sets, locate the **Styles group** on the **Home tab**, click "**Change Styles**," then position your mouse pointer over "**Style Set**." A fly-out menu displays the various Style Sets that are available. If you have some text on your screen, moving the mouse pointer over a Style Set name provides a preview of how the text formatting would change if you selected that particular Style Set.) In fact, there's even a "**Word 2003**" Style Set that looks perfectly serviceable. (It applies single-spacing and zero spacing after the paragraph.) Why not simply use that?

You can, but the Word 2003 Style Set ordinarily works together with the Office Theme, which means that unless you also create and apply your own Theme Fonts, you'll still end up with Calibri as your default font for regular (body) text (and Cambria as your default font for heading styles).

To modify the default Style Set, just open the Default.dotx file as if it were a regular document.[7] (It's actually a template, as you might have figured out from the file extension.) Click the **Office button**, **Open** or press **Ctrl O**, then navigate to the following location (it should be the same regardless of whether you have Windows XP, Vista, or Windows 7):

C:\Program Files\Microsoft Office\Office 12\1033\QuickStyles

Locate Default.dotx and open it. With the blank file on your screen, do the following:

Open the Paragraph dialog, either by clicking the dialog launcher in the **Paragraph group** in the **Home tab** (or the one in the Page Layout tab) or by pressing **Alt O**, **P**. When the

---

[6] **NOTE** for IT people and Firm Administrators: There is a setting that allows you to prevent users from changing Style Sets. See the Sidebar that follows this section.

[7] Ordinarily I avoid modifying built-in files, for two reasons: (1) doing so could cause the program to work abnormally; and (2) I might decide at some point that I want to use them. Rather than overwriting the existing Default.dotx, it might be wise to open the file and save a backup copy with a different name, such as DefaultOriginal.dotx (so that you can restore the original later on if necessary), then close the copy and reopen the Default.dotx for editing.

dialog appears, make any changes you desire (you'll probably want to reset the "after" spacing and the line spacing. Then click the "Default" button at the bottom of the dialog to save your settings. Word will prompt you to confirm these changes—and have them affect all new documents based on the Default template. If you want to save your changes, click "Yes."

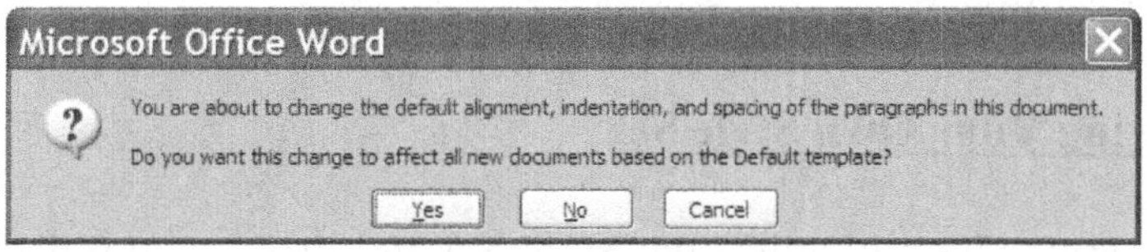

Next, open the Fonts dialog by either clicking the **dialog launcher** in the **Font group** on the **Home tab** or pressing **Ctrl D**.

Note the "+ Body" font

and the "Automatic" color

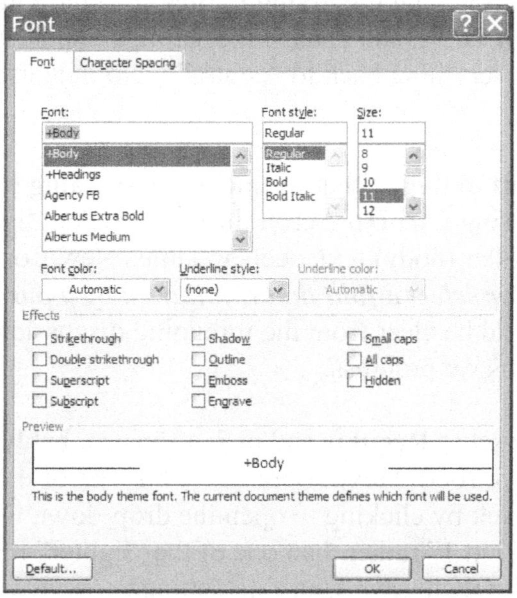

You might notice that instead of a definite font face such as Times New Roman or Arial, the Font box shows "**+Body**." This designation is a placeholder or variable; when it is specified, the font for regular (body) text will change ***depending on which Theme is applied to your document*** (a more detailed explanation follows). It is important that you choose a particular font instead of the +Body placeholder, especially since you are about to set the default font. Note also that you probably need to change the font size (from 11 to 12). Also make sure to change the Font color from "Automatic" to black by clicking one of the black squares (preferably one where a pop-up label displays "Black, Text 1" when you position the mouse pointer over it).

Make the changes you wish, then click the "Default" button. Word will prompt you to confirm these changes—and have them affect all new documents based on the Default template. If you want to save your changes, click "Yes."

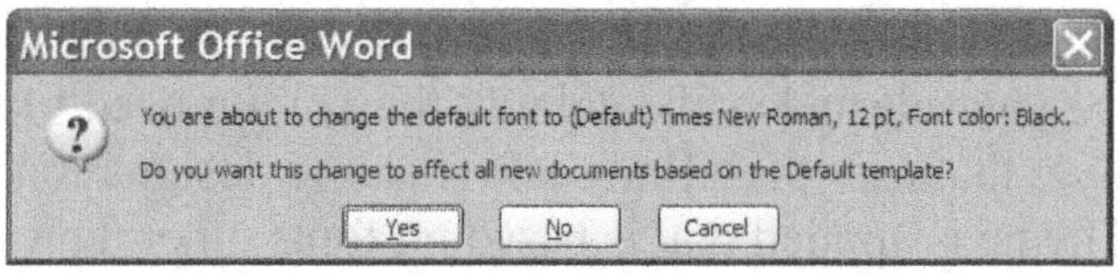

Finally, close the Default.dotx file. If Word prompts you to save the changes to the file, click "Yes."

These modifications should produce regular (body) text that reflects your preferred font and paragraph format settings.[8]

Creating and Applying Your Own Style Set

If you prefer, you can build your own Style Set and then make it the default. Here's how to do so:

In a blank document to which you haven't applied any Style Set or Theme, launch the **Paragraph dialog** (either by clicking the **dialog launcher** in the **Paragraph group** on the **Home tab** or by pressing **Alt O**, **P**), and change the settings to match your preferences. Most likely you will want to put everything back to "neutral": No indents, single-spacing, no before or after spacing.

Next, launch the **Font dialog** (either by clicking the **dialog launcher** in the **Font group** on the **Home tab** or by pressing **Ctrl D**). Scroll through the Font list until you locate the font face you want to use for regular (body) text, such as Times New Roman or Arial. **CAUTION**: ***Do not use the +Body font or select a font that is followed by a parenthetical stating (Heading) or (Body)!*** The reason should be clear from the foregoing discussion about the default Style Set; it will become even clearer as we progress.

Leave the Font style set to **Regular** and pick a **size** (probably 12 points) that you want to use as your default for regular (body) text. Before you OK out of the dialog, change the **Font color** from Automatic to **black** by clicking to open the drop-down list and then clicking a black square (preferably "Black, Text 1" rather than one of the "lighter" blacks) in the color palette. When you've finished, click **OK** to save your font settings.

Locate the **Change Styles drop-down** at the right side of the **Styles group** in the **Home tab** and position the cursor over **Style Set** to open the menu. Click "**Save as Quick Style Set...**" When the "**Save Quick Style Set**" **dialog** opens, navigate to the **File name:** box at the bottom and type a descriptive name, such as TNR12 (for Times New Roman 12). You don't have to add an extension; Word automatically affixes the .dotx extension (it saves the Style Set as a template). Then click the "**Save**" button.

---

[8] Note that these changes constitute a good start, but they might not be sufficient. One reason is that many built-in styles, including heading styles, specify a particular font size and/or apply font attributes such as bolding, italics, and/or underlining. As a result, although those styles might make use of the font ***face*** you selected as the default, they might need further tweaking. And keep in mind that any style that uses the +Body or +Heading designation instead of a definite font will "morph" if a Theme is applied that is based on fonts other than your default.

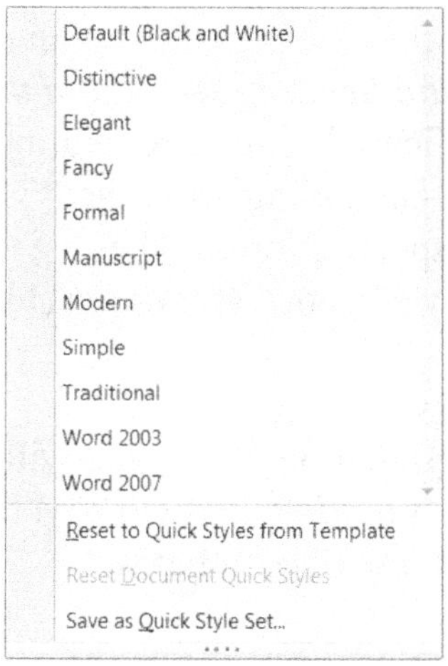

Save as Quick Style Set...

Save Quick Style Set dialog

Now click **Change Styles** again, open the **Style Set menu**, and click to apply your new Style Set. Finally, click **Change Styles**, and this time click the **Set as Default** command. That will make your custom Style Set the default for all future documents.

Applying Themes / Creating Your Own Theme Fonts

Changing the default Style Set will go a long way toward giving you back control over your document formatting. However, so far we haven't changed the default Theme (or the Theme Fonts). As a result, you still could end up with a font setting you don't want, depending on the situation. (If, for example, you apply a Style Set that uses a specific font for regular [body] text, such as Times New Roman, and then apply a Theme that uses a different font for regular [body] text, such as Calibri, ***the Theme font will govern***.) The solution is to set up a customized Theme (or set of Theme Fonts) and make it the default.

You can tell which Theme is active in the current document by navigating to the **Page Layout tab** and holding the mouse pointer over the **Themes drop-down** in the **Themes group**.[9]

When you position the mouse pointer over the Themes drop-down in the Themes group...

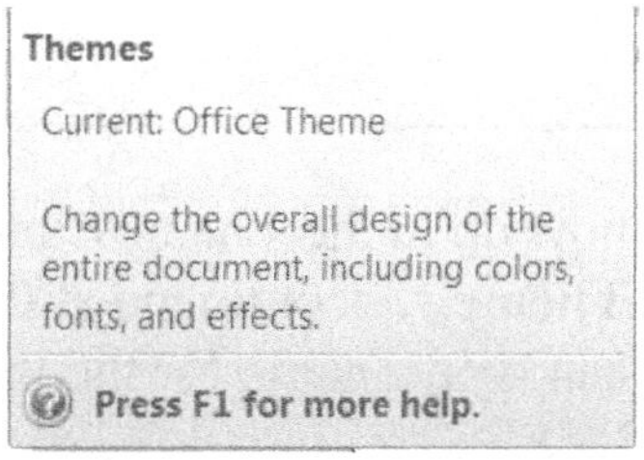

...a pop-up shows the Current Theme (in this case, Office)

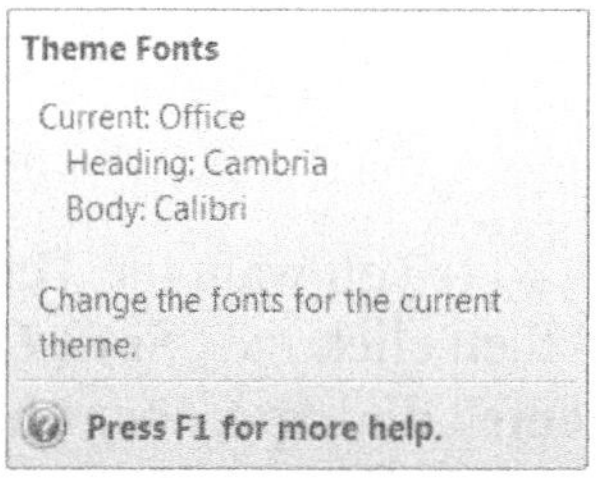

Pointing to the "A" icon (Fonts) in the Themes group shows the Current Theme Fonts (in this case, Office)[10]

---

[9] The ***current*** Theme might or might not be the same as the ***default*** theme, but if you haven't deliberately applied a specific Theme, chances are that it is.

[10] Note that you can have one Theme active and a different set of Theme Fonts active.

As mentioned previously, each Theme employs distinct fonts for headings and regular (body) text. When a Theme is applied, its fonts affect ***all body text and heading styles that do not have a predefined font***, such as Arial or Helvetica. That is significant because, reiterating an important point, many of the built-in paragraph styles in Word 2007—including all of the Heading styles—are set up with ***variables*** or ***placeholders*** in lieu of specific fonts. These variables or placeholders use the designation **+Body** (for regular body text) or **+Headings** (for heading styles).

Keep in mind that any time there is a +Body or +Headings designation associated with a style, the font for that style ***will change depending on which Theme is applied***. Obviously, that can present problems when it comes to formatting legal documents, many of which must conform to strict requirements regarding the font face, size, and color.

There are a couple of possible workarounds (you might want to employ both):

(1) You can create a new Theme (or set of Theme Fonts) and set it as the default; and/or

(2) You can modify any "variable" styles you wish to use so that they are based on a particular font rather than a +Body or +Headings placeholder font.[11]

To create your own Theme Fonts, navigate to the **Page Layout tab**, **Themes group**. Click the **Fonts drop-down**, then click **Create new theme fonts**. You'll see a **Create New Theme Fonts dialog** like the one immediately below. Using the drop-downs, select a **Heading font**, select a **Body font**, type a succinct and descriptive **name** for the new Theme (I've chosen "TNR" for mine), then click **Save**.

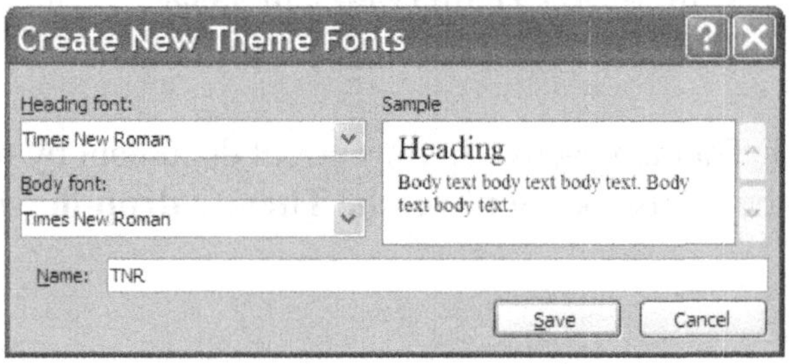

If you want the Theme to show up in the Themes "menu," click the **Themes drop-down** and then click the "**Save Current Theme...**" command at the bottom. A "**Save Current Theme**" **dialog** opens, where you can type a name for the theme and save it permanently to your Document Themes folder.

With the Theme applied, navigate to the **Styles group** in the **Home tab**, click **Change Styles**, then click **Set as Default**. Now your new Theme, as well as your new Style Set, will be applied to new documents.

---

[11]**CAUTION**: When you modify styles, always make sure to save the modified styles to the underlying template.

Changing the Default Font for Headings (and Other Styles)

Even after you have made the changes described in this section—creating a new Style Set and a new set of Theme Fonts and making them the defaults as well as changing the default font for regular (body) text—you might find that certain styles, including heading styles, continue to use a font you don't want. If that is the case, you'll have to modify those styles manually (to change the font from a +Headings or +Body font to whichever specific font you wish to use). For instructions on how to modify a style, see the section immediately below, as well as the section starting on page 118.

Modifying the Normal Paragraph Style

You might want to modify the **Normal paragraph style**, as well. As noted throughout this section, in most versions of Word the Normal paragraph style controls the default line spacing, justification, first-line indent (if any), left and right indentation (if any), before and/or after spacing (if any), and tab settings for regular (body) text, as well as for all styles that are based on the Normal style. In Word 2007, the Normal paragraph style performs a similar role—when all other things are equal.[12] Keep in mind that you can have different Normal paragraph styles for different templates.

To modify the Normal paragraph style, navigate to the **Home tab**, **Styles group** and click the **dialog launcher** to open the **Styles pane** (or press **Ctrl Alt Shift S**). Scroll down to the "**Normal**" style and right-click it.

When the **Modify Style dialog** appears, ***immediately*** go to the bottom of the dialog and click the "**New documents based on this template**" radio button. Otherwise, any changes you make to the Normal paragraph style will be saved ***only in the current document***, not in the template itself.

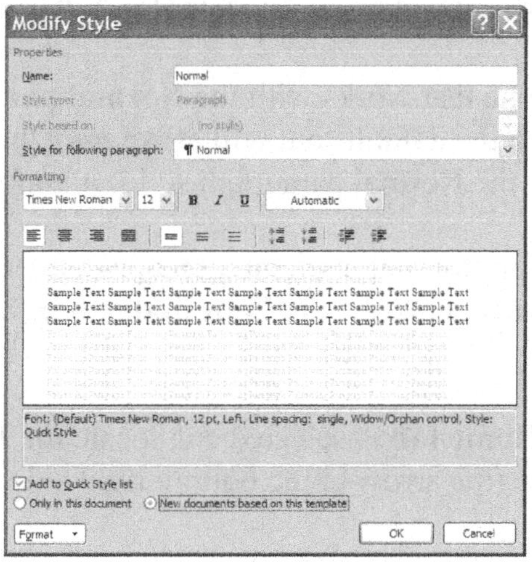

[12] At times, Style Sets and Themes seem to "hijack" the settings in the Normal paragraph style and/or the default font, a fact that underscores the importance of changing the default Style Set and Theme in addition to changing the Normal paragraph style, the default font, and other settings. The Word developers describe the Normal paragraph style in Word 2007 as "empty," which might explain its chameleon-like behavior.

Next, click the "**Format**" **button** in the lower left-hand corner of the dialog. Then click "**Font**." When the **Font dialog** appears, choose a specific font face (***don't use the +Body setting***, or Word will select the font for body text based on the Theme that is in effect in a given document), a specific font size, ***and*** a specific font color. Again, ***don't leave the color set to Automatic*** unless you want Word to choose a color for you based on Themes. Click **OK** to save your Font settings.

Before OK-ing out of the dialog, click the **Format button** again, and this time click "**Paragraph**." Go through every setting in the **Paragraph dialog**—both tabs—to make sure that alignment, indentation, spacing (including line spacing and before and after spacing), and pagination are configured to your liking. Click **OK** to save your Paragraph settings, then click **OK** to save the modified Normal Paragraph style.

Changing the Default Paragraph Formatting Via the Paragraph Dialog

Of course, you also have the option of changing individual settings such as line spacing or before and after spacing from within the Paragraph dialog and then clicking the "**Default**" button at the bottom of the dialog. However, the method described in the previous section obviously is preferable when you need to modify other aspects of the Normal paragraph style (such as font attributes) that aren't available from the Paragraph dialog.

Changing the Default Font

If you modify the Document Defaults by editing the default Style Set as well as creating and applying your own set of Theme Fonts, you might never need to change the default font—at least, the one associated with the NORMAL template. I'm providing instructions regardless, in part so that you'll know how to set a new default font in any custom templates that you create, such as templates for pleadings, estate documents, letterhead, faxes, and the like.

The default font is the one that works with the **Normal paragraph style** in a particular template. Changes you make to the default font will affect ***only*** that one paragraph style (as well as any others that are ***based on*** the Normal paragraph style) in ***only*** that one template.

To change the default font for a given template, open either the template itself or a document based on the template and invoke the **Font dialog box**, using either of the following methods:

(1) Make sure the **Home tab** is selected and locate the **Font group**, then click the **dialog launcher** (the arrow at the bottom right side of the group); ***or***

(2) Press **Ctrl D**.

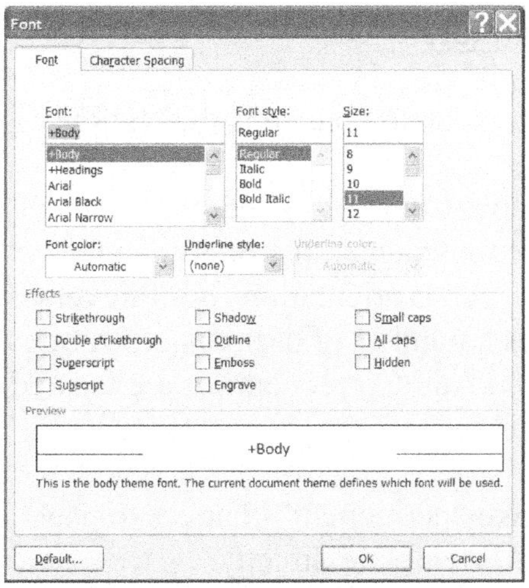

Font dialog
(Note the +Body designation under "Font" and
the Automatic designation under "Font color")

Depending on which Style Set is active, you might notice a +Body designation at the top of the Font list. As noted throughout this section, you definitely should ***avoid using the +Body placeholder*** for your default font.

Instead, select a specific font, such as Times New Roman, Courier New, or Helvetica. Make sure that it is set to use the Regular style (as opposed to Italic, Bold, or Bold Italic) and that the font size is set appropriately for your default regular (body) text (12 points?). **CAUTION**: Again, you might not think to do so, but you also need to check the font color settings. Locate the **Font color drop-down** underneath the font list and, if it says "**Automatic**," click the drop-down and then click one of the black squares ("Black, Text 1") to ensure that the default color will be black. Otherwise, the font color could change depending on which Theme is applied to a particular document.

When everything looks correct, click the **Default button** at the bottom of the dialog box. Word should prompt you to confirm that change. If in fact you want all new documents based on the template to use the font face and size you've just selected, click the **"Yes" button**.

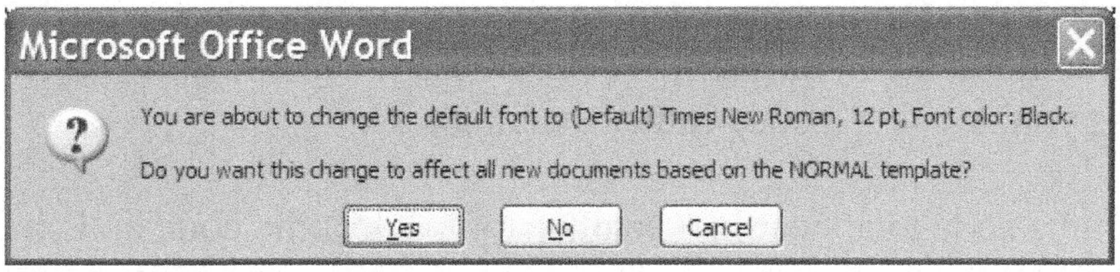

It is important to recognize that modifying the default font in a particular template will not have an effect on the default font in your other templates. You might need to repeat the above steps for other templates you use.

Modifying the NORMAL Template

One final item you might wish to change is the NORMAL template.[13]

Each user has his or her own NORMAL template. Under most circumstances, this template is the basis for all new documents. It stores page formatting settings—default margins, margins for headers and footers, paper orientation (portrait versus landscape), and so forth. In addition, the normal.dotm stores a number of user customizations, including formatted AutoCorrect entries (unformatted AutoCorrect entries are located in each user's *.acl file); styles; keyboard shortcuts; and macros.

Should you wish to make "permanent" changes to page formatting or any of these other items, you can edit the NORMAL template directly.

To open an individual's NORMAL template, simply click the **Office Button**, **Open**. In the **Open dialog**, click "**Trusted Templates**" at the top of the navigation bar on the left side of the dialog.[14] You should see a file called "**Normal.dotm**." If you also work with documents in Compatibility Mode (Word 97-2003 format), you might see a file called "Normal.dot," too. The one you want is Normal.dotm.

Just open that template, modify it as you wish, and save it as you would save any other document.

Although ordinarily you wouldn't insert text in the NORMAL template—remember that this template is the basis for all new documents—some people like to add a code for the file name and path, often in a footer (which means it will appear on every page). It's easy to do because Word comes with built-in "Quick Part" entries (formerly called AutoText) that consist of codes for the file name and the file name and path, respectively.

To insert and expand one of the entries, position the cursor where you want the code to appear—perhaps at the end of the document or in a footer (**Insert tab**, **Header & Footer group**, **Footer**, **Blank**)—then type **filename** or **filename and path** (depending on whether you want the code to contain only the name of the file or also its location/path in the computer) and **press F3**, the keyboard shortcut for expanding Quick Parts entries. Note that Word will insert the file name or file name and path for the template, but when you open and save a document based on the template, the information will change to reflect the actual name and path of the specific document (because you're using a code rather than hard text).

If you want the code to appear in a smaller font, select the code and change the font via the Font Dialog (Ctrl D) or via the font size drop-down. Then **save and close** the template.

---

[13] **NOTE**: the NORMAL template and the default Style Set are not the same thing, although they appear to work in concert. Among other differences, the latter does not hold customized styles, macros, or keyboard shortcuts.

[14] These instructions are based on Windows XP.

CAUTION: Before you save the NORMAL template, be very careful to delete any text you might insert while you are making your changes, unless you want all new documents to contain that text.

FURTHER CAUTION: If you create or modify any styles from within the NORMAL template, it's a good idea to go through the template methodically before saving it to make sure you haven't inadvertently applied any of those new or modified styles to blank paragraphs, which could wreak havoc with your future documents. An easy way to check is to switch to **Draft view** and look in the **Style Area** at the left margin. (**NOTE**: If you don't see anything in the left margin when you switch views, you'll need to configure Word to show the Style Area in Draft view. To do so, click the **Office button**, **Word Options**, **Advanced**, scroll down to **Display**, and make sure the **Style Area Pane width in Draft and Outline views** is set to a minimum of 1". Then **OK** out of Word options.)

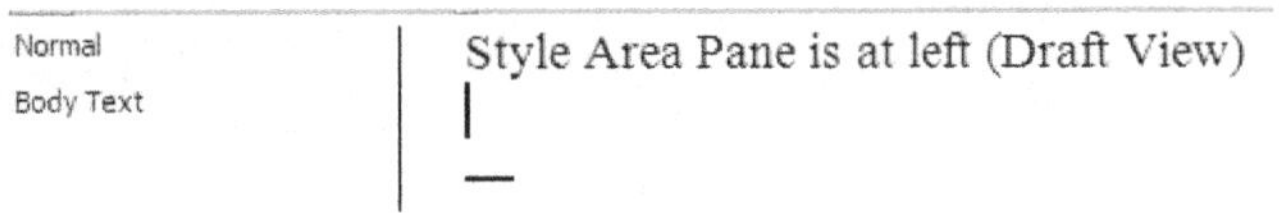

Draft View Showing Style Area Pane in Margin (Document is at Right)

If any style name other than Normal is displayed in the Style Area, double-click it. A Style dialog will open.

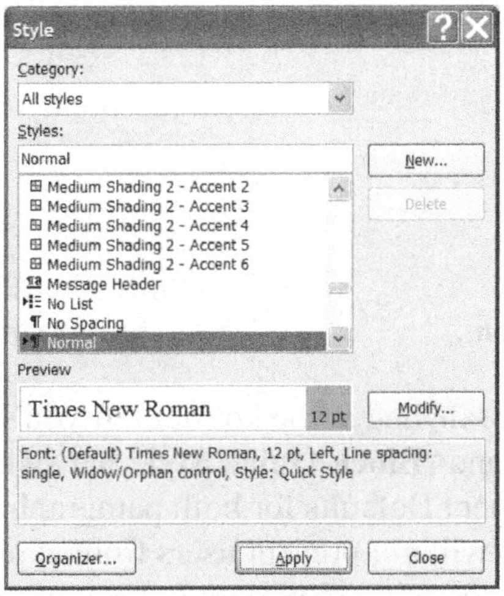

Style Dialog

Scroll down to **Normal**, **click** to select it, and click the **Apply button**. Repeat these steps for every style you see in the Style Area Pane, then **save and close** the modified NORMAL template.

There are other ways to clear styles, of course. One simple method is to select the entire template by pressing **Ctrl A**, then press **Ctrl Shift N** to impose the Normal paragraph style. But the Style Area Pane comes in handy from time to time, and now you know how to use it!

SIDEBAR: Block Quick Style Set and/or Theme Switching

IT people and firm administrators might be interested in using the "**Block Quick Style Set Switching**" and/or the "**Block Theme or Scheme Switching**" options in the **Manage Styles dialog box**. If you have distributed to all users a new Default.dotx or other Style Set that contains your preferred paragraph settings, along with a new set of Theme Fonts, and have made those the defaults, you can prevent users from switching to a different Style Set or Theme.

To open the **Manage Styles dialog**, click the **dialog launcher** in the **Styles group** on the **Home tab** (or press **Ctrl Alt Shift S**). When the **Styles Pane** opens, click the "**Manage Styles**" **button** at the bottom right.

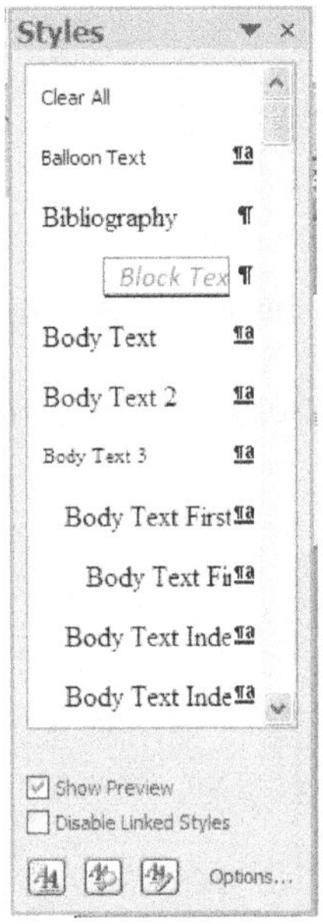

The right-most button...

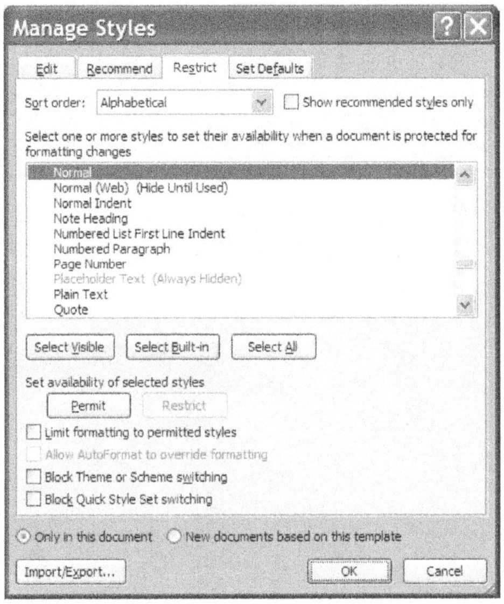

...opens the Manage Styles dialog

Navigate to the **Restrict tab**, and at the bottom left you'll see checkboxes labeled "**Block Theme or Scheme switching**" and "**Block Quick Style Set switching**." If you want to keep users from switching the Document Defaults for both paragraph settings and font settings, check both boxes. (Note that doing so will ***not*** prevent users from applying different fonts manually or changing the fonts in various styles.) It's important to keep in mind that if you check only the first option, users will be able to apply different Style Sets, and if you check only the second option, users will be able to switch Themes and Theme Fonts.

Be sure to click the "**New documents based on this template**" radio button before **OK**-ing out of the dialog.

Needless to say, savvy users (including those who read this book!) will be able to circumvent these restrictions. Even so, blocking Style Set and/or Theme switching might prove useful in certain circumstances.

Taming the New Default File Format

As you know, Word 2007's default file format, .docx, is not backwards compatible with earlier versions of Word, and isn't readable in versions of WordPerfect prior to X4 (14). So how do you share files with clients, co-counsel, and others who don't have Word 2007? Here are a couple of suggestions.

Saving in Compatibility Mode

You can save individual documents in "Compatibility Mode"— i.e., in .doc format, also known as Word 97-Word 2003 format—so that you can share them easily with others.

Alternatively, you can configure Word 2007 to save ***all*** new documents in Compatibility Mode. To do the latter, click the **Office button**, **Word Options**, **Save**, choose **Word 97-Word 2003 format**, then **OK** out.

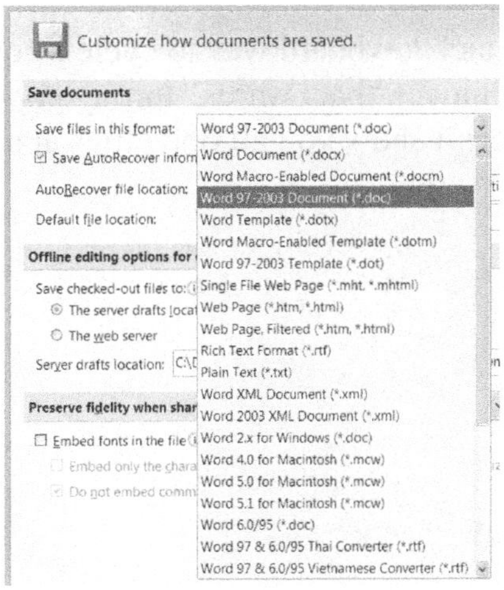

Should you choose to continue to use the .doc format, just be aware that certain features introduced in Word 2007—including Themes—either won't work at all or will work with somewhat limited functionality.

Sharing .docx Files With Others

If you regularly share documents with others who might not have Word 2007, consider saving those documents in .doc format. (If your contacts don't need to edit the documents, you can use Word 2007's new "Save As PDF" option to create a PDF copy. See the instructions on page 223.) Alternatively, you might point them to a utility they can download that will allow them to read native Word 2007 documents (i.e., .docx files). You can even send them a link. The utility, called a "Compatibility Pack," is available here:

"How to use earlier versions of Excel, PowerPoint, and Word to open and save files from 2007 Office programs": http://support.microsoft.com/kb/924074

WHERE DID IT GO? "Switch Windows"

In previous versions of Word, it was convenient to use the Window menu to see all open documents at a glance and switch back and forth between them. The menu bar was stationary, so the Window drop-down was available regardless of the task you were performing or the position of the cursor.

In Word 2007, there is a **Switch Windows** command available in the **Window group** on the **View tab** (which certainly is a logical place for it). However, if you need to work with a command on a different tab or, perhaps, to edit a footer, you lose access to the Switch Windows command. That's why I added a Switch Windows icon to my QAT. (**Office button**, **Word Options**, **Customize**—or ***right***-click the QAT and click the "**Customize Quick Access Toolbar...**" **command**— then click to change the **Choose commands from: drop-down** to display "**All Commands**," scroll down to **Switch Windows**, click the "**Add**" **button**, and click **OK**.)

You might recall that a quick keyboard way to cycle through your open documents is by pressing **Ctrl F6**. (Ctrl Shift F6 moves "backwards" through open document windows.) That's a handy shortcut, although it doesn't show you all open files at a glance.

Customizing Word 2007 to Make It More User-Friendly

It's just a fact of life that Word 2007 isn't as easily customizable as previous versions. Indeed, users who wish to modify the Ribbon or any of its tabs will be disappointed to learn that they can't do so themselves without mastering XML coding.[1]

Still, there are a couple of customizable elements in this version: the **Quick Access Toolbar** and the **Status Bar**. The Quick Access Toolbar comes in very handy because you can add icons for frequently used commands; the Status Bar can be modified to show additional information you might find useful.

Customizing the Quick Access Toolbar

Some people who have adopted Word 2007 say they miss the customizable toolbars available in earlier versions of Word (and in WordPerfect). Happily, Word 2007 still has one versatile toolbar, the **Quick Access Toolbar** (sometimes referred to as the **QAT**). And happier still, it can be customized in a couple of ways that make Word 2007 significantly more functional.

First, you can move the QAT below the Ribbon, where it expands to fill the entire width of the screen. (In its original form, the QAT is teeny-tiny and it contains only a few icons.) That makes it easier to see, and it gives you extra room to add icons and drop-down lists so you have ready access to the features and commands you use most often.

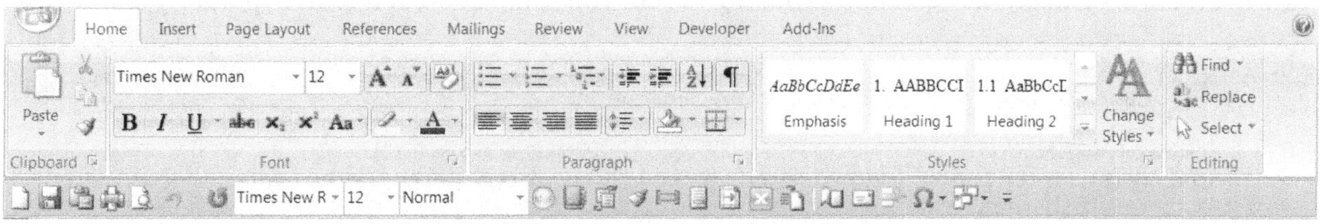

My Customized QAT (Below the Ribbon)

Moreover, the QAT remains stationary—which means your frequently used icons are always available, regardless of which tab of the Ribbon is active at any given time. That fact can be a tremendous boon. For instance, you can attach boxes that display the font face, the font size, and the style of the paragraph your cursor is in (items that were available at all times on the Formatting toolbar in previous versions of Word). I'll provide instructions on the following pages.

---

[1]**NOTE**: You can, however, purchase a "Ribbon Customizer" add-in, available here: http://pschmid.net/office2007/ribboncustomizer/index.php The Customizer has received favorable mention on the Word MVPs site, which means it's a legitimate and well-designed utility. (Word MVPs are highly skilled experts who volunteer to provide assistance to other users via various online newsgroups. They work ***with*** Microsoft to some extent but are ***not*** employed by the company.) The MVP page discussing customization of the Ribbon is located here: http://word.mvps.org/FAQs/Customization/CustomizeRibbon.htm.

There are lots of other possibilities. I have added, among other things, icons for starting a new blank document or opening a template, for using Paste Special, for gaining access to Proofing Options (so that I can make changes to my AutoCorrect options), for opening the Building Blocks organizer, for closing the header or footer editing screen when the Header and Footer Tools tab isn't at the forefront, for inserting a symbol, for addressing an envelope, and for switching windows (so that I can see at a glance which documents I have open).

To move the QAT below the Ribbon, **right-click** anywhere within it and choose **Show Quick Access Toolbar Below the Ribbon**. (To put it back above the Ribbon, **right-click** it and choose **Show Quick Access Toolbar Above the Ribbon**.)

To add icons or drop-down boxes to the QAT, **right-click it** and choose **Customize Quick Access Toolbar**. When Word Options opens, click ***the drop-down list at the top left side*** and select **All Commands** (so that you can see all of your choices). In the command list immediately below the drop-down, the icons and drop-down boxes are listed in name (alphabetical) order. After locating one that you wish to add, **click it** and click the **Add button.**

To add boxes for the font face and font size, use the scrollbar in the command list to locate the icon labeled "Font" that displays both an arrow pointing down and what looks like an I-beam pointer. In the screenshot below, it's easier to figure out which one to use by looking at the right side, where it shows the icons I've added to my QAT. Click the icon in the command list, then click the **Add button.** You can add a Font Size and Style box in the same manner (you can't select more than one icon at a time, however; you must add each icon separately).

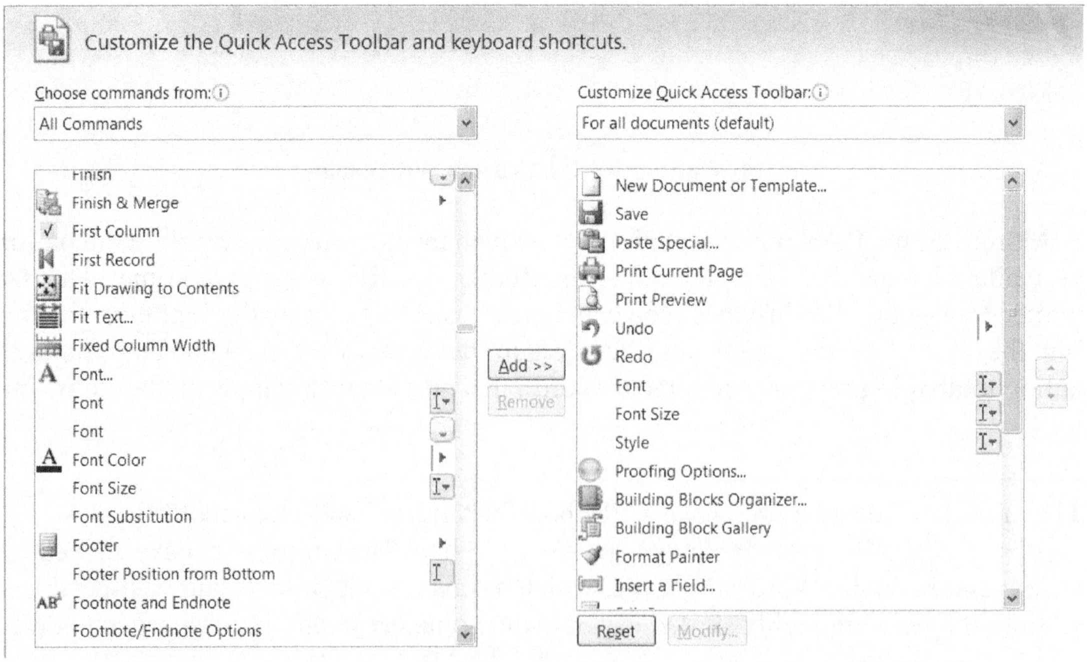

Click to select an icon from the "Command List" on the left, then click "Add"

Note that after you've added an icon, you can move it up or down (i.e., left or right on the QAT) by clicking one of the arrow buttons to the right of the "Customize Quick Access Toolbar" box (they become active when you click one of the icons).

When you have finished customizing the QAT, click **OK**.

Note that you can remove icons and drop-downs from the QAT by following the same steps, except that you'll select an item from ***the box on the right*** and then click **Remove**. Or you can simply **right-click** a button on the QAT, then click **Remove from Quick Access Toolbar**.

The QAT has a couple of built-in limitations: (1) There is no way to display more than one row, no matter how many icons you add (you can view any "excess" icons by clicking the double-arrows / chevrons at the right side of the QAT); and (2) you can't change the size of the buttons without tinkering with your screen resolution, which usually isn't advisable.

<u>Customizing the Status Bar</u>

You can customize the Status Bar by adding such useful information as Section number (which, in a departure from previous versions of Word, is not displayed by default), Overtype mode, Track Changes, and—perhaps in a nod to WordPerfect users—Vertical Page Position. The full range of options, and the status of each item (On or Off, etc.) is shown below.

To add or remove Status Bar icons/text, ***right***-click within the Status Bar, then **click** to check or uncheck individual items.

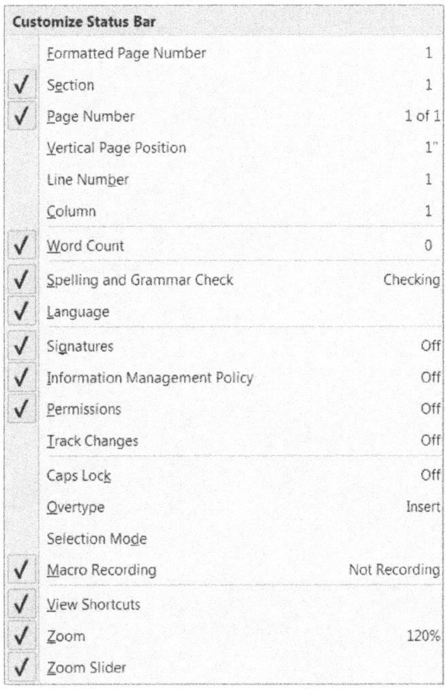

Just press the **Esc key** or click somewhere outside the menu in order to close it.

SIDEBAR: Minimizing the Ribbon

You can change the appearance of Word 2007 in yet another way: by minimizing or hiding the Ribbon.

A quick way to do so is to double-click any tab heading. Then double-click a tab heading to display the full Ribbon again.

Another method: Right-click somewhere within the tab headings or the QAT, and select "Minimize the Ribbon." When you have minimized the Ribbon, the command doesn't change (there is no "Maximize the Ribbon" command), but it has a check next to it to show that it has been hidden. Just click to uncheck, and the Ribbon will be its normal size again.

Disabling or Enabling Certain Features

Microsoft has chosen to enable (or disable) certain features by default that you might prefer to turn off (or on). These features include the new paragraph option, "Don't add space between paragraphs of the same style," which is turned ***off*** by default in the Normal paragraph style but turned ***on*** by default in numbered and bulleted lists and certain other styles—meaning that Word might prevent you from adding space between paragraphs of the same style by changing Before and/or After spacing. Also, if you use the new .docx format rather than the older (.doc) file format, you might find your settings for the font face, font size, and font color of body text and headings hijacked by Word 2007's built-in "Themes." This behavior can be unsettling, mystifying, and frustrating—and can have a negative impact on productivity.

The following chart provides some tips about changing the default settings of a few features operating in the background that might make it more difficult for you to format your document to your (or your firm's) specifications.[1]

Feature	**Comments**	**How to Disable (or Enable)**
Don't add space between paragraphs of the same style (Paragraph dialog)	This new Paragraph formatting option is ***unchecked*** (***disabled***) by default in the Normal paragraph style and ***checked*** (***enabled***) by default in list styles and certain other styles. That means that Word might prevent you from adding space between paragraphs by using the Before and/or After setting(s) in the Paragraph dialog unless you specifically turn this option off.	If necessary, ***select the affected paragraphs***, then launch the **Paragraph dialog** and click to check or uncheck the "Don't add space between paragraphs of the same style" option (depending on whether you want to enable or disable it) and click **OK**. You can change the default settings for this option (as it affects the Normal paragraph style) in at least two different ways: (1) by turning it on or off, clicking the "Default" button at the bottom of the Paragraph dialog, then clicking OK; or (2) by opening your NORMAL template for editing, enabling or disabling the option, clicking OK, and then saving the revised NORMAL template. **CAUTION**: You probably will need to disable this setting on ***a style-by-style basis***.

[1] Thankfully, the ubiquitous Clippy has been removed from Word 2007, so it is no longer necessary to include instructions for disabling him.

Feature	Comments	How to Disable (or Enable)
Themes	By default, Word applies a Theme to every new .docx. Each Theme uses a certain font face, size, and color for body text and for heading styles. These choices are predetermined for you and, if you're not well versed on Themes and how they behave, it can be frustrating to try to work around them.	The only sure-fire way to disable Themes altogether is to work in Compatibility Mode (i.e., use the .doc format rather than .docx). If you need to use the .docx format, a reasonably good workaround is to create a custom Theme that uses your preferred fonts (making sure to configure the specific font face, size, ***and*** color you want) for body text and for heading styles, and then make that Theme the default. Or you can create a custom Theme Fonts set and make that set the default. See the instructions on page 30.
Paste Options Button	On by default in Word 2007 Some people find this pop-up distracting.	**Office button**, **Word Options**, **Advanced**, **Cut, copy and paste**, ***un*****check** **Show Paste Options buttons**.
Set Left- and First-Indent With Tabs and Backspaces	On by default in Word 2007 With this setting enabled, pressing the Tab key results in a first-line indent and or a left indent rather than a simple tab. Pressing the Enter key copies the first-line indent or left indent to the following paragraph.	**Office button**, **Word Options**, **Proofing**, **AutoCorrect Options**, **AutoFormat As You Type tab**, ***un***check Set left- and first-indent with tabs and backspaces.
White Space Between Pages	Unlike in prior versions, this feature is turned ***off*** by default in Word 2007. When white space is hidden, *headers and footers also are hidden* (though footnotes and endnotes are not).	**Office button**, **Word Options**, **Display**, **Show white space between pages in Print Layout view**, ***check*** to enable. You also can this setting turn on and off (temporarily) by clicking gray area / division between pages.

Feature	Comments	How to Disable (or Enable)
Reviewing toolbar—Final Showing Markup	With this feature enabled, revision marks, comments, and other interlineations inserted in a document via "Track Changes" or "Compare Documents" are visible. Note that Microsoft has chosen to make this setting the default so that you are less likely to send a document containing metadata to people who are not supposed to see such information.	I don't know how to change this setting so that Final Showing Markup isn't the default (there's probably a kludge available on the Internet), but you can prevent hidden markup from displaying when you open a document by clicking **Office button**, **Word Options**, **Advanced**, **Editing Options** and ***unchecking*** **Keep Track of Formatting**. If you are sending the document to outside counsel or anyone else you don't want to see the markup, you should make a copy of the document and ***accept or reject each (all) of the changes*** before forwarding that copy of the doc. That is the ***only*** sure way to keep others from seeing the revisions.
Use Balloons	"Balloons" are used for revision marks (Track Changes) and comments. They appear in the margins and ***they print with the document*** (unless you remember to change the **Balloons** setting in the **Tracking group** on the **Review tab** to **Show All Revisions Inline** ***or*** change the **Display for Review** options on the **Review** tab to show **Final** rather than **Final Showing Markup**).	To configure balloons, click the **Review tab**, **Tracking group**, **Balloons**. You have three options for using balloons: • Show Revisions in Balloons • Show All Revisions Inline (this option effectively turns balloons ***off***; they won't display or print with the document) • Show Only Comments and Formatting in Balloons

Miscellaneous Tips for Working Smarter and Faster

Saving Time by Using Keyboard Shortcuts

As a legal word processor (and a fast typist—I can bang out documents at 85-95 wpm when I'm really cranking), I rely heavily on keyboard shortcuts. They allow me to work much more quickly and efficiently than if I were using the mouse to click my way around the Ribbon, tabs, groups, icons, and dialog boxes. Every time I take my hands off the keyboard, my productivity drops. I couldn't tell you precisely how much, though I remember reading efficiency studies years ago that suggested that people who use keyboard shortcuts shave 20% to 40% off their time. That sounds about right to me.

In any case, fast typists will be pleased to know that Word offers lots of built-in keyboard shortcuts. And it's easy to set up additional shortcuts of your own.

For Users of Prior Versions of Word

Keyboard shortcuts also come in handy because the interface has changed so drastically in Word 2007. Without the familiar menus and toolbars, you might feel a little lost trying to determine where a particular feature went. Luckily, one of the best ways to invoke dialog boxes and carry out commands in Word is with keystrokes. Most of the shortcuts you learned for prior versions of Word still work in Word 2007 (and if you never learned them, you'll be glad to learn of them now).

Note, too, that you can use most of the familiar keyboard shortcuts to work with "File" commands (now accessible through the Office button). So, for example, **Alt F** opens the drop-down equivalent of the File menu; **Alt F, S** is Save; **Alt F, A** is Save As; **Alt F, C** is Close; **Alt F, O** is Open (as is **Ctrl O**); **Alt F, P** is Print, as is **Ctrl P** (both key combinations open the print dialog); **Alt F, X** is Exit (i.e., from Word).

And the Paragraph dialog, which will come to be an old friend, can be opened from just about anywhere in the program by pressing **Alt O, P**. Who needs to remember which tab(s) it's on?

For WordPerfect Users

For the most part, Word's standard keyboard shortcuts differ from those you might be accustomed to in WordPerfect. The good news is that many of them are simple to remember because they are mnemonic (i.e., they use the Ctrl key plus a letter of the alphabet that is the first letter of the command, such as Ctrl P for Print). Others will become second nature because you will use them every day.

Should you wish to assign familiar WordPerfect keyboard shortcuts to Word functions, be sure to read the next section, "How to Create Your Own Keyboard Shortcuts."

All Manner of Shortcuts

I have provided lists of keyboard shortcuts that are organized in a few different ways. The first list represents many commands that make use of the Ctrl key plus a letter or number; the second offers keyboard commands that use various function keys; the third is organized by feature or function; and the fourth contains keyboard shortcuts for access to tabs of the Ribbon and to dialog boxes. The lists aren't exhaustive, and there is some overlap. My intention and hope in including these lists is that they will familiarize you with the keyboard shortcuts you will use most often.

How to Create Your Own Keyboard Shortcuts

Setting up your own keyboard shortcuts for nearly any function is a relatively simple matter.

First, do one of the following:

(1) click the **Office button**, **Word Options**, **Customize** or

(2) right-click the **Quick Access Toolbar** (or the **Ribbon**), then click **Customize the Quick Access Toolbar**.

Next, scroll to the bottom of the **Word Options dialog** and click the **Keyboard Shortcuts: Customize button**. You'll see the **Customize Keyboard dialog** (screenshot below).

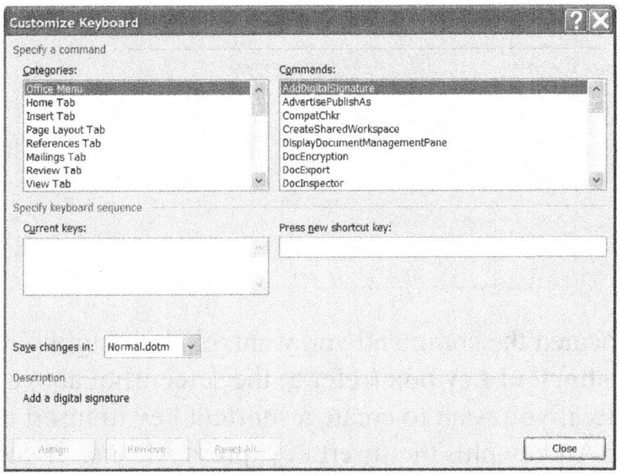

Customize Keyboard dialog

Note the **Categories list** on the left and the **Commands list** on the right. What you highlight in the **Categories list** determines the commands that are displayed in the **Commands list**. (In the screenshot, the Office Menu is highlighted on the left, which means that all of the commands displayed on the right are items accessible through the Office button.)

The Categories are organized roughly by tabs of the Ribbon (though the first item in the box is the Office button, which is labeled here as the Office Menu). As you scroll down, you'll see as well the context-sensitive tabs, and then, toward the bottom, **All Commands**. Below **All Commands** there are a few other miscellaneous categories, including **Fonts**, **Macros**, **Styles**, and **Common Symbols**.

Depending on which feature(s) you wish to assign a keyboard shortcut, scroll down to the appropriate category in the **Categories box**.

TIP: If you're not sure which tab a particular feature is associated with, scroll down to the **All Commands** category. That category can be somewhat overwhelming, but it's probably your best bet for finding a specific item. Keep in mind as you scroll through the commands that they are listed in alphabetical order. Also keep in mind that Microsoft often uses a verb—and not necessarily the verb that first comes to mind—where you might assume a noun as the name of a command. So, for example, GrowFont and ShrinkFont are the commands to increase and decrease font size, respectively.

ANOTHER TIP: You can search through the commands by pressing a letter of the alphabet, such as "S," to see all of the commands that begin with that letter. That may or may not speed up the process of looking for a particular command. Be sure to click in the Command list first.

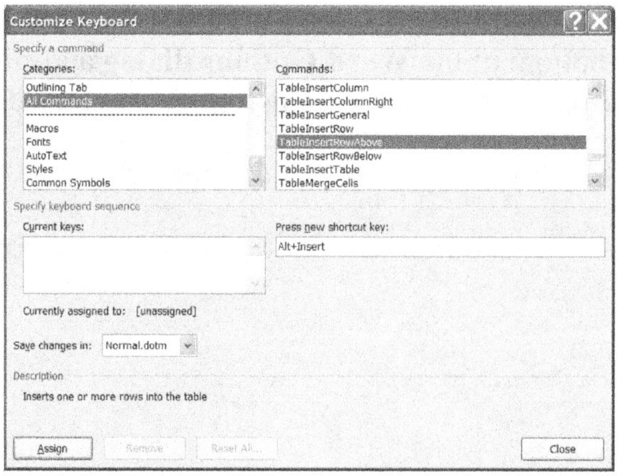

Once you have located the command you want, click to highlight it. Then position your cursor in the **Press new shortcut key** box (refer to the screenshot above) and press the keys you wish to use. For example, if you want to create a shortcut key to insert a table row above the cursor position using the Alt key plus the Insert key, press Alt Ins. If you want to create a shortcut key for the section sign (§) using the Alt key plus the letter "S," press Alt S. If you want to use the key combination Alt Ctrl F1, press those keys in sequence.

If the keyboard shortcut you type in the **Press new shortcut key** box is already assigned to a Word feature or function, you'll see "**Currently assigned to:**" underneath the **Current keys:** box on the left side of the dialog. (See screenshot below for an example.)

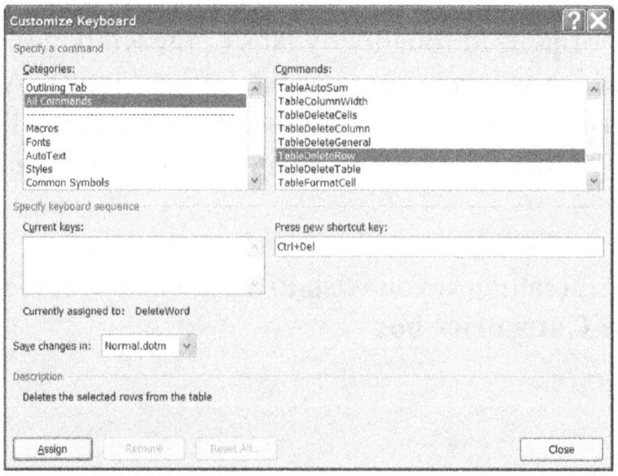

If you want to use a keyboard shortcut that is assigned to another feature, just click the "**Assign**" button in the lower left-hand corner of the dialog. That will remove the key assignment from the feature it was associated with previously and associate it with the feature you have highlighted instead. **CAUTION**: Word will make this change without warning you, so don't click the Assign button unless you're certain you want to reassign the key combination. Should you wish to remove a key assignment, **select** the keys in the "**Current keys**" box, then click the "**Remove**" button.

If you don't want to use keystrokes that have been assigned to a different function, simply type another key combination in the **Press a new shortcut key** box. If that combination isn't already assigned to a feature, click **Assign**.

Once you have finished setting up your own keyboard shortcuts, simply **Close** the dialog box and **OK** out of **Word Options** (don't click the Cancel button).

It's always a good idea to test your keyboard shortcuts to make sure they work as you intended. Also, keep in mind that by default, you are saving your customized keystrokes in your **Normal template** (**Normal.dotm**).

SIDEBAR: Some Cool Built-In Keyboard Shortcuts

Here are a few keyboard shortcuts you might not know about—but you'll definitely appreciate. I've chosen them somewhat randomly. To me they're cool because they make it easy to perform tasks I actually use in my legal word processing work.

Did you know that Word 2007 comes with a keyboard shortcut you can use to apply highlighting? It's Alt Ctrl H. Just be sure to select the text first. (After applying highlighting, you can turn it off by selecting the text and pressing Alt Ctrl H again.)

Alt Ctrl C inserts the copyright symbol (©); Alt Ctrl R inserts the registered symbol (®); and Alt Ctrl T inserts the Trademark symbol (™).

Alt Ctrl F inserts a footnote reference in the text and positions the cursor in the footnote pane. Alt I, N, N does the same thing.

Ctrl Shift A applies the ALL CAPS attribute to text (if subsequent text takes on all caps formatting, select the text and use Shift F3 to change case ***or*** press Ctrl D to open the Font dialog and deselect All Caps, then OK out of the dialog, to change back to lower case). To remove the attribute, press Ctrl Shift A again (the following three keyboard shortcuts also work as toggles).

Ctrl Shift K applies the SMALL CAPS font attribute.

Ctrl Shift W underlines words (but not spaces or tabs).

Ctrl Shift D applies double underline.

Ctrl Spacebar removes ***character formatting*** (such as the font attributes applied by the four previous keyboard shortcuts).

Alt Ctrl P switches to Print Layout view.

Alt Ctrl N switches to Draft view (formerly called "Normal" view, which explains the mnemonic).

F7 starts the Spell-Checker and Shift F7 opens the Thesaurus, while Alt Shift F7 opens the Dictionary / Translator.

Shift F5 moves the cursor to the previous editing position. Very useful!

There is no built-in keyboard shortcut for the section sign (§), but it's easy to create one. Open the Symbols dialog (Insert tab, Symbols group, Symbol drop-down, More Symbols), then click the Special Characters tab. Click the symbol and then click the Shortcut Key button and proceed as described in the section above. See also the discussion about symbols on page 66.

Keyboard Shortcuts That Use the Control ("Ctrl") Key

Keystrokes	Function	Comments
Ctrl A	Select All (i.e., the entire document ***or*** an entire header or footer ***or*** an entire table)	
Ctrl B	Bold	
Ctrl C	Copy	
Ctrl D	Font dialog	
Ctrl E	Center	In Word 2007, toggles Center Justification on and off
Ctrl F	Find	
Ctrl G	Go To	
Ctrl H	Replace	
Ctrl I	Italics	
Ctrl J	Justify (Full Justification)	In Word 2007, toggles Full Justification on and off
Ctrl K	Insert Hyperlink	
Ctrl L	Left Align (Left Justification)	
Ctrl M	Indent Paragraph (i.e., indent entire paragraph from the left) Each time you press Ctrl M, it indents by one additional tab stop	Ctrl Shift M = Decrease Indent
Ctrl N	New Document (blank screen)	
Ctrl O	Open Document	
Ctrl P	Print	
Ctrl Q	Remove Paragraph Formatting (i.e., formatting applied through the Paragraph dialog)	
Ctrl R	Right Align (Right Justification)	In Word 2007, toggles Right Justification on and off

Keystrokes	Function	Comments
Ctrl S	Save	
Ctrl T	Hanging Indent Each time you press Ctrl T, it increases the hanging indent by one additional tab stop	Ctrl Shift T = Decrease Hanging Indent
Ctrl U	Underline	
Ctrl V	Paste	
Ctrl W	Close (Document Window)	
Ctrl X	Cut	
Ctrl Y	Repeat Action	
Ctrl Z	Undo	
Ctrl 0 (Zero)	Add/Close Space Before Paragraph	Adds or removes extra points before a paragraph.
Ctrl 1	Single Spacing	
Ctrl 2	Double Spacing	
Ctrl 5	One-and-One-Half Spacing	
Ctrl Alt V	Paste Special dialog	
Ctrl Alt Enter	Style Separator	Used to prevent the text of a paragraph from being inserted into a generated TOC along with the paragraph heading.
Ctrl Shift * (asterisk)	Display (or hide) Non-Printing Characters (Hidden Text)—a toggle	
Ctrl Shift D	Double Underline Words	
Ctrl Shift A	All Caps	
Ctrl Shift K	Small Caps	
Ctrl Shift N	Applies the Normal paragraph style for the template you're using	

Keystrokes	Function	Comments
Ctrl Shift = (equal sign)	Superscript	
Ctrl = (equal sign)	Subscript	
Ctrl - (hyphen)	Soft Hyphen	
Ctrl Shift - (hyphen)	Hard (Non-Breaking) Hyphen	
Ctrl Shift Spacebar	Hard (Non-Breaking) Space	
Ctrl Delete	Deletes the word to the right of the cursor	Cursor must be on the first letter of the word
Ctrl Backspace	Deletes the word to the left of the cursor	Cursor must be to the right of the last letter of the word
Ctrl] (close bracket)	Increase font size by 1 point	Select text first
Ctrl [(open bracket)	Decrease font size by 1 point	Select text first
Ctrl Shift > (greater than / close chevron)	Increase font size by 2 points	Select text first
Ctrl Shift < (less than / open chevron)	Decrease font size by 2 points	Select text first

Favorite Ctrl Key Tips

Everyone—or nearly everyone—knows that Ctrl B applies boldface, Ctrl I applies italics, Ctrl U applies underlining, and Ctrl A selects the entire document. But not everyone knows about the following Ctrl key shortcuts, which come in very handy. I use them almost every day!

Applying the Normal Paragraph Style

The key combination **Ctrl Shift N** applies the Normal paragraph style (for whichever template your document is based on; different templates can have different Normal styles). It wipes out any formatting that has been applied manually via the Paragraph dialog: justification, line spacing, indentation, first-line indent, before and/or after spacing, line and page breaks, tab settings. It also restores the default font face and size (and color) for the Normal style.

Just insert your cursor within a paragraph that you want to strip of formatting, press **Ctrl Shift N**, and the paragraph should go from fancy to plain vanilla.

NOTE: Ctrl Q also removes paragraph formatting, ***with the exception of formatting that has been applied via a style***. If you attempt to use Ctrl Q to strip a paragraph's formatting and it doesn't work, try Ctrl Shift N instead.

Using Keystrokes for Indent and Hanging Indent

In Word, **Ctrl M** (M for Margin?) is like Indent in WordPerfect (F7 or, for those of you who still use the DOS-compatible keyboard, F4). **Ctrl T**, on the other hand, creates a hanging indent (T for indenT?). Each time you press Ctrl M or Ctrl T, you increase the indentation by one tab stop. To reverse the amount of indentation, press **Ctrl Shift M** or **Ctrl Shift T**.

Increasing or Decreasing Font Size on the Fly

A quick way to increase or decrease font size by **1 point** is to select the text and press **Ctrl]** (close bracket—increase) or **Ctrl [** (open bracket—decrease). While the text is selected, you can continue pressing Ctrl] or Ctrl [until the text attains the desired size.

To increase or decrease font size by **2 points**, select the text and press **Ctrl Shift >** (increase) or **Ctrl Shift <** (decrease). **NOTE:** In Word 2007, this shortcut appears to increment or decrement font sizes below 12 points by 1 point, and to increment or decrement font sizes from 12 points and above by 2 points.

Other Faves

I also regularly use **Ctrl D** to open the Font dialog and **Ctrl H** for Find and Replace. And I often insert non-breaking spaces with **Ctrl Shift Spacebar**, as well as non-breaking hyphens with **Ctrl Shift -** (hyphen).

Selected Keyboard Shortcuts That Use Function Keys
(Listed by Keystrokes)

Keystrokes	Function	Comments
F1	Help	
Shift F1	Reveal Formatting	
Ctrl F2	Print Preview	Toggles between Print Preview and regular view
Shift F3	Change Case (of selected text)	Toggles among ALL CAPS, lower case, and Initial Caps or Sentence Case (depending on context)
Alt F3	Opens Quick Parts / Building Blocks dialog	Must select text first
F4	Repeat Previous Command	
Ctrl F4	Close Document Window	
Alt F4	Exit Word	
F5	Go To (page, section, line, footnote, comment, etc.)	Ctrl G performs the same function
Shift F5	Go To Previous Cursor Position	
Ctrl F6	Next Document Window	Like F3 (Switch Screen) in WordPerfect
F7	Spell-Check	
Shift F7	Thesaurus/Research	
F9	Update Field Codes	(To update an individual field, put the cursor into the field and press F9; to update all fields in document, select the entire document with Ctrl A and press F9)
Alt F9	Toggle Between Field Codes and Field Results in Document	

Keystrokes	Function	Comments
Shift F10	Display Shortcut Menu	
F12	Save As	
Shift F12	Save	
Ctrl Shift * (asterisk)	Display (or hide) Non-Printing Characters, including Hidden Text	This is a toggle; press once to display and a second time to hide
Ctrl Shift D	Double Underline Words	
Ctrl Shift A	All Caps	
Ctrl Shift K	Small Caps	
Ctrl Shift N	Applies the Normal paragraph style for the template you're using	
Ctrl Shift = (equal sign)	Superscript	
Ctrl = (equal sign)	Subscript	
Ctrl - (hyphen)	Soft Hyphen	
Ctrl Shift - (hyphen)	Hard (Non-Breaking) Hyphen	
Ctrl Shift Spacebar	Hard (Non-Breaking) Space	

Selected Function Key and Ctrl Key Shortcuts (Listed by Feature)

Feature	Keystrokes	Comments
Help	F1	
Reveal Formatting	Shift F1	
Change Case (selected text)	Shift F3	
Close Document Window	Ctrl F4 *or* Ctrl W	
Go To	F5 *or* Ctrl G	
Go To Previous Cursor Position	Shift F5	
Next Document (Switch Screen)	Ctrl F6	
Previous Document	Shift Ctrl F6	
Spell-Check	F7	
Thesaurus	Shift F7	
Update Field Codes	F9	
Toggle Between Codes and Results	Alt F9	
All Caps	Ctrl Shift A	
Small Caps	Ctrl Shift K	
Double Underline	Ctrl Shift D	
Normal Paragraph Style	Ctrl Shift N	
Display Non-Printing Characters	Ctrl Shift * (asterisk)	
Soft Hyphen	Ctrl - (hyphen)	
Hard (Non-Breaking) Hyphen	Ctrl Shift - (hyphen)	
Hard (Non-Breaking) Space	Ctrl Shift Spacebar	
Superscript	Ctrl Shift = (equal sign)	

Feature	Keystrokes	Comments
Subscript	Ctrl = (equal sign)	
Increase Font Size by 1 Point	Ctrl] (close bracket)	See * below.
Decrease Font Size by 1 Point*	Ctrl [(open bracket)	See * below.
Increase Font Size by 2 Points*	Ctrl Shift > (greater than / close chevron)	See * below.
Decrease Font Size by 2 Points*	Ctrl Shift < (less than / open chevron)	See * below.
Style Separator	Ctrl Alt Enter	Used to prevent the text of a paragraph from being inserted into a generated TOC along with the paragraph heading.

*Be sure to select the text first. Note that Ctrl Shift > (greater than / close chevron) and Ctrl Shift < (less than / open chevron) change the text size by 2 points only for font sizes from 12 points and up; below 12 points, they change the text size by 1 point.

Keyboard Shortcuts for Access to Tabs and Dialog Boxes

The following keyboard shortcuts provide quick access to tabs on the Word 2007 Ribbon and to certain dialog boxes. (This list is not intended to be comprehensive.)

First, note that tapping the **Alt key by itself** displays mnemonics (shortcut keys) for opening the Office button, the tabs on the Ribbon, and icons/drop-downs and other commands on the Quick Access Toolbar (QAT).[1] Some people refer to these mnemonics as "**badges**." You might see them referred to elsewhere as **KeyTips**.

Note, too, that once you have pressed the Alt key, pressing the **Tab key** moves the cursor in sequence from icon to icon on the Ribbon and then moves from icon to icon on the QAT. To use a highlighted icon, simply press the **Enter key**.

Displaying the Mnemonics (Badges) on the Various Tabs

Alt H—Displays mnemonics (badges) for commands on the Home tab

Alt N—Displays mnemonics (badges) for commands on the Insert tab

Alt P—Displays mnemonics (badges) for commands on the Page Layout tab

Alt S—Displays mnemonics (badges) for commands on the References tab

Alt M—Displays mnemonics (badges) for commands on the Mailings tab

Alt R—Displays mnemonics (badges) for commands on the Review tab

Alt W—Displays mnemonics (badges) for commands on the View tab

Alt L—Displays mnemonics (badges) for commands on the Developer tab (if displayed)

Alt X—Displays mnemonics (badges) for commands on the Add-Ins tab (if displayed)

Using Keyboard Shortcuts to Open Various Dialog Boxes and Panes

Alt O, P—opens the Paragraph dialog (works regardless of which tab is active)

Alt P, M, A or Alt P, S, P—opens the Page Setup dialog

Alt Ctrl Shift S—opens the Styles Pane (you can press the first three keys in any sequence; just keep them depressed and then tap "S")

---

[1] To stop the mnemonics from displaying, either press the Alt key again or press the Esc key.

Ctrl D—opens the Font dialog

Alt I, T or Alt N, D—opens the Date and Time dialog

Alt I, S—opens the Symbols dialog

Alt I, N, N—opens the Footnote dialog

Alt V, Z—opens the Zoom dialog (for changing magnification of the document on the screen)

Alt V, Z, E—opens the Zoom dialog and positions the cursor in the Percent box so you can change the magnification easily

Alt H, F, O—opens the Clipboard

Shift F1—opens the Reveal Formatting pane

Miscellaneous

Alt N, H, E—puts the cursor in the Header editing screen

Alt N, O, E—puts the cursor in the Footer editing screen

Tips Based on Frequently Asked Questions[1]

Since I first began providing training services for law firms, corporate legal departments, and government agencies some 15 years ago, certain questions have come up again and again. Although not all of these "Frequently Asked Questions" (sometimes referred to as "FAQs") fall into the category of legal document formatting, the frequency with which they arise suggested to me that it might be worthwhile to address them in the book. That is the reason I've created this separate "catch-all" section.

The tips in this portion of the book are presented in a somewhat random order, though I have attempted to keep related topics (issues related to fonts, for example) together.

NAVIGATION: Moving Up or Down One Page at a Time

In Word 2007, you can move up or down one full page at a time by pressing **Ctrl Page Up** or **Ctrl Page Down**. (Page Up and Page Down move you up or down one ***screen*** at a time.) Of course, you can also click the Page Up / Page Down arrows toward the bottom of the vertical scrollbar.[2]

FONTS: Changing Case

To change case, **select** the text and press **Shift F3**. If you press Shift F3 repeatedly, the text will alternate among UPPER CASE, lower case, and either Initial Caps or Sentence case (depending on the context—i.e., whether the selected text includes a period, which will trigger Sentence case). Note, as well, that there is a Change Case drop-down in the bottom row (toward the right) of the **Font group** on the **Home tab**. The drop-down includes Sentence case and tOGGLE cASE, additional options that are not available with the keyboard shortcut.

FONTS/FORMATTING: Inserting Symbols

In Word 2007, the **Symbol dialog** is available from the **Insert tab**, **Symbols group**. Clicking the **Symbol drop-down** opens the **Most Recently Used** (**MRU**) **list**, giving you easy access to the last 20 symbols you used. (When you first install the program, you'll see an MRU list that contains 20 symbols chosen by Microsoft, but the list changes to reflect your personal choices as you insert different symbols.) To open the **Symbol dialog**, click the **More Symbols** label at the bottom of the **MRU list**.

---

[1]**NOTE**: This material was written specifically with Word 2007 in mind. Some of the tips ***do not apply*** to earlier versions of the program.

[2] **Watch out!** If the "**Browse by Object**" feature is active, it will attempt to perform a Find when you press the Page Up/Page Down keystrokes or click the Page Up/Page Down arrows. To disable it, click the round **"Browse by" button** near the bottom of the vertical scrollbar (between the Page Up and Page Down arrows), then click the Page icon. See "'Find' Triggers 'Browse by Object,'" page 79.

When the dialog opens, you can choose symbol sets by selecting a Font (at the upper left) and/or a sub-set of symbols for that font (at the upper left). To insert a symbol, either double-click it or click once, then click the **Insert button**. After you've done so, the label on the **Cancel** button changes to **Close** so that you can close the dialog box if you wish. The dialog box also has buttons that make it easy to set up a keyboard shortcut for any of the symbols.

Note that there is a second tab to the dialog box (labeled "**Special Characters**") that displays commonly used symbols, such as the paragraph mark (pilcrow) (¶), the section sign (§), the copyright symbol (©), non-breaking hyphens, and em-dashes (among others). Most of those symbols already have keyboard shortcuts assigned to them, but you can add or change the assignments by using the **Shortcut Key…** button at the bottom of the dialog (on both tabs).

There is also an **AutoCorrect** button that allows you to create AutoCorrect entries. For example, when you click on the symbol for ½ and click the AutoCorrect button, Word opens the AutoCorrect dialog with the cursor positioned in the "Replace" box so that when you type 1/2 and press the Spacebar, Word automatically converts the numbers-plus-forward-slash into the smaller fraction. This feature can come in very handy and is worth exploring.

BASIC FORMATTING: Adjusting Line Spacing

Remember that line spacing in Word is considered an attribute of a paragraph. Therefore, the Line Spacing controls are located in the Paragraph dialog. (See the left-hand screenshot on page 3.)

If you haven't started typing your document, you can set line spacing at the beginning and the spacing will continue from paragraph to paragraph until you change to a different setting.

If you need to change the line spacing of existing text, ***you have to select the text first***.

For simple single- or double-spacing, you can use the keyboard shortcuts **Ctrl 1** (single spacing) and **Ctrl 2** (double spacing). For 1.5 spacing, you can press **Ctrl 5**.

For anything more complex, you need to use the Paragraph dialog and choose one of the other options. If you need triple spacing, for example, click **Multiple** and then enter the number 3 and OK out of the dialog.

Line spacing in pleadings can be complex because of the way that the line numbers in the pleading paper are generated. If necessary, you can specify an exact number of "points" for single and double spacing in pleadings. ("Points" has to do with the height of the characters you type.) Normal single spacing with a standard 12-point font is 12 points; normal double spacing with a standard 12-point font is 24 points. However, in pleadings you might need to set single spacing at a fraction such as 11.375 points and double spacing at an Exact fraction such as 22.75 points. To do so, use the "**Exactly**" setting in the Paragraph dialog.

This issue is discussed in more detail in other sections of the book, including "Aligning Text With Pleading Line Numbers." If you don't work with pleadings or if your pleading template is set up in such a way that you're able to use standard single and double spacing, you might never encounter this situation.

NOTE: "**Before**" and "**After**" spacing control the amount of spacing that is inserted automatically before and/or after a paragraph. Many people use these controls to put 12 points of space between paragraphs—eliminating the need to press the Enter key twice after typing a paragraph. (To do so, you can set both "Before" and "After" to 6 points or simply set "After" to 12 points.) Some users—particularly people who have worked with WordPerfect for many years—dislike "Before" and "After" paragraph spacing and prefer to keep both settings at 0 (zero). Either way, it is important to understand these options for troubleshooting purposes—i.e., in case you encounter paragraph spacing that appears to be "off" in some way and you're not sure why, or if a certain section of your document requires more or less space between paragraphs. For more about this aspect of paragraph formatting, see the "Paragraph Formatting" section of the book.

BASIC FORMATTING: Setting Line Height

In Word, you can approximate the "Line Height" feature found in WordPerfect by using "Exactly" line spacing. As noted in the previous tip, this option—found in the Paragraph dialog on the Line Spacing drop-down—lets you fine-tune character height down to fractions of a point. (For what it's worth, there are 72 points per inch; one point is one-twelfth of a pica.) You might have to experiment somewhat to get the precise measurement you want.

BASIC FORMATTING: Combining Left, Center, and Right Justification on One Line

WordPerfect's text-stream formatting makes it easy to put left-aligned, centered, and right-aligned text on the same line. In Word, this task is complicated by the fact that Word considers all text part of a paragraph—and, not surprisingly, the program can't figure out how to format one paragraph so that it uses three different types of justification.

Fortunately, there are a couple of reasonably good workarounds available. To left-justify, center-justify, and right-justify text on the same line in Word, ***either***:

1. Create a three-column table and use different justification in the three cells (**NOTE**: You will have to turn off the table border to prevent it from printing along with the text. To do so, insert your cursor into a table, then click the **Borders drop-down arrow** at the right side of the **Table Styles group** and click **No Borders**); ***or***

2. Set a center tab and a right tab at appropriate intervals. If you are using 1" left and right margins, the center tab should be at approximately 3.25" and the right tab at approximately 6.5". You might have to position the right tab shy of the 6.5" mark and then drag it over. (**NOTE**: It's best to set the tabs ***before*** you begin typing; that way, your settings will apply to the entire document.)

A corollary to this tip: Headers and footers in Word are automatically configured with a center tab and a right tab, so all you need to do to center and/or right-align text in a header or footer is press the Tab key the appropriate number of times.

CAUTION: The header/footer tab settings are based on Word's default margin settings of 1.25" left and 1.25" right. If you change the L/R margin settings (for a pleading) to 1.5" and .5", the header/footer tab settings will **not** adjust automatically—even if you make the new L/R margin settings the default for new documents. Thus, you could end up with a situation in which text in the document uses a center point of (approximately) 3.25", whereas text in the footer (incorrectly) uses a center point of 3".

You can change the tab settings within headers and footers easily by turning on the Ruler and dragging the tab markers—if you do, be sure to change the settings in both the header(s) and the footer(s)—but if you want to use the new tab settings in all future documents, you must either (1) modify the Footer style and save the modified style to the template or (2) modify the default template.

BASIC FORMATTING: Setting Indents / Working With the Ruler

As you probably know, you can set certain indents via the Indents and Spacing tab of the Paragraph dialog box (which you can launch from the **Home tab**, **Paragraph group**, **dialog launcher** ***or*** simply by pressing **Alt O**, **P**). By default, the dialog box opens with the Indents and Spacing tab active (as opposed to the Line and Page Breaks tab). For more details, see the screenshot below; both tabs of the Paragraph dialog are shown on page 3.

You can, for example, set the Left indent of a paragraph and/or the Right indent of a paragraph. Doing so is particularly useful for block quotes in a pleading.

Left indent
Right Indent

Before spacing
After spacing

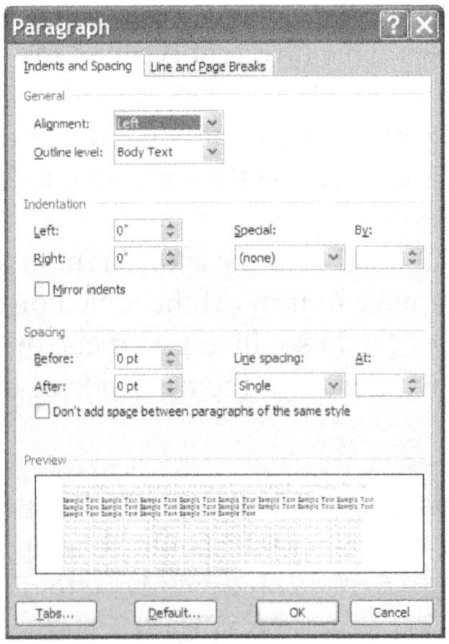

"**Special**" controls the indentation of the first line (none, First line, Hanging)

Line spacing

There is no single key combination in Word for setting a left and right indent, as there is in WordPerfect. However, you can create ***a style*** to set a left and right indent and then assign a keyboard shortcut to that style. See the section entitled "Setting Up a Simple Style (and Keyboard Shortcut) for Indented Quotes in Word 2007," starting on page 181.

To indent ***from the left only***, you can use the Paragraph dialog ***or*** the keyboard shortcut **Ctrl M**. Each time you press Ctrl M, the left indent increases by one tab stop. (This function is similar to using the F7 key in WordPerfect.) To reverse the indent by one tab stop, press **Ctrl Shift M**.

The Paragraph dialog also has a drop-down under "Special" where you can choose to format a paragraph so that the first line automatically indents by half an inch (or .25 inches or one inch or some other amount). This is the "**First line**" option.

The other choice you have under "Special" is **Hanging Indent**. With a hanging indent, the first line is "outdented"[3]—i.e., it begins one tab stop or more to the left of the rest of the paragraph. This paragraph style is commonly used in bibliographies. It is seldom used in legal document formatting, but be on the alert for it because it is the default setting for numbered lists and certain other items in Word. When you encounter it, you might have to change the setting, either from within the Paragraph dialog or from the Ruler.

You might find that you prefer using the Paragraph dialog to adjust indents because it is somewhat more precise than using the Ruler. With the Ruler, you position your cursor in the paragraph you want to adjust and drag one or more of the **Indent Markers**.

First Line Indent Marker

Hanging Indent Marker (triangle)
Left Indent Marker (rectangle)

The down-pointing triangle at the left side of the Ruler (see screenshot above) controls the first line of the paragraph your cursor is in. You can drag that triangle—called the **First Line Indent Marker**—to indent the first line of the paragraph by as much as you like.

The up-pointing triangle at the left side of the Ruler controls the indentation of the remainder of the paragraph—i.e., every line except the first. It is the **Hanging Indent Marker**. You can drag it by itself (leaving the First Line Indent Marker where it is) when you want the second line of a paragraph to indent an inch more than the first line, for example.

By contrast, the rectangle at the bottom left of the Ruler (the **Left Indent Marker**) controls the indentation of the entire paragraph. When you drag it, the First Line Indent and the Hanging Indent markers move accordingly, but they retain the same relationship with each other.

CAUTION: It is easy to click and drag the Left Indent Marker by accident when you are trying to drag the Hanging Indent marker. It takes a certain amount of practice to get it right.

---

[3] I don't like that term—it strikes me as "technobabble"—but it gets the point across.

To see how these indent markers work in practice, experiment with them. You'll quickly see their utility.

AUTOMATION: Inserting a Date Code

Word's default date format is MM/DD/YYYY, so before inserting a date code, you'll probably want to select a different format. Click the **Insert tab**, **Text group**, **Date and Time** (or press **Alt I, T**), select a format you like, and click the "**Default**" button. That format will be used as the default from now on.

Once you have chosen a default format, it's easy to insert a date code by using the keyboard shortcut **Alt Shift D**. This code will update automatically whenever you open or print the document.

Note that you can insert the date (or date and time) as text rather than a code by ***unchecking*** the "**Update Automatically**" checkbox in the lower right-hand corner of the **Date and Time dialog**. Also, it's easy to open the **Date and Time dialog** by using the keyboard shortcut **Alt I, T**. This key combination works regardless of which tab of the Ribbon is active.

Another alternative is to insert a **CREATEDATE** field (**Insert tab**, **Text group**, **Quick Parts drop-down**, **Field**, then scroll to **CREATEDATE**, select the date format you want, and click **OK**). The CREATEDATE field reflects the date a particular document was created; it won't update automatically every time you open or print the file. **CAUTION**: You do need to be careful not to re-save a file containing the CREATEDATE field if you open it after the original creation date, or the field ***will*** update, which likely is not your intention.

NOTE: If Word inserts a leading zero before dates, you need to edit Regional Settings in Windows. To do so in Windows XP, click the **Windows Start menu** > **Settings** > **Control Panel**, and double-click **Regional and Language Options**. Click the **Customize** button, then click the **Date** tab. Navigate to the **Long date format** drop-down at the bottom of the tab, and select the option you want (**MMMM dd, yyyy**). Since "dd" produces the leading zero, click directly in the box and ***delete one of the d's***, then click "**Apply**" and **OK** out of the dialog box.

AUTOMATION: Inserting the File Name and Path

To insert a code for the file name, position the cursor where you want the file name to appear, type "**filename**" (without quotation marks), and press **F3**. (If you haven't named the document yet, you'll see a temporary name, like Document5.) To insert a code for the file name and path, position the cursor, type "**filename and path**" (without quotation marks), and press F3. Note that you can change the font size (and/or font face) by selecting the code, then clicking **Ctrl D** to open the Font dialog and apply any font size and/or font face you like.

You can also insert the file name or file name and path via the **Insert tab**, **Text group**, **Quick Parts**, then click **Building Blocks Organizer**. Because the list in the Organizer is very lengthy, press the letter F to take you to the Filename entry (and, a couple of lines below it, the Filename and Path entry), then click "**Insert**."

AUTOMATION: Updating Field Codes

You can update an individual code by placing the cursor within the code and pressing the **F9** key. To update all field codes in your document (date code, file name/path, Page X of Y, Table of Contents, SEQ codes and other automatic numbers, etc.), select the entire document by pressing **Ctrl A**, then press **F9**.

NOTE: Header and footer codes usually do not update unless you go into the editing screen for the header or footer (**Insert tab**, **Header & Footer**, click **Header** or **Footer**), select the header or footer (with **Ctrl A**), and press **F9**.

NOTE ALSO: It is possible to lock codes so that they don't update unless they're unlocked. To unlock a field code (assuming it's actually locked), click the code and press Ctrl Shift F11.

COPYING AND PASTING: Using Paste Special

When you need to move or copy text but you don't want to retain its formatting, use Paste Special, Unformatted Text rather than the regular Paste command. In Word 2007, you can find the Paste Special command at the left side of the **Home tab** in the **Clipboard group**. (Alternatively, **Ctrl Alt V** opens the Paste Special dialog.) In most instances, you'll choose Unformatted Text so that whatever you are pasting takes on the formatting of the destination document (or portion of a document). Note that this feature is particularly useful if you need to copy and paste text from a WordPerfect document or from the Internet into a Word doc.

A couple of other pasting tips:

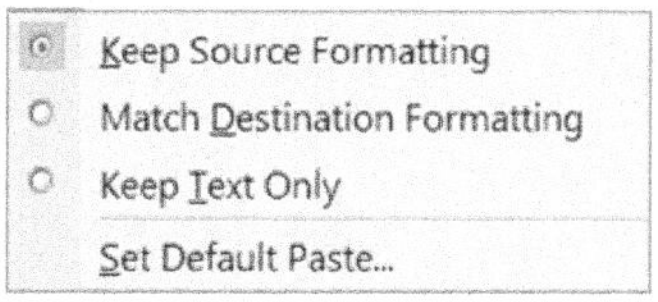

In recent versions of Word, when you paste text that you have copied or cut, a **Paste Options button** pops up.  If you click the button, you can choose among different options for how the text will be pasted, as shown in the screenshot to the right of this paragraph.

The default, **Keep Source Formatting**, means that the item you are pasting will retain the formatting of the document or portion of the document you took it from.

Match Destination Formatting means that the item you are pasting will take on the formatting of the document or portion of the document into which you're inserting it.

Keep Text Only means the item will be pasted as text (and/or numbers or other characters) without any formatting whatsoever.

In Word 2007, clicking **Set Default Paste** opens **Word Options**, **Advanced**, where you can change the way that pasting operations work in various situations: when you paste within the same document, when you paste between documents, when you paste from other programs (such as WordPerfect or the Internet), and so on.

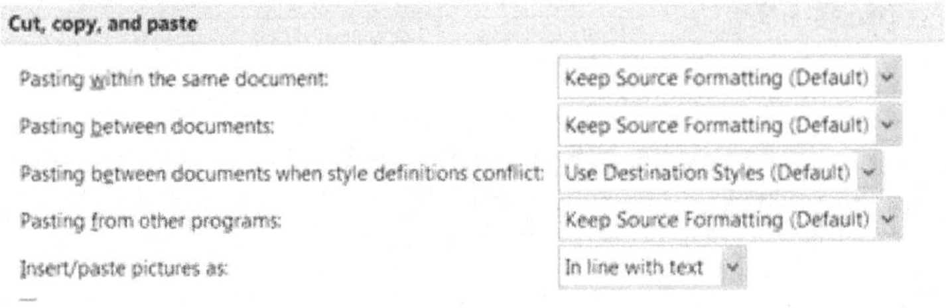

Of course, you can modify these settings at any time by clicking the **Office button** and going to **Word Options**, **Advanced**, **Cut, copy, and paste**.

TROUBLESHOOTING / UNDER THE HOOD: Showing the Non-Printing Characters

There are several non-printing characters that ordinarily are not displayed on the screen. These include the paragraph symbol (pilcrow), tabs, spaces between words or letters (created by pressing the spacebar), end-of-cell markers in tables, hidden text, and more.

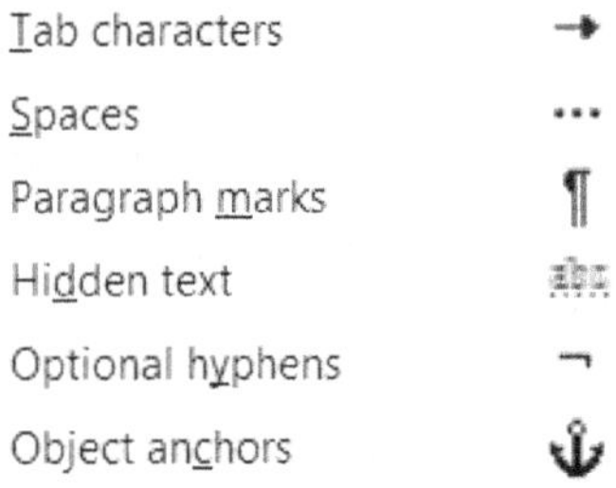

The Non-Printing Characters
(End-of-Cell Markers Not Shown)

Displaying those characters can be useful for troubleshooting purposes (e.g., to determine if you really did press the spacebar twice between two words, when you meant to press it once). Also, it's useful when you want to copy one paragraph's formatting to another paragraph—remember that the formatting codes for any given paragraph are contained within the paragraph symbol at the end of that paragraph.

You might want to hide the non-printing characters in certain circumstances, too. When you mark headings for inclusion in a Table of Contents or citations for inclusion in a Table of Authorities, Word displays the non-printing characters and TOC/TOA field codes. Those characters and codes actually take up space in the document, such that they can bump headings or citations down to the next page. As a result, when you generate the TOC and TOA, the generated page numbers will be incorrect. In order to avoid that problem, you need to hide the non-printing characters before generating a TOC or TOA.

To display the non-printing characters, either

(1) click the **paragraph symbol** in the **Paragraph group** on the **Home tab** ***or***

(2) press **Ctrl Shift * (asterisk)**.

Repeat either of those steps to hide the non-printing characters again (it's a toggle).

TABLES: Tabbing Within a Table Cell / Creating a New Row at the End of a Table

In both Word and WordPerfect, ordinary tabbing within a table cell moves the cursor into the next cell. To insert a "hard tab" within a table cell, press **Ctrl Tab** instead of the Tab key alone.

Both programs also allow you to add another row at the end of a table simply by positioning the cursor in the **last (bottom right-most) cell** of the table and pressing **Tab**. This feature can be useful, but if you didn't intend to add another row, you can just click the **Undo** icon, which is located on the **Quick Access Toolbar** (or press **Ctrl Z**, the keyboard shortcut for Undo) immediately after pressing Tab.

STYLES: Modifying the Footer Style

To modify the Footer style as suggested in another tip, locate the **Styles group** on the **Home tab** and **click the dialog launcher**. The **Styles Pane** should open.

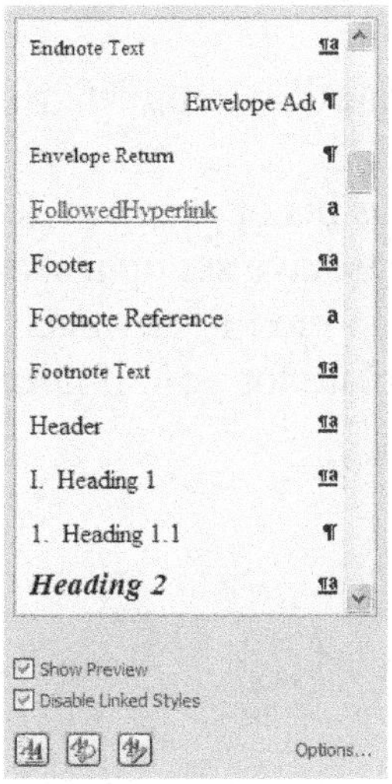

Find and select the **Footer style** in the Styles list, then either (1) position the cursor within the name of the style, ***right***-click and click the "**Modify**" button, ***or*** (2) click the **drop-down arrow** —the paragraph symbol and letter "a" turn into a drop-down when you hover the mouse over the style name—and then click "**Modify**." The **Modify Style dialog** should open.

Click the **"Format" button** in the lower left corner of the Modify Style dialog, then click **"Tabs."** When the Tabs dialog appears, type the desired number for a center tab (probably 3.25") in the "Tab stop position" box, make sure the Alignment is set to Center and Leader is set to None, and click **"Set."** Then click the 6" setting, type 6.5 in the Tab stop position box, and click **"Set."** Finally, click the 3" setting (if any) and click **"Clear,"** click the 6" setting (if any) and click **"Clear,"** then click **"OK."** Before clicking "OK" a second time, be sure to click the **"New documents based on this template"** radio button, or the changes will take effect ***only*** in the current document.

TEMPLATES: Modifying the Default Template[4]

To modify the default template (called **Normal.dotm** in Word 2007—note the "dotm" extension, which is different from the "dot" extension used in earlier versions), you can open it as if it were any other document, make your changes, and save the file. To locate the template, click the **Office button**, **Open**, then navigate (in Windows XP) to the **menu bar** at the left-hand side of the Open dialog and click **Trusted Templates**. You should see Normal.dotm in the dialog.

CAUTION: You should ***close all other documents*** prior to opening the default template for editing.

In Windows XP/Word 2007, the default template is usually located in the following path:

C:\Documents and Settings\YourName\Application Data\Microsoft\Templates

In Windows Vista and Windows 7 you can find it here:

C:\Users\<UserName>\AppData\Roaming\Microsoft\Templates

NOTE: Although each user ordinarily has his or her own default template (located on the hard drive on that user's machine), some offices have set up a shared default template on a network drive. It is unlikely that you will be able to modify any such shared template. Your network administrator can modify the shared template for you, if necessary.

[4] See also pages 34 and following.

Get Smart: Understanding Word 2007's "Smart" Features

Smart Cursoring

When you scroll through a document, you might find that the cursor doesn't follow you. Instead, it remains in the original position, where you can't see it. Of course you can reposition it by clicking at the new location, but Word offers you another option, as well. That option is called **Smart Cursoring**. When that option is enabled, pressing any of the arrow keys brings the cursor to your current position (unless you have selected some text at the prior position).

Smart Cursoring should be turned on by default in Word 2007, but if for some reason it isn't, you can enable it by clicking **Office button**, **Word Options**, **Advanced**, **Editing options**, **Use smart cursoring**.

For more information, see:

http://office.microsoft.com/en-us/word/HP051893871033.aspx

Smart Paragraph Selection

When this option is enabled, Word automatically includes the paragraph symbol when you select a paragraph by using keystrokes, by dragging with the mouse, by double-clicking in the margin to the left of the paragraph, or by triple-clicking within the paragraph. The assumption is that you wish to include the formatting instructions for the paragraph when you move or copy the text to another location in the document. (Remember that formatting codes are contained within the paragraph symbol, also known as a pilcrow.) [1]

To turn **Smart Paragraph Selection** off (it's enabled by default), click the **Office button**, **Word Options**, **Advanced**, **Editing options**, and uncheck **Use smart paragraph selection**.

Smart Cut and Paste

The **Smart Cut and Paste** options control the appearance and formatting of sentences, words, paragraphs, bulleted and/or numbered list items, tables, and content from a PowerPoint presentation or from an Excel spreadsheet that you cut (or copy) and paste into a Word 2007 document.

---

[1] There is a similar feature called "**When selecting, automatically select entire word**." With this option turned on (as it is by default), double-clicking a word selects both the word itself and the space after the word, something you may or may not intend to do. To disable the option, click the **Office button**, **Word Options**, **Advanced**, **Editing options**, and uncheck the **When selecting, automatically select entire word** checkbox.

Smart cut and paste options are set by clicking the **Office button**, **Word Options**, **Advanced**, **Cut, copy, and paste** and clicking the **Settings button** to the right of the **Use smart cut and paste** checkbox. Make any changes you like in the **Settings dialog**, shown below, and **OK** out.

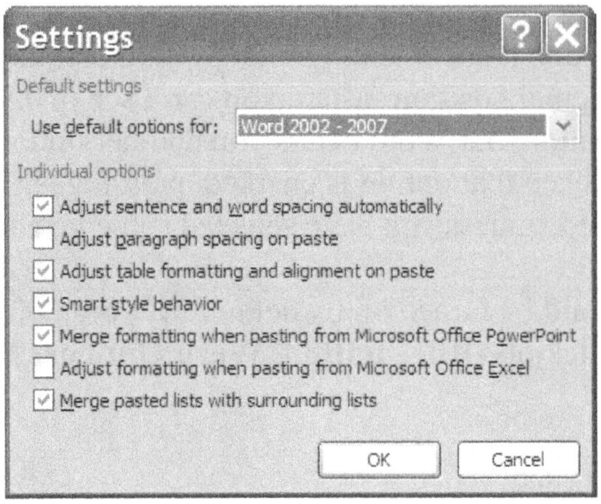

The setting for sentence and word spacing is intended to ensure that there is adequate—but not excessive—white space between pasted text and any surrounding text into which it is inserted. (This setting also controls the amount of space left between words and sentences when you **delete** text.)

The setting for paragraph spacing is intended to avoid inconsistently formatted paragraphs and/or empty paragraphs when you cut (or copy) paragraphs.

According to Microsoft, when the table adjustment option is enabled, "single cells are pasted as text, table portions are pasted as rows into an existing table (rather than as a nested table), and tables added to an existing table are adjusted to match the existing table."

Microsoft says that the Smart Styles option "has no effect." Rather, it is the "**Pasting between documents when style definitions conflict**" option (also under **Word Options**, **Advanced**, **Cut, copy, and paste**) that determines which style takes precedence—the one in the source document or the one in the destination document—when the styles have the same name but are formatted differently.

For more information on **Smart Cut and Paste** options in Word 2007, see Microsoft's online article, "Control the formatting when you paste text," available here:

http://office.microsoft.com/en-us/help/HA102157081033.aspx#6

Smart Tags

Word can be set up to recognize certain types of information, such as contact names and addresses, so that you can perform actions such as adding a contact to Outlook, sending e-mail to an individual, or looking up driving directions—all from within your Word document.

In order to make use of these **Smart Tags**, you must enable Smart tags by clicking the **Office button**, **Word Options**, **Advanced**, **Show document content**, and checking "**Show Smart Tags**."

Then you have to tell Word which **Smart** Tags to identify. To do that, go into **Word Options**, **Proofing**, **AutoCorrect Options**, click the **Smart Tags tab**, and click the "**Label text with smart tags**" checkbox. Once you have done so, click to check any of the individual "**Smart Tag Recognizers**" you wish to use. Also, make sure that "**Show Smart Tag Action buttons**" at the bottom left side of the **AutoCorrect dialog** is checked.

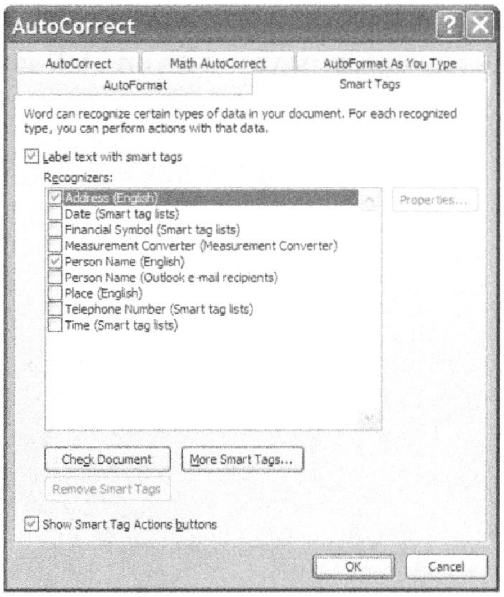

Before clicking **OK**, click the **Check Document button**. Word needs to go through your document and look for "Recognizers." If it finds any, it highlights them with a purple dotted underline.[2] Assuming you checked **Show Smart Tag Actions buttons**, a button should appear when you position the mouse pointer over one of the Recognizers. Clicking the button opens a list of possible actions you can take, such as the one in the screenshot below (the Recognizer in this case was Person Name, and Word tagged my own name).

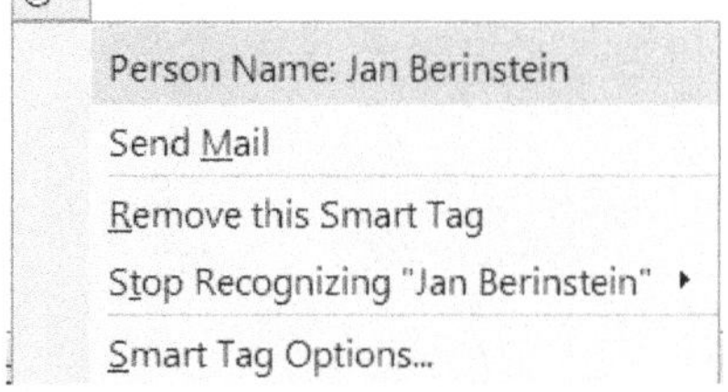

Because I don't use Outlook on this computer, the list of actions doesn't include options such as Schedule a Meeting, Open Contact, Add to Contacts, or Insert Address, any or all of which might appear if I did use Outlook.

---

[2] If it doesn't find any Recognizers, you might have to click **Recheck Document**.

You can have Word stop recognizing individual smart tags in your document and/or you can turn off Smart Tags altogether. To have Word stop recognizing individual smart tags, position the cursor over a tag and, when the **Options button** appears, click it and click "**Stop Recognizing <Smart Tag identifier>**."

To have Word stop recognizing ***all*** Smart Tags in the document, you need to uncheck two boxes in the **AutoCorrect dialog** for Smart Tags: (1) **Label text with smart tags**; ***and*** (2) **Show Smart Tag Actions buttons**. **NOTE**: Unchecking the Show Smart Tags box under Word Options, Advanced, Show document content appears to have little, if any, effect on whether the program identifies Smart Tags and displays a Smart Tags Options button. So be aware that unless you actually uncheck the two boxes in the AutoCorrect dialog, Word might continue to recognize Smart Tags and present you with an Options button.

Troubleshooting Tips: A Few Glitches and "Gotchas"

Both personal experience and questions from my training clients prompted me to incorporate into the Tips section of the book a few warnings about potential pitfalls. These "oopsies" can take you by surprise.

"Find" Triggers "Browse By Object"—and Disables the Keyboard Shortcuts for Page Up and Page Down

After you use "**Find**" (or "**Find and Replace**") to look for a word, phrase, or object, the keyboard shortcuts for Page Up (**Ctrl Page Up**) and Page Down (**Ctrl Page Dn**) stop working as navigation keys (and the Page Up and Page Down buttons in the scrollbar stop working as expected). This seemingly arbitrary change in functionality actually happens by design, but it can be disconcerting if you're not expecting it. It has to do with the "**Browse by Object**" feature and the fact that this feature is linked to "**Find**."

"**Browse by Object**," which is invoked by clicking a circular button at the bottom of the vertical scrollbar, can be quite useful. Related to "Go To," it allows you to search through your document according to any of the following criteria:

Browse By

Go To	(opens the Go To dialog box[1])
Find	(opens the Find dialog)
Edits	(allows you to search by edits if you are using Track Changes)
Heading	
Graphic	
Table	
Field	
Endnote	
Footnote	
Comment	
Section	
Page	

[1]Note that the "Go To" dialog, which you also can invoke by pressing Ctrl G, allows you to search for all of the above, as well as by Line, Bookmark, Equation, and Object. And, of course, the "Special" button in the Find dialog offers many additional searchable objects.

Here's where things get tricky. For some reason—perhaps because the default search object is "Page"—Microsoft assigned the key combination for **Page Up (Ctrl Page Up)** and **Page Down (Ctrl Page Dn)** to the Browse by Object feature.

That fact, in and of itself, doesn't present a problem—unless and until you use "**Find**" or "**Find and Replace**." When you use Find or Find and Replace to search for text, the "Browse by" default search object ***changes from "Page" to "Find."*** Thus, when you try to go to the previous page or the next page by pressing Ctrl Page Up or Ctrl Page Dn—***or when you click the Page Up or Page Down arrows on the scrollbar***—Word stops browsing by page and instead browses by the word or phrase you last typed into the Find box![2]

If Word doesn't find any more instances of the word or phrase you last searched for, you might get a rather mystifying error message similar to the one in the screenshot below.

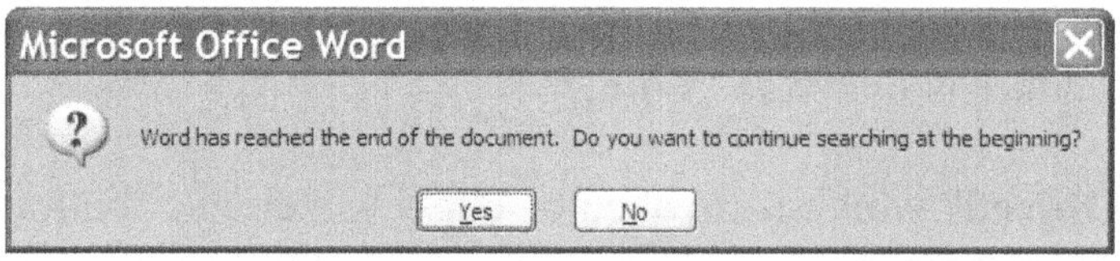

The thing to keep in mind is that whatever object you last used as your search criterion — whether you used one of the "Find" dialog boxes or "Browse by Object"—will become the new "Browse by Object" default. This new default will stick ***until (1) you close out of and reopen Word*** (the program restores the "Browse By Object" default settings when it reopens) ***or (2) you specifically click the "Browse By" button and then click Page to reset the default object.***[3]

TIP / WORKAROUND: One workaround for the Browse By issue is to assign a different keyboard shortcut to the Page Up and Page Down commands and use that shortcut instead of Ctrl Page Up and Ctrl Page Dn .

To assign a new key combination to the Page Up and Page Down commands, click the **Office button**, **Word Options**, **Customize**, then click **Keyboard shortcuts: Customize**. In the **Categories box**, scroll down to and click on **All Commands**. In the **Commands** box, scroll down to and click **GoToNextPage**.

Next, click in the **Press new shortcut key:** box and press a new key combination, such as Ctrl Shift Page Dn. If that key combination isn't already assigned to another function in Word, click the **Assign** button.

---

[2] In fact, the same problem occurs if you use the Browse by Object feature to search by anything other than Page—such as Comment.

[3] Alternatively, you can open the **Go To dialog** by pressing Ctrl G, click **Page**, click **Next** (or **Previous**), then click **Close**. **CAUTION**: Simply clicking Page in the Go To dialog and then clicking Close without clicking Next or Previous ***does not*** re-set the default search object.

Then, in the **Commands** box, scroll down to and click **GoToPreviousPage**. In the **Press new shortcut key:** box, press a different key combination, such as Ctrl Shift Page Up. If that key combination isn't already assigned to another function in Word, click the **Assign** button. When you've finished, click **Close**, and then be sure to click **OK** (not Cancel) to close out of Word Options.[4]

Now, when you wish to move up or down one full page, use your new keyboard shortcuts. They'll work regardless of whether you have recently used "Find," "Find and Replace," or "Browse by Object."

Where'd That Line Come From??

If automatic borders is turned on—which it appears to be by default in this version of Word—pressing the hyphen key three times, then pressing Enter, produces a horizontal line. That's great if you intended to create a line, but it can be disquieting if you didn't! To turn off automatic borders, click the **Office button**, **Proofing**, **AutoCorrect Options**, **AutoFormat As You Type tab**, and ***uncheck*** **Border lines**.

To delete the line, click the **paragraph symbol** (¶) in the **Paragraph group** (***or*** press **Ctrl Shift * [asterisk]**), which will turn on **Show Non-Printing Characters**, and delete the paragraph symbol ***above*** the line. (If that doesn't work, delete the paragraph symbol *below* the line.)

NOTE: Be sure to explore the AutoCorrect Options on the AutoFormat As You Type tab and uncheck any that you don't want (note that some options appear on both that tab and the AutoFormat tab; the options on the AutoFormat tab don't go into effect automatically, however, so you don't need to uncheck any of them). If you're unsure what a particular option does, click the question mark in the upper right-hand corner of the AutoCorrect dialog, then click the option.

The Curious Case of Mutating Section Breaks

Perhaps the most confounding aspect of working with section breaks is their tendency to mutate spontaneously from one type of break to another (for instance, from a "next page" break to a "continuous" break), which can create all sorts of headaches. Trying to delete the offending section break often makes things worse; you might find that section breaks that had been formatted correctly suddenly go bad, too.

---

[4] If you prefer, you can remove the Ctrl Page Up and Ctrl Page Dn keystrokes from Browse Object and assign them, instead, to GoToPreviousPage and GoToNextPage, respectively. In some ways, that might be a better option because you won't have to memorize a new keyboard shortcut for those functions.

What makes things particularly confusing is that each section break stores the formatting for the document section that ***precedes*** it. So when you delete a section break, the text ahead of it takes on the formatting of the section that comes immediately ***after***.[5]

But, complicating the situation further, the information that determines each section break's ***type***—that is, whether an individual section break is a "Next Page" or "Continuous" break—actually is stored in the section ***after*** that specific break. (***Huh?***) What that means is that when you delete a section break, the prior section break takes on the characteristics of the one you deleted. (In other words, although it is completely counter-intuitive, deleting a rogue "Continuous" section break doesn't help matters because it ***turns the previous break into a "Continuous" section break***.) Are you tearing your hair out yet?

Not to worry. Here's a workaround: First, switch to **Draft view** so that the section breaks in the document are easier to see / identify. Suppress your impulse to delete the misbehaving section break. Instead, put your cursor on—or, better yet, select—the ***next*** section break.[6] Open the **Page Setup dialog**, click the **Layout tab** and click to open the **Section start drop-down**. Select the type of section break you want, which probably is "**New page**." Make sure that choice is displayed, then click **OK**.

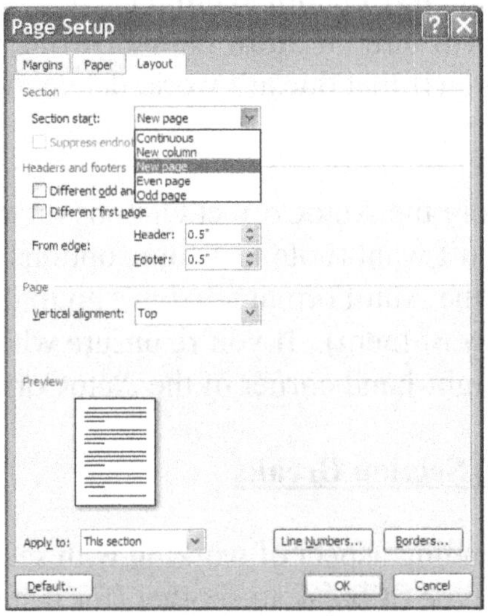

Page Setup dialog

The "bad" section break should change to reflect your "Start type" choice. Problem solved!

[5] In this regard, section breaks are similar to paragraph marks, which store the formatting information for the preceding text.

[6] Alternatively, you can double-click the section break, which will open the Page Setup dialog.

Demystifying Everyday Features

Changing Margins

Changing Margins for the Entire Document

The first thing to keep in mind about margins is that in Word, document margins are considered an attribute of ***page layout***. That means that you set margins for the entire document—as opposed to only a few paragraphs—via **Page Setup** on the **Page Layout tab**.

From the **Page Layout tab**, you can either (1) click **Margins**, then click **Custom Margins** at the bottom of the drop-down, or (2) click the **dialog launcher** at the lower right-hand side of the **Page Setup group**. (Or, as a quick alternative, you can open the **Page Setup dialog** from anywhere within Word by using the keyboard shortcut **Alt P, M, A** or **Alt P, S, P**.)

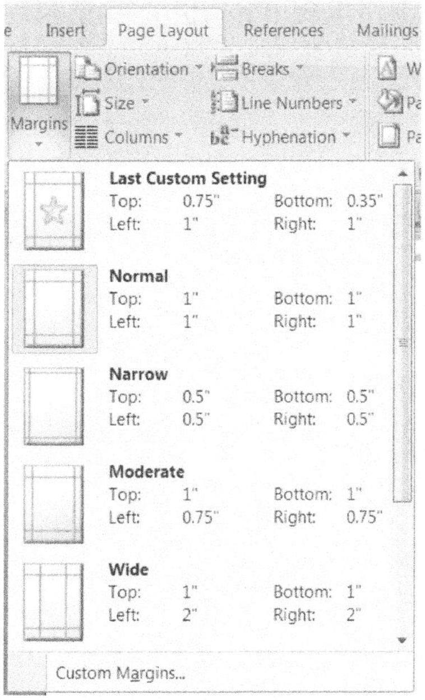

Page Layout, Custom Margins...

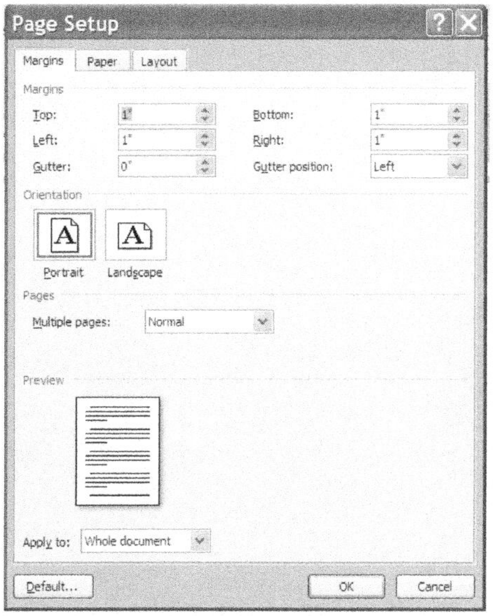

Page Setup Dialog

Once the **Page Setup dialog** is open, you can simply type numbers for the Top, Bottom, Left, and/or Right margins directly in the respective boxes. (Some people click the up/down arrows—known as "spinners"— but I find it faster to type the numbers in the boxes.) Note that you don't need to add quotation marks for inches after the digits; Word automatically inserts those for you. To save your settings, be sure to click **OK** rather than pressing Cancel or Esc.

If you want your new settings to apply to all future documents—i.e., to become the default settings—click the "**Default**" button at the bottom of the dialog before OK-ing out.

To display page margin borders, click the **Office button**, **Word Options**, **Advanced**, and under **Show document content**, click to check **Show text boundaries**, then click **OK**. (**CAUTION**: This setting will not affect other documents you have open on your screen, but will affect documents you open in the future.) These guidelines will not print with the document.

Changing Margins for Only Certain Paragraphs

Should you wish to change margins for only a few paragraphs—without changing the margins for the entire document, or for a section—just select the paragraphs and use the Paragraph dialog to change the left and/or right indent. (If the paragraphs are not contiguous, you will have to select them separately, rather than as a group.)

Alternatively, if the paragraphs are contiguous, you can do the following: **Select the text**, launch the **Page setup dialog**, and **change the margin settings**. ***Before clicking OK***, navigate to the **"Apply to:" drop-down** at the lower left-hand side of the dialog box and make sure it is set to "**Selected Text**." Then **OK** out of the dialog.

Because Word applies page margins on a section-by-section basis, the program automatically inserts section breaks before and after the text you selected in order to set that portion of the document off from other portions that use different margin settings.

Inserting Footnotes

1. To **create** a footnote in Word 2007, position the cursor where you want to insert a footnote and click the **References tab**, **Insert Footnote** (toward the left side of the Ribbon). Word inserts a footnote number code in both the body of the document (the footnote reference number) and the footnote area, and it puts the cursor in a special footnote editing screen so you can begin typing the note.

2. To move the cursor back to the document at the point where you left off, click the **Show Notes** button. (This button acts as a toggle that moves the cursor between the footnote reference in the document text and the footnote text itself.) **CAUTION**: Word normally puts the cursor ***to the left of*** the footnote number, not to the right of it. Be sure to move the cursor past the footnote number before you continue typing.

3. Note that you can see the text of the footnote without scrolling down to the footnote screen. Just position the mouse pointer over the footnote reference number in the document and Word will display a pop-up box containing the text of the footnote.

4. Should you wish to change any of the footnote options, click the arrow in the lower right-hand corner of the Footnotes group (the dialog launcher) to launch the Footnote and Endnote dialog.

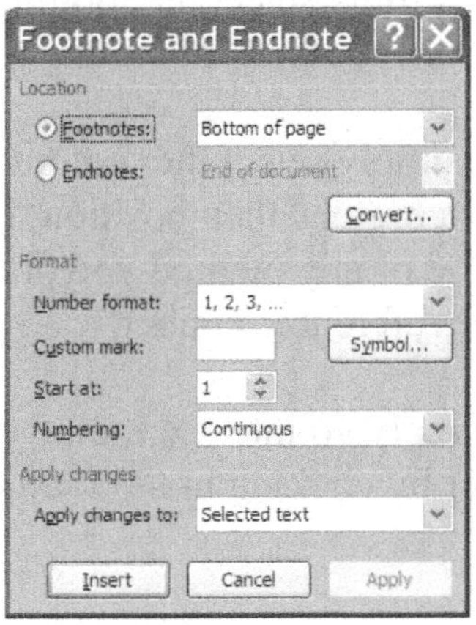

5. When the Footnote and Endnote dialog box appears, you can change the placement of the footnotes, the number format, the starting number, and whether numbering is continuous (the norm in legal documents) or restarts on every page or in every section of the document.

NOTE ALSO: If you switch to **Draft View** (by clicking the View tab, Draft View or clicking the Draft View button in the Status Bar), you can click the **Show Notes button** to display a footnote bar that splits the screen so that you can see both the footnote editing screen (sometimes called the note pane) and the document at the same time. Switching back to Print Layout view closes the note pane. (There's also an X at the far-right side of the note pane that you can click to close it.)

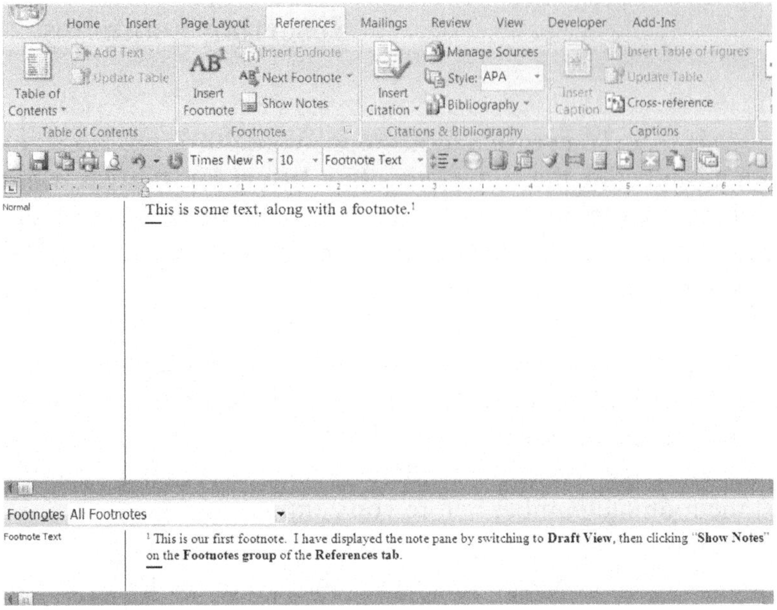

Document editing screen

Footnote bar

Footnote editing screen (note pane)

Note that you can drag the footnote bar up or down in order to view more or less of the footnote text / document text.

6. To **delete** a footnote, simply select the footnote number ***in the text*** and press the Delete key (or cut it using Ctrl X or any method for cutting text that you prefer).

7. To **move** a footnote, simply select the footnote reference number in the text and cut it (with Ctrl X or any method you prefer), then position the cursor where you want the number to be and paste it (with Ctrl V or any method you prefer). Alternatively, if you are good at using the mouse, you can drag the reference number.

8. To **edit** a footnote, simply go into the footnote (by double-clicking the footnote reference number in the document or by clicking in the footnote editing screen) and make your changes.

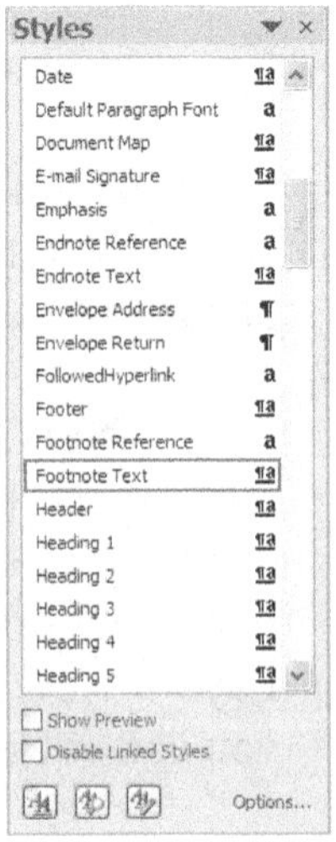

9. If you like, you can **change the appearance** of the footnote (such as the font face or size or the line spacing) by modifying the Footnote Text style. Navigate to the **Home** tab, **Styles** group and click the dialog launcher to open the **Styles Pane**.

10. When the Styles Pane appears, scroll down to **Footnote Text** and **right-click** it. Click **Modify** and, when the **Modify Style dialog** opens, make any changes you desire. If you want your changes to take effect in all new documents, be sure to follow Step 11 (on the next page).

11. Before closing the dialog box, click the "**New Documents based on this template**" radio button. That will ensure that the modifications you have made will apply to footnotes in future documents. (If you don't click that radio button, the changes will apply only in the current document.

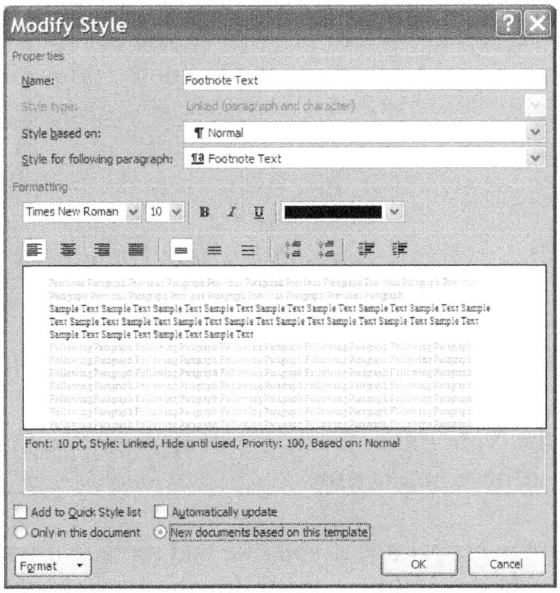

12. Once you have finished, **OK** out of the dialog and then click the **X** at the upper right-hand side of the Styles Pane to close it.

NOTE: If for some reason you need footnotes to start re-numbering with the value of 1 at some point in your document, you must insert a section break (next page) on the page before where the numbering should re-start. Otherwise, the note numbers will be continuous throughout your document.

SIDEBAR: Changing the Footnote Separator

If you have attempted to change the footnote separator line in Word 2007, you might have noticed that you can't select the line with the mouse. Left-clicking, right-clicking, and double-clicking are exercises in frustration; they move you between the note text and the note reference or they offer a command for opening the footnote options dialog, but they don't let you anywhere near the line itself.

To delete or change the separator line, you need to do the following:

1. Switch to **Draft view**. (**View tab**, **Document Views**, **Draft** or click the **Draft icon** in the **View Mini-Toolbar** in the Status Bar.)

2. Click the **References tab**, **Footnotes group**, **Show Notes**.

3. In the **Note Pane**, locate the **drop-down** and change it to display "**Footnote Separator**."

Now you can delete the separator if you like and replace it with a different line. There are various ways to insert a horizontal line; the following is a relatively simple method that also gives you control over the length and/or width of the line:

Navigate to the **Home tab**, **Paragraph group**, and click the **Borders button**, then click **Horizontal Line**. When the horizontal line appears, you can edit the length and width by ***right***-clicking the line, then clicking **Format Horizontal Line**. The resulting dialog box lets you change the width of the line (note that you can change the unit of measurement from percent to inches), the height of the line, the color, and/or the alignment (left, center, or right). **CAUTION**: By default, the line is center aligned. You'll probably want to switch to left alignment.

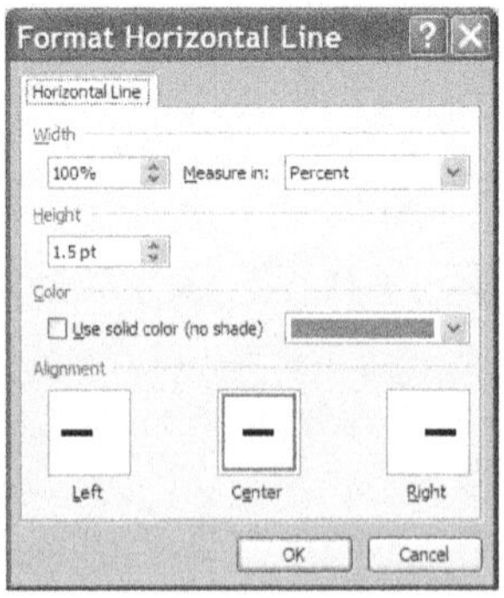

Make any changes you desire, then **OK** out. The change should persist throughout your document. (I'm not sure if there is a way to make the change permanent. Separator lines are stored in your **Normal style**, but it isn't readily apparent where or how to effectuate the change.)

If you decide you don't like your custom line, click the **Reset button** in the note pane.

Setting and Deleting Tabs

There are a couple of ways to set tabs in Word 2007. You can set them directly on the **horizontal Ruler**, or you can use the **Tabs dialog box**.

The horizontal Ruler is displayed by default. If you don't see it, click the **View tab** and make sure there is a check in the **Ruler** checkbox in the **Show/Hide group**.

The Tabs dialog is accessible from the **Paragraph dialog**, which in turn can be opened from the dialog launcher in either (1) the **Home tab**, **Paragraph group** or (2) the **Page Layout tab**, **Paragraph group**. (The keyboard shortcut to open the Paragraph dialog—regardless of which tab is active—is **Alt O, P.**)

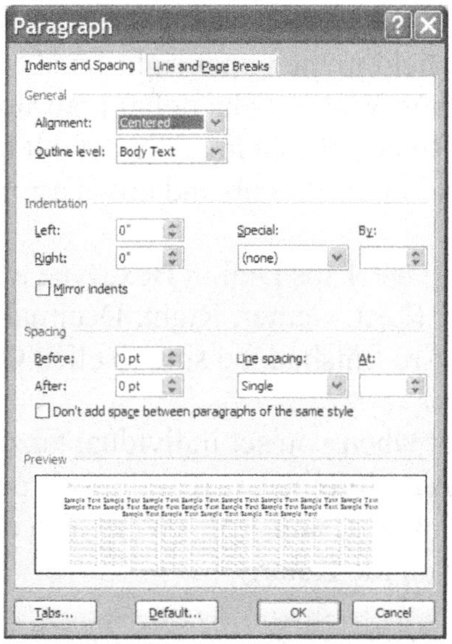

Note as well that you can open the Tabs dialog directly by double-clicking a tab stop within the Ruler (if you click the top border of the Ruler or a portion of the Ruler that is within the margins, the Page Setup dialog opens instead).

Keep in mind that in Word, tab formatting is associated with ***paragraphs***. Thus, if you change tab settings before you start typing or while you are typing, the new settings will be copied to successive paragraphs when you press the Enter key. However, if you need to adjust tab settings in a portion of the document you have already typed, ***you must select the paragraph(s) you want the new settings to affect***.

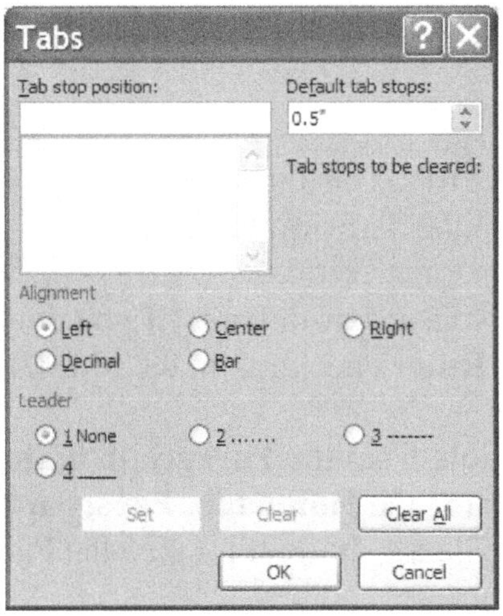

Tabs Dialog Box

Note the Default tab stops field in the upper right-hand corner of the Tabs dialog box. By default, tabs are set every half inch in Word. (The default tab stops appear as short vertical marks in the gray area below the Ruler.) To change the default tab setting, just type a new setting in the Default tab stops field or use the up and down arrows to adjust the setting.

To set custom tabs by using the Tabs Dialog Box, type a setting in the Tab stop position box, set the alignment if necessary (Left, Center, Right, Decimal, or Bar[1]), set any desired Leader, then click Set. When you're finished, be sure to click OK.

CAUTION: Be aware that when you set individual tabs, ***any existing tabs to the left of your custom settings will be cleared***. In other words, if you type 1.75 in the Tab stop position box, Word will delete the tabs set at .5, 1, and 1.5! (Word also clears tabs to the left of your first custom tab if you set tabs directly on the Ruler.)

Another way to clear individual tabs from within the dialog box is by clicking the setting in the Tab stop position box and then clicking the Clear button.

To insert custom tab settings directly on the Ruler, first click the Tab type button at the far left of the Ruler to change to the appropriate tab type. The "L" symbol sets Left tabs; the upside-down "T" symbol (⊥) sets Center tabs; the backwards "L" symbol sets Right tabs; and the inverted "T" with a period to the right of the bar of the "T" sets Decimal Tabs. Once you have the Tab type button set the way you want, just left-click at the point on the Ruler where you want to insert a tab stop. (To clear tab settings, just drag the tab symbols off the Ruler.)

TYPES OF TABS

(NOTE: In the following examples, **X** marks the location of the tab stop.)

---

[1]Definitions of Left, Center, Right, Decimal, and Bar tabs follow below.

Left tabs (the most commonly used type): Text moves *to the right* from the tab stop.

X

This is an example of a Left tab.

Right tabs: Text moves *to the left* from the tab stop.

X

This is an example of a Right tab.

Center tabs: Text *centers around* the tab stop.

X

This is an example of a Center tab.

Decimal tabs: Text (consisting of numbers) *aligns at a decimal point*.

.**X**

This is an example of a Decimal tab 1,279,567.85

734.27

Bar tabs[2]: Word inserts *a vertical line* at the tab stop.

This is an example of a Bar tab. Note: Word extends the bar when you press Enter (which copies the paragraph formatting containing the bar tab to the next paragraph) or if you press the Tab key continuously.	You can type text on either side of the "bar."

TYPES OF LEADERS

NOTE: Leaders work with **Right tabs**. They move *to the left* from the leader tab stop to the previous tab stop.

Dot...**X**
Dash --**X**
Underline____**X**

[2] Not to be confused with your running account for drinks you've bought at the local tavern.

<u>WHERE DID IT GO?—Spell-Checker</u>

The **Spelling & Grammar** command has been moved to the left-hand side of the **Review tab,** in the **Proofing group**.

Note that you still can use the **F7** keystroke to start the **Spell-Checker**, as in previous versions of Word.

Creating and Using "Quick Parts" (Formerly Called AutoText)

Word's Quick Parts feature allows you to insert commonly used phrases, boilerplate paragraphs, signature blocks, and other frequently used text and graphics into your documents with just a few keystrokes. Note that Quick Parts are referred to at times as Building Blocks.

To create a Quick Parts entry, first type and format the text, and insert any graphics you wish to use. Then select everything—including any tabs or other formatting you wish to incorporate[1]—and click the **Insert tab**, **Text group**, **Quick Parts**, **Save Selection to Quick Part Gallery...** Alternatively, once you have selected the text, you can bring up the Create New Building Block dialog simply by pressing **Alt F3**.

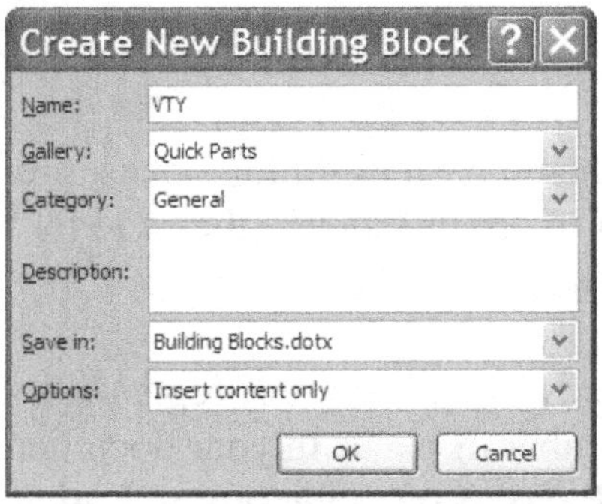

At this point, type an abbreviation in the "Name" field. This abbreviation, plus the F3 key, is what you will use to insert the Quick Parts entry into your document. Note that the Quick Parts feature ***is NOT case-sensitive***—in other words, the abbreviation VTY is the same, in effect, as vty, and Vty (and all other permutations).

You can add a brief description in the Description field if it will help you remember what your abbreviation does, but that step is optional. If you like, you can change the gallery, as well.

Note that the default "Save in" location is the Building Blocks.dotx template—each user has one.[2] Quick Parts stored in that template will be available to the user regardless of which template he or she is using at any given time (such as a pleading template or letterhead). Should you wish to create Quick Parts for use only with one specific template, you can change the "Save in" location to that template.

---

[1] Also, if you wish to preserve any paragraph formatting, be sure to select the paragraph symbol at the end of the paragraph along with any text and graphics. To ensure that you select the paragraph symbol, tab indicators, and the like, be sure to turn on Show Non-Printing Characters by clicking the **paragraph icon** on the **Home tab**, **Paragraph group** (or pressing **Ctrl Shift ***) before selecting the text (and graphics).

[2]There actually are two copies of the Building Blocks template on each machine. One, located under Programs\Microsoft\Office 12, is the generic template that comes with Word; the other, located in the individual user data folder, is the working copy. The latter is the one where the user's customized entries are stored. **NOTE**: It is a good idea to back up this customized template to another location from time to time because it occasionally gets corrupted.

After creating your Quick Parts entry, click **OK**.

To insert your Quick Parts entry at the cursor position, either (1) click the **Insert tab**, **Quick Parts**, locate your entry in the list, and click **Insert**, ***or*** (2) simply **type the abbreviation** (assuming you remember it!) and press **F3**.

Creating a Page X of Y Quick Part

In a blank document, type "Page" (without quotation marks) and press the Spacebar.

Next, press **Alt Shift P** (which will insert a page number code for the current page) and press the Spacebar.

Type "of" (without quotation marks) and press the Spacebar.

Press **Alt I, F**, and when the **Field dialog** opens, press the letter "**N**" as many times as necessary to move the cursor to "**NumPages**" (the code for the total number of pages in the document), and then click **OK**.

You should see "Page X of Y," where X represents the page number of the current page and Y represents the total number of pages in your document. Select the text (and codes) and click the **Insert tab**, **Quick Parts**, **Save Selection to Quick Part Gallery**. When the **Create New Building Block dialog** appears, type an abbreviation such as PXOY, then click OK.

To insert the Page X of Y entry, position the cursor where you want the text and codes to appear, then **type your abbreviation** and **press F3**.

Managing / Deleting Quick Parts Entries

When you click Insert, Quick Parts, then click Building Block Organizer, you will see that there are already a number of Quick Parts entries that come with the program. Microsoft organizes them into Galleries and Categories (a Category, such as AutoText or Built-In, can span multiple Galleries). By default, your new entries go in the Quick Parts gallery, but you can create your own galleries and assign existing or new Quick Parts to one of those galleries if you like. It's basically a matter of organization and how the entries appear when you open the Building Block Organizer.

Note that clicking the Gallery heading sorts the entries alphabetically by Gallery name; clicking the Category heading sorts the entries alphabetically by Category name; and clicking the Name heading sorts the entries alphabetically by name (abbreviation). You might have to click a heading twice; one click sorts in descending order and another click sorts in ascending order (or vice versa).

Because there are so many entries in the Organizer, you might choose to create, and assign your entries to, a new gallery called AAA (or that starts with an underscore character), then sort by Gallery. That way, your most frequently used entries will be easier to locate in the Organizer.

Of course, if you remember the abbreviations, you can insert entries simply by typing the abbreviation and pressing the F3 key.

And you can delete entries that you are unlikely to use. Doing so has the added benefit of making it easier to find your own entries in the list. Just go into the Organizer, click to select an entry, and click the Delete button. Word will prompt you to make sure you wish to delete the entry. If you're sure, click Yes. Unfortunately, you can't select multiple entries; you have to select and delete one at a time.

Sharing Quick Parts

To share Quick Parts with other users, create a new blank template. Then create Quick Parts from within that template, making sure the "Save in" field displays the name of the new template rather than the Building Blocks template or any other default. Continue creating your entries in and saving them to the new template.

Before distributing the template to others in the firm, delete any content (i.e., the "expanded" Quick Parts) and save the blank template. Even though you have deleted the content, the Quick Parts remain stored in the template.

When you give the template to others, instruct them to store it in the "language" subfolder (1033 for American English) in their Building Blocks folder (in Windows XP, the path is: C:\Documents and Settings\<User Name>\Application Data\Microsoft\Document Building Blocks\1033; in Vista and Windows 7, it is C:\Users\<User Name>\AppData\Roaming\Microsoft\Document Building Blocks\1033). Note that they might have to close and reopen Word before the entries will appear in the Building Blocks Organizer.

To share ***existing*** Quick Parts, create a new template and then, one by one, edit the properties of the Quick Parts entries to change the "Save in" location to the new template. (From the Building Blocks Organizer, click to select an entry, click the "Edit Properties" button, and click the "Save in" drop-down. Select the new template. Repeat those steps for each Quick Parts entry you wish to distribute to other users.)

Note that you are ***moving***, ***not copying***, the Quick Parts entries to the new template, which means they might not be globally available to you (if you are working on a document created with a different template).

Importing Your Word 2003 AutoText Entries into Word 2007

Unless you have made a point of saving your Word 2003 AutoText entries to one or more customized templates, they are stored in your old Normal.dot template from that version. To import them into Word 2007, you'll need to copy that template into the same folder where your personalized Building Blocks template (Building Blocks.dotx) is located. That way, the AutoText entries will load when you open the Building Blocks Organizer.

First, locate the Word 2003 NORMAL template. (Note that if you installed Word 2007 on the same computer with Word 2003, the installation process changed the name of your original Normal.dot template to "Normal11.dot.") Make a copy of the old template and rename the copy "AutoText.dot" or "AutoText.dotx."

Next, paste the renamed template into the folder containing the user-specific Building Blocks template, as detailed on the previous page in the section about sharing Quick Parts. (In Windows XP, the location is C:\Documents and Settings\<User Name>\Application Data\Microsoft\Document Building Blocks\1033. In Windows Vista and Windows 7, it is C:\Users\<User Name>\AppData\Roaming\Microsoft\Document Building Blocks\1033.)

The next time you open the Building Blocks Organizer, you should see your AutoText entries under an AutoText Gallery. (If you click the Gallery heading to sort the entries alphabetically, all of the AutoText entries will be displayed together.)

Working With Headers and Footers

As you might know already, headers and footers work very differently in Word from the way they work in WordPerfect. In WordPerfect, it is relatively easy to insert two separate headers and two separate footers (actually, more than two); each can be formatted independently of the other(s).

In Word, although you can create multiple headers and footers, there is a bit of a trick to doing so. First, you have to break the document into ***sections***. After you do so, all headers and footers in the various sections are ***linked together***, such that if you change one, the others change as well. In order to insert a different header (or footer), you must navigate to the document section where you want to create a new header (or footer) and ***break the link*** to the header (or footer) in the previous section. I'll provide step-by-step instructions below.

In Word, headers and footers are considered "hidden text" or a separate "layer" of the document. (You'll notice that they appear grayed out when you are working in the normal document editing screen.) That "hidden" attribute might explain why the Headers and Footers command was found on the View menu in previous versions of Word.

To insert a header or footer, click the **Insert tab**, **Header & Footer** group, and click either **Header** or **Footer** (as appropriate). A drop-down opens. You can select one of the pre-formatted header or footer styles ***or*** simply click "**Edit Header**" (or "**Edit Footer**") at the bottom of the drop-down. When you do so, Word puts you in the header or footer editing screen, and the Ribbon morphs into a context-sensitive **Header & Footer Tools Design tab** (shown below).

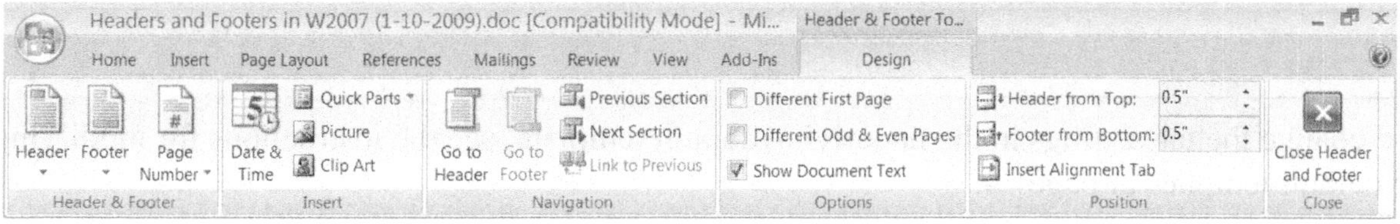

Note that this tab makes it easy to change the header or footer margins (see the **Position group**) and to choose various formatting options.

In the screenshot above, in the **Navigation group**, "Go to Header" is active and "Go to Footer" is grayed out because I chose to insert a footer rather than a header (and my cursor was in the footer editing screen when I took the screenshot). If I had inserted a header or moved my cursor to the header editing screen, the reverse would be true.

You can move between the header and footer editing screens by either (1) clicking "Go to Header" (or "Go to Footer") in the **Navigation group**, ***or*** (2) by pressing the down arrow or the up arrow on the keyboard as appropriate (down arrow to move from the Header screen to the Footer screen, up arrow to move from the Footer screen to the Header screen).

Headers and footers in Word are pre-configured with a center tab at the 3" mark and a right tab at the 6" mark. That makes it easy to insert a centered page number and a right-aligned file name and path code. However, be aware that if you use L/R margins that differ from the default margins in Word (1.25"), 3" won't be true center and 6" won't be the true right margin. In order to compensate, you'll have to drag the tab markers on the ruler bar in both the header and the footer editing screens.[1]

If all you want to do is insert one header and/or one footer, just type the text you want (and/or insert the codes you want), and click the **Close** button, and you're done.

Using the "Different First Page" Option

But let's say you want to do something more complex. For example, you plan to type a multi-page letter that will go on your firm's letterhead, and you want to insert a header on every page except the first. Word provides a couple of fairly easy ways to accomplish this task.

Method 1:

Assuming you have created at least one page break in your document, click the **Insert tab**, **Header & Footer**, click **Header**, then click **Edit Header** and click to put a check in the "**Different First Page**" box.[2]

---

[1] To change the tab settings in the underlying default template, see the instructions for modifying the default template at page 74.

[2] One caution about using the "Different First Page" option: If you decide to use it to "suppress" page numbering on the first page of pleadings, you might find that the pleading paper disappears, as well. The reason is that the pleading paper is within the header (which might be a confusing concept, since the lines and numbering appear at the sides of the page), and using the different first page option for a header ***or for a footer*** essentially deletes the code that creates the pleading paper. The problem occurs because headers and footers are linked together in Word.

There is another workaround for the vanishing pleading-paper problem (see the Sidebar on page 104).

Another caution: If you decide to use the "Different First Page" option, be sure to ***turn that option off*** (i.e., uncheck it) in the other sections of the document. (Make sure your cursor is in the correct header or footer when you disable the option.) Otherwise, ***each section*** will have both a regular Header/Footer ***and*** a First Page Header/Footer—which can be very confusing.

Look at the header editing screen and note whether your cursor is in the **First Page Header** or the main **Header**. If necessary, move the cursor from the First Page Header to the Header by clicking the **Next Section** button on the ribbon. To move back to the First Page Header, click the **Previous Section** button.

If in fact you are working on a multi-page letter, remember to leave the First Page Header blank (because the first page will be printed on letterhead).

Method 2:

With your cursor somewhere in the first page of the letter, click the **Page Layout tab** and launch the **Page Setup** dialog. Click the **Layout tab** of the dialog box, then click to check the "**Different First Page**" option and click **OK**. Note that you can select this option even if you haven't yet typed more than one page of text (or created a hard page break in the document by pressing Ctrl Enter), but you must insert at least one additional page before setting up the main header (the one that will go on all pages but page 1).

Once you have done so, click the **Insert tab**, **Header & Footer group**, and click **Header**, **Edit Header**. Look at the lower left side of the header editing screen to see if it is labeled **First Page Header** or simply **Header**. If the former, be sure to click **Next Section** in order to move the cursor to the editing screen for the main **Header**. Then type the text of the header and click the **Close Header and Footer** button.

TIP: An easy way to make space for the letterhead—and ensure that the text on page 1 starts in the right place—is to insert the cursor into the First Page Header and press the Enter key several times. You might have to experiment to get the right amount of space.

NOTE: If you are creating a more complex document that requires multiple headers and footers, check the Status Bar to see which section your cursor is located in before launching the Page Setup dialog. [3] Either enable or disable the "**Different First Page**" option as appropriate, making sure that the "**Apply to:**" **drop-down** at the bottom of the dialog is displaying "**This section**." Then **OK** out of the dialog and repeat these steps, if necessary, for the other sections of the document.

[3] In previous versions of Word, "Display Section" was enabled on the Status Bar, making it easy to see which section your cursor was in. (Every blank Word document already comprises one section.) However, Display Section is disabled by default in Word 2007. You can change this setting easily by right-clicking within the Status Bar and checking Section, then clicking anywhere outside the pop-up menu to close it.

Creating Multiple Headers and/or Footers

If you want to create more than one header or footer, things become a little more complicated. In Word, in order to have different headers and footers, you must create—and put the separate headers or footers in—different ***sections***.

Let's assume you want to create two different footers. First, you need to insert a section break, which will split the document into two sections. Position the cursor at the bottom of the page ***immediately before*** the page where you want the new footer to go into effect. Then click the **Page Layout tab, Breaks, Section Break, Next Page.**[4]

Next, click the **Insert tab, Header & Footer group**, **Footer**, **Edit Footer**. Note which footer editing screen you're in (it should say **Footer -Section 2-** or **Footer -Section 1-**). Note as well whether the words "Same as Previous" appear at the right-hand side of the footer editing screen (just below it).

Make sure your cursor is in the Section 2 footer editing screen, and, if the words "Same as Previous" do appear, click the **Link to Previous** button (labeled "Same as Previous" in some earlier versions of Word). Doing so will ***UNLINK*** the Section 2 footer from the Section 1 footer—allowing you to create two different footers. After breaking the link, you can type the text for the Section 2 footer.

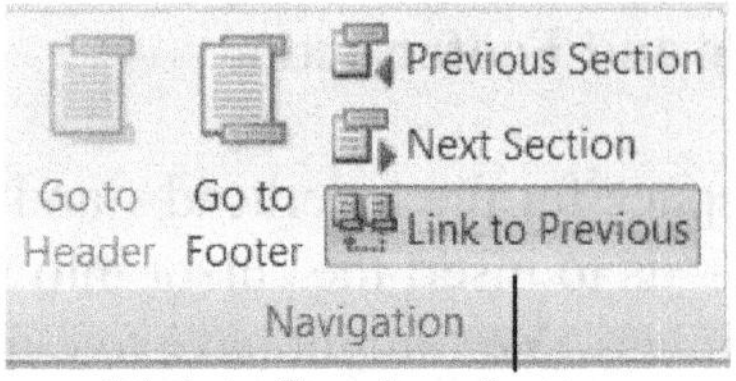

Link to Previous button

NOTE: This is a critical step. If you don't turn off "Link to Previous," whatever you type in the Section 1 footer will replace what you have typed in the Section 2 footer—and vice versa.

When you have finished typing the text in the Section 2 footer (and the Section 1 footer), click the **Close Header and Footer** button.

If you want to create another (different) footer, you need to insert another "Next Page" section break on the page before the page where you want the new footer to start. Before you start typing the text for the additional footer, be sure to position your cursor in the footer editing screen for the new section, and then turn off "Link to Previous" by clicking the Link to Previous button.

The same general steps, and precautions, apply to the creation of multiple headers.

---

[4] Assuming you have enabled "Display Section" per the instructions in footnote 3, the Status Bar should indicate that your cursor is in Section 2.

CAUTION: Sometimes Word will change a "Next Page" section break into a "Continuous" section break with no warning and for no apparent reason. If that happens, it can cause problems with your document. (To see which type of section breaks exist in your document, switch from Print Layout view to Draft view by clicking the **View tab, Draft.**[5]) For a solution, see the tip on page 81.

ANOTHER CAUTION: Formatting for each section of your document is contained in the section breaks. (Each section break stores the formatting codes ***for the section preceding the break***.) If you accidentally delete a section break, the text will take on the formatting of the ***following*** section (i.e., it will be affected by the codes within the next section break). So be sure to click the **Undo button** on the **Quick Access Toolbar** (or press **Ctrl Z**) as soon as you realize what happened.

---

[5] **TIP**: You might find it helpful to switch to Draft view whenever you are working with section breaks. In Draft view, section breaks are graphically represented as double lines that extend across the page.

SIDEBAR: Tips for Working With the "Different First Page" Option

Creating and Editing a Second-Page Header (or Footer) in a Template

Many people use the "Different First Page" option to set up a letterhead template. It's an ideal method because it allows you to have a blank header on the first page (a placeholder for the firm's printed letterhead) and a header starting on page two and continuing on all subsequent pages (if any) that contains the recipient's name, the date of the letter, and a page number code.

In order to create a header for the second section, you'll need to insert a page break in the body of the letter. However, you should delete the page break (and any extra hard returns) in the final draft of the template, since many, if not most, letters are limited to a single page. But what if you need to edit the second header in the template at some later point? Is there an easier way to do so than to create another hard page break that you'll have to remove?

Indeed there is. Just go into the header editing screen (**Insert tab**, **Header**, **Edit Header**) and click to ***uncheck*** "**Different First Page**." When you do, Word should put the cursor in the main (second-page) Header editing screen, as opposed to the First Page Header editing screen. Make any desired changes, then click to ***check*** "Different First Page," close out of the Header editing screen, save the template, and close it.[1]

Note that this principle works exactly the same way with respect to setting up and editing a pleading footer where the page number is "suppressed" on (or deleted from) the caption page but not on the other pages of the document. Just make sure that your cursor is in the ***footer editing screen*** when you click the "Different First Page" checkbox.

How to Prevent the Pleading Paper Lines From Disappearing

As discussed in footnote 2 on page 100 above, using the "Different First Page" option in a pleading can cause the pleading lines and numbers to disappear. If you're concerned about that possibility, go into the header editing screen on the first page of the document and copy the very first paragraph symbol. That symbol contains the formatting codes for the header, including the graphics (pleading lines and numbering).

Next, click the "Different First Page" option. Don't panic if the pleading paper disappears. Instead, simply paste the paragraph symbol at the top of the first-page header. The pleading paper should come back. Once it does, you should be able to create a first-page footer with a "suppressed" page number (i.e., a placeholder instead of a page number code) and a different footer for the second and following pages that has a page number code above the horizontal line.

---

[1] **CAUTION:** When "Different First Page" is checked, sometimes the main header or footer editing screen becomes hidden. This odd, rather unexpected behavior can be confusing. If you are working with headers or footers and you are having trouble finding the main header or footer editing screen, try unchecking "Different First Page"—if only temporarily. The hidden header or footer editing screen should reappear.

Using Field Codes/Fill-in Fields

Field codes have many uses in MS Word. For example, as shown in the section that starts on page 151, you can insert ***SEQ codes*** from the Fields dialog box to produce automatic numbers such as those used in headings for discovery and discovery responses (e.g., Interrogatories and Responses to Interrogatories, or Requests for Production of Documents and Responses to Requests for Production of Documents).

Another example is ***Fill-In fields***, which you typically embed in templates to prompt the person working on the document to enter variable information at certain points in the document. (Fill-In fields are somewhat akin to variables in keyboard merges in WordPerfect.)

The Fields Dialog Box

Most people insert field codes via the **Fields dialog box**. Because the user interface has changed dramatically, perhaps the easiest way to open the **Fields dialog box** in Word 2007 is by using the key combination **Alt I, F**.

In this version of Word, the Fields command—which used to be on the Insert menu—has been moved and renamed. It now appears in a couple of places: (1) on the **Insert tab**, on the **Text Group**, under **Quick Parts** (toward the bottom of the drop-down), and (2) on the **Mailings tab**, on the **Write & Insert Fields group**, under **Rules**.

As for option (2), specific Field codes are available from Rules (which opens the Fields dialog), but note that Rules is grayed out—i.e., not activated—unless you are in a merge document (a document that contains merge codes)! So if you want to use a Field code without beginning a merge or opening a merge document, you should use the keyboard shortcut.

Using Fill-In fields

As mentioned above, Fill-In fields in Word are somewhat comparable to keyboard merges in WordPerfect.

In order for Fill-In fields to work properly, you need to do the following:

(1) embed them in a template;

(2) put the template in the default template location in Word (note that you might have to copy the templates to each staff member's computer or put them in a shared network location); and

(3) open a new document based on the template by using the **Office button**, **New**.

Note that after clicking Office button, New, users might have to click "**My templates….**" in order to locate the template that contains the Fill-In fields (depending on where you've stored the template).

Creating a Template With Embedded Fill-In fields

You can start with a blank document or with a form you're already using. In either case, position the cursor at the first point where you want variable information to be inserted. Then open the **Fields dialog** (again, an easy way is by using the keyboard shortcut **Alt I**, **F**) and locate the **Fill-In fields** command. One quick way to get to that command is by pressing the letter "F" as many times as necessary to move the cursor down through the Field names. In this case, pressing "F" three times took me to the Fill-In field.

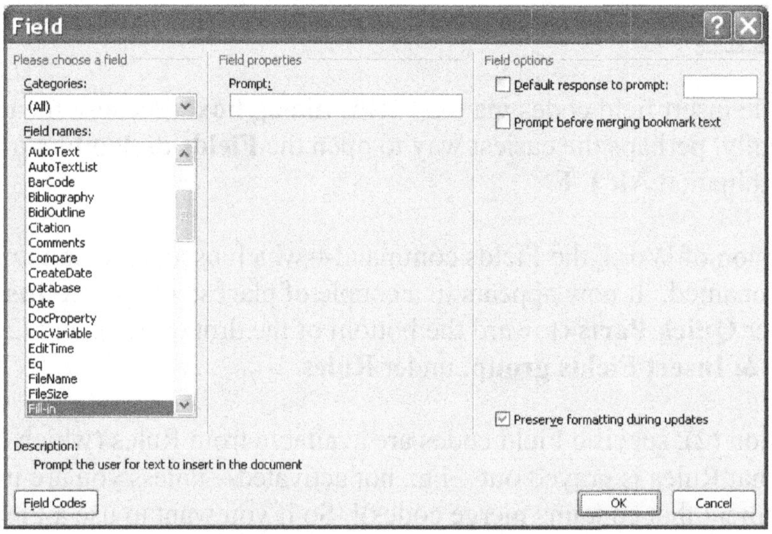

At this point, you have the option of **adding a specific prompt** to help guide the users (see the top center of the dialog box). You also have the option of setting up a **default response** (see the upper right-hand corner of the dialog box), which will be inserted automatically into the document if the person filling in the fields in response to the prompts leaves that field blank.

When you are ready to insert the field code into the document, click **OK** ***or*** press the **Enter key**.

A **prompt box** will appear. Since you are still in the process of creating the template, don't type anything in the box. (If you like, you can type a placeholder such as an "X," which users will be able to type over when they are prompted to enter text in the box.) Simply click "**OK**," and the code will be inserted at the cursor position.

Note that unless you specifically choose to display the codes while creating the template, you won't be able to see them, which can make things somewhat challenging. In order to display the codes, press **Alt F9**. To hide the codes, simply press Alt F9 again (it's a toggle).

Continue inserting fill-in field codes at appropriate places in the document. Then, when everything is to your liking, save it as a template.

To save the template, click the **Office button** (*or* press Alt F), then click **Save As** (*or* press the letter A). Navigate to the folder where templates are stored. If you are using Windows XP, it is likely to be something like the following:

C:\Documents and Settings\<User Name>\Application Data\Microsoft\Templates

In Windows Vista and Windows 7, the templates folder usually is located here:

C:\Users\<UserName>\AppData\Roaming\Microsoft\Templates

Be sure to save the document as a template. Note that you have a choice of saving the template as a **Word 2007 template (*.dotx)** or as a **Word 97-2003 template (*.dot)**. If you think you might also use the template in an earlier version of Word, you should save it as the latter, since the dotx format isn't backwards compatible.

Using a Document Based on the Template

Once you've saved the template, users should open it by clicking the **Office button, New**. If the template is not visible in the **Blank and recent** areas, they can try the **My templates....** link. In either case, to open a doc based on the template, double-click the template or click "Create" or "OK" (as appropriate).

When the doc opens, the first prompt will pop up. **Type the information** and click **OK**. (**NOTE**: pressing Enter won't dismiss the prompt. Rather, it will merely move the insertion point down to the next line within the prompt.)

The next prompt (if any) will pop up. Continue as in the previous paragraph.

When you have filled in the last prompt, you'll be returned to the document, where you can make any necessary changes.

Note that if you close the document and reopen it, you won't be prompted to fill in the fields. ***Prompting occurs only when you open a new document based on a template that was created with Fill-In fields embedded in it.*** However, you can press F11 to move your cursor to the first field in the document, then press F9 to open the pop-up for that field, type any text you want, and click OK to dismiss the pop-up. To continue, repeat the F11, F9 sequence.

WHERE DID IT GO? Macros

If you've scoured the Ribbon for a Macros command, you're probably completely at a loss. Where the heck did it go?

For some reason, Microsoft moved the Macros command(s) to the **View tab**. There's a **Macros group**, with a **Macros drop-down** that you can use to record macros (or to view the built-in macros), at the far-right side of the tab.

In addition, Microsoft added icons for Macros, Record Macro, and Macro Security to the **Developer tab** (in the **Code group**), which by default doesn't display in the Ribbon. However, it's surprisingly easy to add the Developer tab to the Ribbon. Just click the **Office button**, **Word Options**, and it's right there in the "**Popular**" category under "**Top options for working with Word**" ("**Show Developer tab in the Ribbon**"). Click to check the box, then **OK** out of Word Options.

So... if it's such a popular option, why not display the tab by default? Hm. Maybe in the next release?

Creating a Simple Macro to Print the Current Page[1]

In Word 2007, there are three different ways to start recording macros:

1. Click the **Macro icon** on the **Status Bar**; ***or***

2. Navigate to the **View tab**, **Macros group**, click the **Macros drop-down** and then click **Record Macro…**; ***or***

3. Display the **Developer tab**, an optional tab that ordinarily is hidden, then click the **Record** button on that tab.

   To display the Developer tab, click the **Office button**, **Word Options**. The dialog should open with the "**Popular**" options at the forefront. Underneath "**Top options for working with Word**" you'll see a checkbox labeled "**Show Developer tab in the Ribbon**." Click to put a check in the box, then click **OK** to close the dialog.

Whichever method you choose, you will see the **Record Macro dialog box**, which looks something like the following:

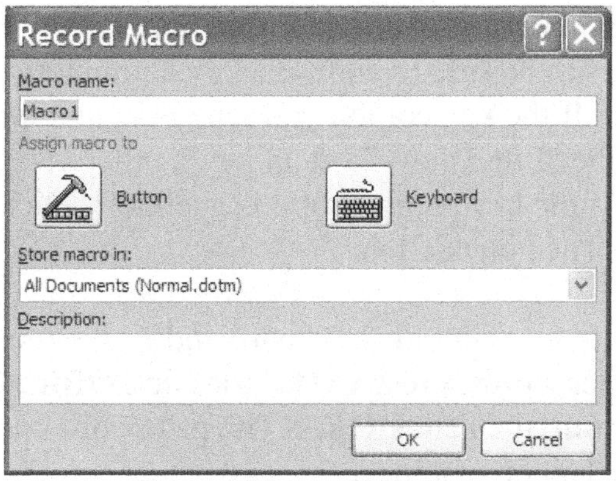

Record Macro dialog box

In the **Macro name** box, type a short name for the macro that identifies what the macro does and is easy to remember, such as PrintCurrentPage. **NOTE**: Spaces are not allowed in macro names.

You can type a description of the macro in the **Description** box. This is an optional step, but it has two advantages: (1) It permits other users who open the Macros dialog box to figure out what the macro does; and (2) if you assign the macro to a toolbar, the description you type will appear on the toolbar button that runs the macro. A good description for our sample macro might be "Prints the current page."

---

[1]This section of the book is intended to introduce you to the process of writing (recording) macros in MS Word. I've deliberately chosen a very simple macro to get you started.

NOTE: By default, the macro will be stored in your NORMAL template. If you prefer, you can use the **Store macro in:** drop-down and choose to store it in the current document.

At this point, you can either create a **button** so that you can run the macro from the Quick Access Toolbar or designate a **keyboard shortcut** for the macro. Let's start by assigning a keyboard shortcut; later on, we'll also put a button to run the macro on the QAT.

First, click the **Keyboard** button in the section of the dialog box labeled "**Assign macro to:**." You will see a **Customize Keyboard** dialog similar to the following:

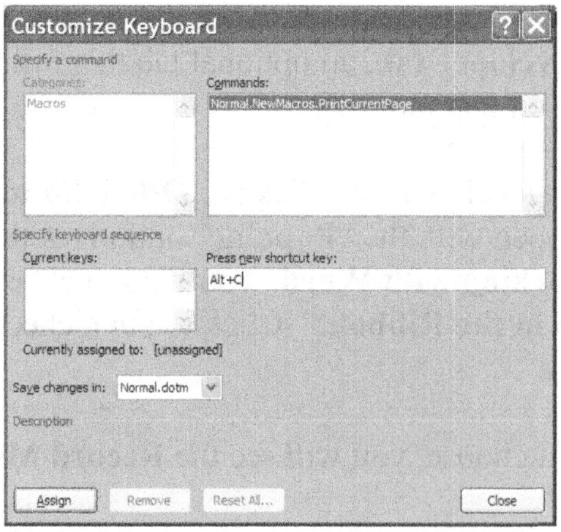

Type a key combination in the "**Press new shortcut key:**" box. In the example above, I used Alt C. The main thing is to be sure to choose a key combination that hasn't already been assigned to another function. If the key combo you type is in use, you'll see "Currently assigned to:" and the function below the "Press new shortcut key"; otherwise, you'll see "Currently assigned to: [unassigned]." If the key combination is available, click the **Assign** button to assign that shortcut to your macro. Then click **Close**.

Now create your macro by using the keyboard and/or the mouse as if you were going to print the current page. In other words, press **Ctrl P** (or click **Office button**, **Print**), then click the **Current Page radio button**, then click **OK**. (The page your cursor is in should print, unless you don't have a printer attached or running.)

Next, stop recording the macro by clicking the **Macros drop-down** in the **Macros group** on the **View tab**, then clicking the "**Stop Recording**" icon (or clicking the "**Stop Recording**" icon in the **Code group** of the **Developer tab.**) Alternatively, you can click the **Macro Recorder** icon in the Status Bar.

To run (play) the macro, you can simply press Alt C (or whatever key combination you assigned to the macro)—***or*** you can open the Macros dialog by pressing **Alt F8** (or clicking the **Macros button** in the **Macros group** on the **View tab *or*** the **Macros icon** in the **Developer tab**), scrolling to the PrintCurrentPage macro, and either clicking **Run *or* double-clicking** the macro name.

You can assign the macro to the Quick Access Toolbar after you have recorded the macro. To do so, click the **Office Button**, **Word Options**, **Customize**, then click the **Choose commands from: drop-down** and select **Macros**.

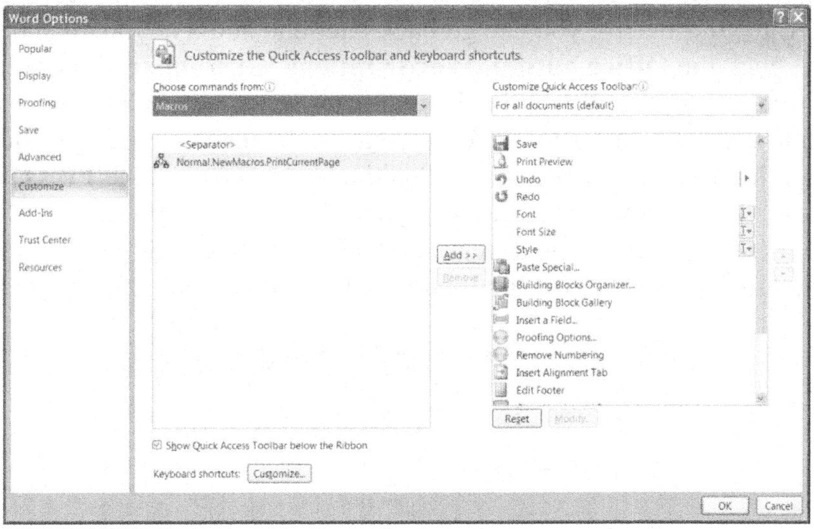

Click to select the macro and then click the **Add button** in the middle column to add the macro to the Quick Access Toolbar. Once you've done so, a grayed-out "**Modify**" button underneath the **Customize Quick Access Toolbar box** will become active. **Click** the "**Modify**" button. A dialog similar to the one shown below will open.

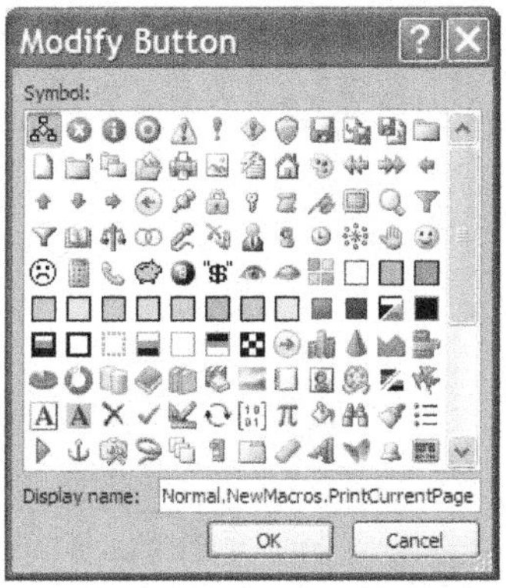

Note that this dialog allows you to type a "**Display name**" for the macro—one that is more user-friendly than the VBA-coded name Microsoft assigns when you record the macro. For example, I've chosen to use the display name "**Print Current Page**" (without the quotation marks). (Display names can have blank spaces between letters.) You can simply put your cursor in the "**Display name**" box and delete or type over the existing name.

Before OK-ing out of the Modify Button dialog, you can select an icon for the macro by double-clicking it. I've chosen one that looks like a printer.

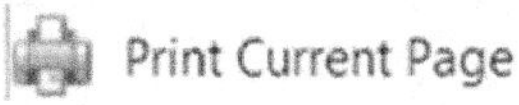

Now I have an icon on the Quick Access Toolbar that I can click to print whatever page my cursor is in.

Note that if you choose to run the macro via a button rather than a keyboard shortcut when you first create your macro, you can go back later and add a keyboard shortcut to the macro. To do so, click the **Office button**, **Word Options**, **Customize**, then click the **Keyboard shortcuts: Customize button**. When the dialog opens, navigate to **Categories** on the left side, then scroll down to and click **Macros**. Next, navigate to **Macros** on the right side and scroll down to and **click the name of your macro**. Position your cursor in the **Press new keyboard key:** box and press a key combination. If the keyboard shortcut you wish to use isn't assigned to another function—or if you're willing to reassign that shortcut to your macro—click the "**Assign**" button. Finally, click **Close** and then **OK** out of the Word Options dialog.

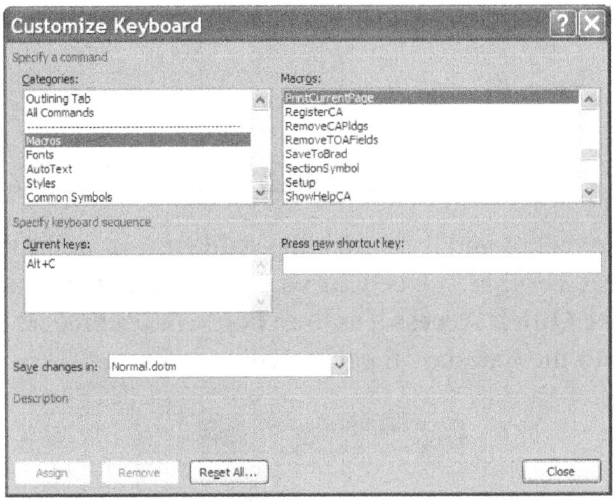

Working With Styles

What Are Styles?

Styles are merely groups of formatting codes that can be applied all at once to a paragraph or series of paragraphs.[1] For example, you could create a style called "Block Quote" that indents a paragraph 1" from the left and 1" from the right and has a first-line indent of .5". Then you could turn on that style before typing a block quotation in a pleading (or apply the style after typing the text of the quotation), rather than applying the various indents separately.

You can configure a particular style so that it is always followed by another particular style. To use a typical example, many people create heading styles that are followed by a text style that indents the first line by half an inch or an inch, so that when they type a heading and press the Enter key, the cursor moves to the next line (or two lines down) and is indented the appropriate amount.

What Are the Advantages of Using Styles?

One advantage of using styles is that they provide a certain uniformity of appearance throughout your documents. If you don't use styles, you might inadvertently indent outline-numbered paragraphs differently; if you use styles, the numbered paragraphs always will be indented the same amount of space.

Styles save you time because you can apply multiple formatting codes all at once, rather than individually.

Also, it's very easy to change the formatting of paragraphs to which styles have been applied. If a particular style needs to be modified—let's say you have set up a heading style that uses boldface type, but you want underlining instead—you can modify the style and choose to have it update automatically, so that all of the paragraphs using that style will reflect the change without your having to go through the document and make changes to individual paragraphs.[2]

If you use one of Word's built-in heading or outline numbered styles, Word will pull your headings into a Table of Contents automatically—without your having to mark the headings for inclusion in the TOC.

---

[1] Actually, Word uses both paragraph styles and character styles, but paragraph styles are the ones most people are referring to when they use the term "styles." Character styles involve formatting attributes such as font face, font size, bolding, italics, small caps, etc. Paragraph styles involve formatting attributes such as alignment (justification), indentation, first-line indent (if any), hanging indent (if any), line spacing, space before, space after, and tabs.

[2] **CAUTION**: The "Automatically Update" option can have unintended, and unwanted, consequences, so use it sparingly if at all.

What Are the Potential "Gotchas" of Using Styles?

1. For one thing, you have to remember that when you create or modify a style, you are creating or modifying a style ***ONLY*** in the current document. This very important point is simply the way styles work in both MS Word and WordPerfect. In order to ensure that your customizations are available in new documents, ***you must check the "New Documents Based on This Template" radio button*** at the bottom of the Create New Style From Formatting dialog box or the Modify Style dialog box (i.e., before you close the dialog after creating or modifying a style).

2. Styles can change unexpectedly. There are a few possible reasons why:

(a) You previously checked the "**Automatically update**" box in the **Create New... or Modify Formatting dialog box** and have **manually reformatted** a paragraph to which that style has been applied in a document you are working on.

(b) You have (or someone else has) modified **an underlying style** that is the basis for your style.

(c) You have (or someone else has) modified **the template** in which your style is stored.

(d) You are working on a different computer, and there is a style in the NORMAL template (normal.dotm) on that machine that has ***the same name*** as your style but ***is formatted differently***. (Your document will reflect the formatting of the style in the normal.dotm of the machine you are working on.)

What Is the "Normal" Style?

The "Normal" style is the ***default paragraph style***—i.e., it uses the default settings in the **Paragraph dialog box (Home tab, Paragraph group, dialog launcher**; alternatively, press the keystrokes **Alt O, P**). The "Normal" style typically inherits the default font face and size specified in your underlying template (usually meaning the **NORMAL template**). So, for example, if your Normal.dotm uses a 10-point Times New Roman font, that is the font you'll get when you apply the "Normal" style to a paragraph.[3] When you do so, you'll also strip out any and all indentation, alignment, space before and after, etc. that you have applied to the paragraph manually via the Paragraph dialog.

CAUTION: In Word 2007, the Normal paragraph style ***does not*** determine the font settings for built-in Heading styles. Those settings are determined by "Themes." For

[3] **NOTE**: Different templates can—but do not necessarily— have different Normal paragraph styles.

instructions on creating a new "Theme" that uses your preferred font for Heading styles, see the "Making Word 2007 Work Like Older Versions" section of the book.

How Do I Use Word's Built-In Styles?

Word comes with a number of built-in styles, including nine heading styles (corresponding to various "levels" of headings). Note that built-in styles are responsible for the appearance of various features of your documents, including footnotes and footers. You can use any of the existing styles as is, or you can modify them to suit your needs.

To use a built-in style, click somewhere within the paragraph to which you want to apply the style (or select contiguous paragraphs), then use one of the following methods:

1. On the **Home tab**, locate the **Styles group** and click the **dialog launcher** (or press **Ctrl Alt Shift S**). When the **Styles Pane** opens, select the style from the Styles list, and click it. Word will apply the style to the paragraph your cursor is in.

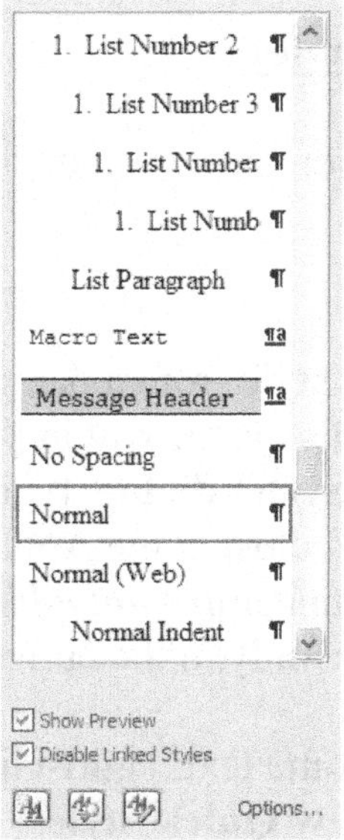

Styles Pane

NOTE: By default, Word 2007 displays only some of the built-in styles. In order to change which styles are displayed, click the **Options** button at the lower right-hand side of the Styles pane and select **All Styles**. If you like, change the order in which the styles are displayed (from Recommended to Alphabetical, for example). Then **OK** out of the Style Pane Options dialog.

2. Alternatively, you can position your cursor to the right of the **Quick Styles Gallery** at the right side of the **Home tab**, click the **up arrow** or **down arrow** to scroll through the gallery row by row and, if you see an icon for the style you want to use, click that icon.

3. You can click the "**More**" button (underneath the up and down arrows) to open the gallery and click "**Apply Styles**" (at the bottom of the gallery), then type a name of the style

you want to use—or click the drop-down and choose a style from the list—and finally click "**Reapply**."

4. If you click "**Change Styles**," you will open a drop-down with a "**Style Set**" option. This option provides a gallery of predefined "**Style Sets**" that you can apply to your document as a whole (as opposed to a paragraph style).[4] ***Use this option with some caution***, for obvious reasons.

5. There is a "mini" style pane called the **Apply Styles dialog** that you can open by pressing the key combination **Ctrl Shift S**. When it opens, you can select a style from the drop-down list (or type the name of an existing style) and apply the style by clicking the somewhat confusingly labeled "**Reapply**" **button** or you can modify the style by clicking the **Modify button**. (The Apply Styles dialog also features a button that opens the full Styles Pane.)

6. If you have assigned a **keyboard combination** to a style, just press that key combination.

How Do I Create My Own Custom Styles?

There are two different ways to create a custom style:

1. **By Example**:

   (a) You can create a style from a paragraph that is already formatted a certain way by placing the cursor within the paragraph, pressing **Ctrl Shift S** to open the **Apply Styles dialog**, typing a name in the **Style Name** box, then clicking **New** and closing the Apply Styles dialog. **NOTE**: Styles created in this manner ***are not added to the default template***, which means they are available only in the current document.

   (b) You can select some text, **right-click**, click "**Styles**," then click "**Save selection as a New Quick Style**." When the **Create New Style from Formatting** dialog opens, type a **unique name** for the style. To add the new style to the default template, click the "**Modify**" **button**, click the "**New documents based on this template**" **radio button**, and **OK** out.

2. **From Scratch**:

   (a) On the **Home tab**, locate the **Styles group** and click the **dialog launcher**. When the Styles Pane opens, click the "**New Style**" button in the lower left-hand corner. That will open an expanded version of the **Create New Style from Formatting dialog box** (see the screenshot on the next page).

---

[4] The Style Sets include one that Microsoft has labeled "Word 2003." As mentioned on page 26, this label is somewhat misleading because when you apply the Word 2003 Style Set, you still get the Calibri font, which was not the default font in Word 2003.

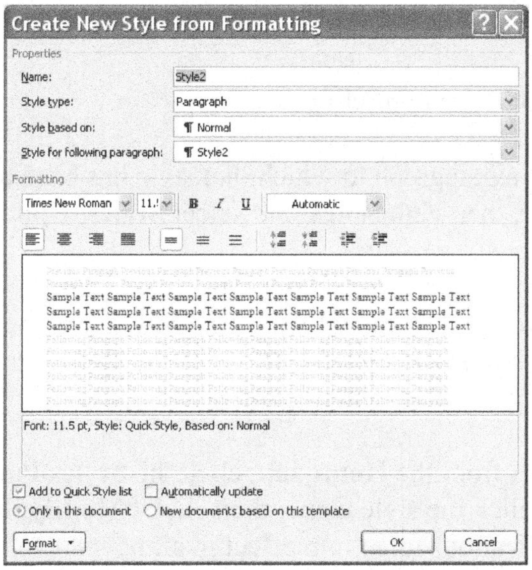

Create New Style from Formatting dialog

(b) When the dialog appears, **type a name** for the style (it must be unique, and it should describe what the style does). Ignore the style type; Word assumes that you're creating a paragraph style, which you are. Therefore, you don't want to change the style type.

(c) You can base the style on an existing style. If you wish to do so, type the name of the base style in the "**Style based on**" field. (**CAUTION**: When you use this option, it's important to remember that ***any modification to the base style will affect your new style as well***.)

(d) Also, you can specify a style for the following paragraph by typing a style name in the "**Style for Following Paragraph**" field. If you don't specify a style, the following paragraph will use the same style.

(e) To specify formatting details, such as font, tabs, numbering, and so forth, click the "**Format**" **button** and choose the appropriate options.

(f) When you have finished, click the "**New documents based on this template**" radio button, then **OK** out of the dialog. (If you don't click the "New documents based on this template" radio button, the style will be available ***only in the current document***.)

(g) Note that if you check "**Automatically update**," any ***manual formatting changes*** you make to one paragraph to which that style has been applied will redefine the style and, as a result, will be reflected in ***all*** paragraphs to which that style has been applied. That option can be useful, but, as mentioned previously, it can produce unexpected results, so ***use it with caution, if at all***.

How Do I Modify Styles?

There are a couple of ways to modify a style:

1. Click within a paragraph to which that style has been applied. Make any formatting changes you like, then **right-click** and select **Styles**, **Update <style name> to match selection**.

The modifications you just made will be incorporated into the style. Note that this method ***does not add your modifications to the default template*** (i.e., it will modify the style only in the current document).

2. Alternatively, from the **Home tab**, click the **Styles Pane launcher**. When the Styles Pane appears, ***right***-click the style name, then click "**Modify**." Make any changes you like. If you want the modifications to go into effect in all new documents, be sure to click the "**New documents based on this template**" radio button before OK-ing out of the dialog.

Can I Copy a Style From Another Document (or Template) into This One?

Yes! Just copy the paragraph symbol at the end of a "styled" paragraph in your "source" document (which can be a regular document or a template) and paste it into your "destination" document (which also can be either a regular document or a template). You can copy some text, too, if you like, but ***the key is to copy the paragraph symbol*** because—as you know—it contains the formatting codes for that paragraph, including the information about the style.

If necessary, turn on **Show Non-Printing Characters** (press **Ctrl Shift * [asterisk]**, or click the **¶ button** in the **Paragraph group** on the **Home tab**) so that you can see the paragraph symbol.

Copying Styles With the Organizer

In addition to the method described above, you can copy styles between documents and/or templates by using the **Organizer**.

There are two different ways to open the Organizer in Word 2007. Either:

(1) Click the **Office button**, **Word Options**, **Add-Ins**, then click the "**Manage**" drop-down and change it to **Templates**, and finally click "**Go**." When the **Templates and Add-Ins dialog** opens, click "**Organizer**"; ***or***

(2) Launch the **Styles Pane**, click **Manage Styles**, then click the **Import/Export button** at the bottom of the **Manage Styles dialog**.

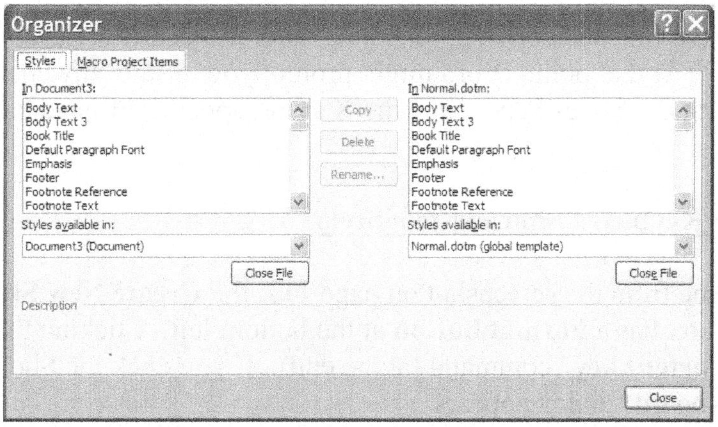

When the Organizer opens, you'll see a box on the left and a box on the right. The left-hand box typically shows the styles available in the document on your screen; the right-hand box typically shows the styles available in your NORMAL template (normal.dotm). To copy a style from one to the other, click the style in the "**source**" document (the one you want to copy ***from***). The "**Copy**" **button** will become active, and will display an arrow pointing left or right, depending on which box you're copying into (the arrow points to the "**destination**" document or template—the one you're copying ***to***). Click the button to copy a style from one document or template to the other. Note that you can select and copy multiple styles all at once (by pressing the **Ctrl key** before clicking the styles you wish to copy).

CAUTION: If a style in the source document or template has the same name as a style in the destination document or template, Word will warn you and ask if you want to overwrite the style in the destination document. Pay attention to this warning; it is designed to prevent you from accidentally overwriting ***a custom style*** that you might have assigned the same name as a style that actually is formatted differently. Styles with the same name ***are not necessarily the same style***!

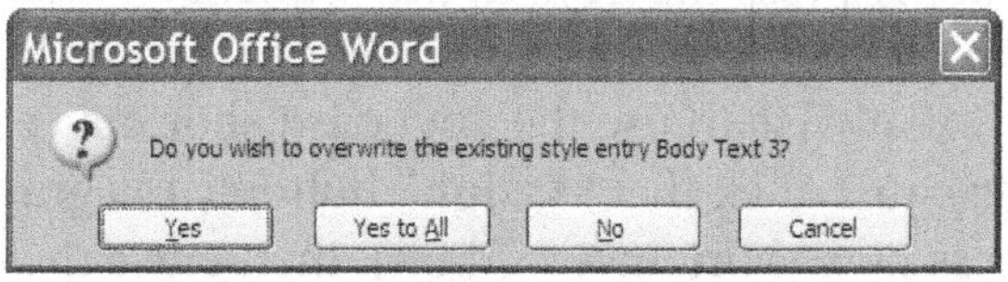

The Organizer lets you delete or rename styles in documents and templates, as well. Again, use caution before deleting or renaming a style, especially from within a template. (On the other hand, people sometimes clutter their documents and templates with lots of styles they never use; if you're sure you don't need particular styles, it's not a bad idea to delete them, since a profusion of styles can lead to document corruption.)

Although the Organizer opens with items in the current document displayed on the left and items in the NORMAL template displayed on the right, you can display a different document or template on either side simply by clicking the "**Close File**" button underneath one of the boxes, which then becomes an "**Open File**" button. Click the "Open File" button and navigate to the document or template you wish to use instead, then click the "**Open**" button. (If you like, you can repeat the process for the other document or template.)

When you have finished copying, renaming, and/or deleting styles, just click "**Close**" to close the Organizer. (At that point, Word might prompt you to save any changes you've made.) If you're through with the Styles Pane, click the X at the upper right-hand side of the Styles Pane to close it.

How Do I Assign a Keyboard Shortcut to a Style?

As you can see from the screenshot on page 117, the **Create New Style from Formatting** dialog box has a **Format button** at the bottom left. Clicking the button opens a menu that has a "**Shortcut key**" command (at the end). If you click the Shortcut key command, the "Customize Keyboard" dialog appears.

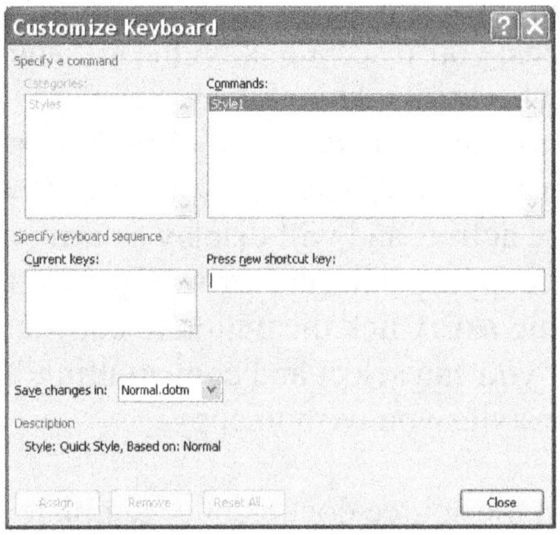

Customize Keyboard dialog

To assign a keyboard shortcut, type the shortcut you wish to use in the "**Press new shortcut key**" box. (For keyboard combinations that use function keys or the Alt key, the Ctrl key, and/or the Shift key, simply press the keys in the sequence you desire.) If that shortcut already has been assigned to another function, you'll see the words "**Currently assigned to**," followed by the function. If you wish to use the keyboard shortcut (even if it is currently assigned to another function), just click the "**Assign**" button (it is grayed out until you insert a key combination in the "Press new shortcut key" box), then **close** the dialog.

As mentioned toward the beginning of the book in the section on keyboard shortcuts, there are a few predefined keystrokes in Word that will apply (or remove) styles. These shortcuts include the following:

Ctrl Q	– removes paragraph formatting (unless applied via a style)
Ctrl Shift N	– applies the Normal paragraph style
Ctrl Shift L	– applies the bulleted list style
Ctrl Alt 1	– applies the Heading 1 style
Ctrl Alt 2	– applies the Heading 2 style
Ctrl Alt 3	– applies the Heading 3 style

How Can I View the Styles in a Document?

First, click the **Office button**, **Word Options**, click **Advanced**, then scroll down to **Display**. In the **Style Area Width** box, set a width larger than 0" (1" is usually sufficient), and **OK** out of the dialog box.

Then switch to **Draft view** (by clicking the **View tab**, **Draft** or clicking the **Draft View icon** on the Status Bar). You should see a **Style Area** at the left-hand side of your document that shows the styles (if any) that have been applied to the various paragraphs in the document.

What Are Those Weird-Looking Styles in the Style Pane?

If an obscure feature called **Keep Track of Formatting** is enabled, the Styles pane will display the name of the style in use in a particular paragraph, ***plus*** any formatting you've applied directly, such as bold, underlining, a first-line indent, or a custom font size (or, as in the example below, only the font attributes, without a style name). This new feature can be both confusing and distracting.

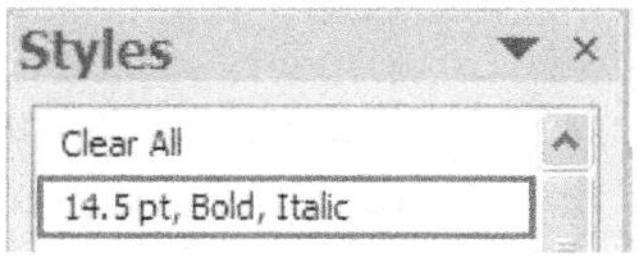

To turn it off, click the **Office button**, **Word Options**, **Advanced**, **Editing**, uncheck **Keep track of formatting**, and **OK** out.

CAUTION: There's another place you might inadvertently turn on this feature. If you click **Options** in the **Style pane**, you'll see an option to "**Select formatting to show as styles**," with checkboxes for Paragraph level formatting, Font formatting, and bullet and numbering formatting. (See the screenshot below.)

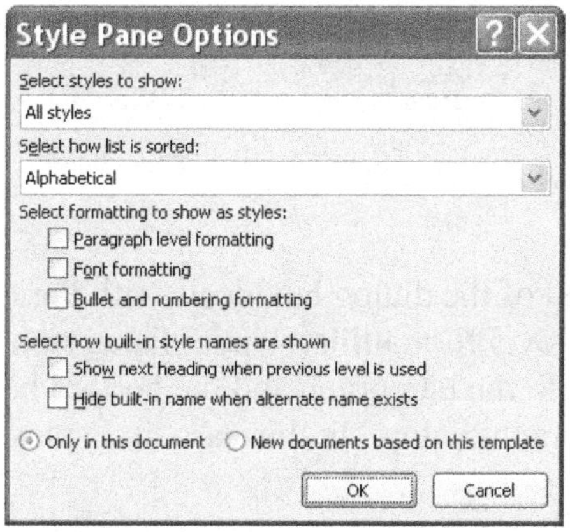

If you check one or more of those boxes and OK out of the dialog, you will in effect enable the Keep track of formatting feature.

SIDEBAR: The Style Inspector

The Style Inspector

Word 2007 contains a new tool called the "**Style Inspector**" that lets you see—and remove—paragraph formatting and character formatting (the latter is referred to in the Style Inspector as Text-level formatting) in a paragraph.

For the example shown below, I typed some text and applied the Body Text Indent 3 style (a paragraph style) to it. Then I went into the Paragraph dialog and manually set the Before Spacing—in this one paragraph only—to 12 points (I did ***not*** modify the style so that it always uses Before Spacing of 12 points).

After that, I selected certain portions of the text and changed the font size to 9 points (the default font size for that style is 8 points), bolded and italicized other portions, and used strikeout (there's a strikeout button in the **Font group** on the **Home tab**, though I could have applied the strikeout attribute from the **Font dialog**).

I clicked in the portion of the text with the various font changes, then launched the Style Pane and clicked the Style Inspector button (the one in the middle at the bottom of the Pane). The result is shown below.

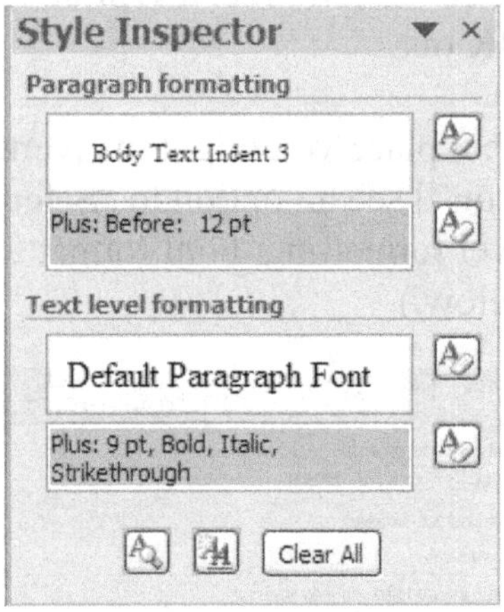

Note that the top portion of the dialog box deals with Paragraph formatting and the bottom with character or Text-level formatting. Under Paragraph formatting, the top box shows any style that has been applied to the paragraph and the bottom box shows any formatting you've applied manually via the Paragraph dialog. In this case, it displays the 12-point Before Spacing I added.

Under Text level formatting, the top box shows the font face that is in use in the paragraph, while the bottom box shows any character or font attributes you've applied to the text. In this case, it displays the change in the size of the text (to 9 points), as well as the Bold Italic, and Strikethrough attributes.

You can clear paragraph or character formatting by clicking one or more of the button(s) at the right side of the dialog—the ones with the eraser on them. Note that if you wish to clear either type of paragraph formatting, it doesn't matter where your cursor is as long as it's somewhere within the affected paragraph. However, if you wish to clear Text-level formatting, you need to select the text before stripping the formatting. (As far as I know, if you've applied several different font attributes, you can't clear only one via the Style Inspector; the "Clear" buttons wipe out all attributes at once. Of course, you always have the option of opening the Font dialog and unchecking one or more individual attributes, leaving the others intact.)

You don't need to select text to use the "Clear All" option. That option works on the entire paragraph.

QUICK TIP: Exploring a Few Advanced "Find" Options

The Find feature in Word 2007 has a few new options that are worth exploring. One is the "**Reading Highlight**" option available in the "Find" box. When you enter a word and click the **Reading Highlight drop-down**, then click "**Highlight All**," Word goes through your document and highlights (normally in yellow) all instances of the word. When you want to turn the highlighting off again, just click "**Clear Highlighting**."

There is also a new "**Find in**" button that lets you specify which part of the document to search: the **Main Document**, **Headers and Footers**, **Footnotes**, or, if you have text selected, **Current Selection**. **CAUTION**: This feature occasionally goes awry, such that you might assume you are searching the entire document, but Word "gets stuck" searching only the footnotes. If you get an error message indicating that the program can't find any more instances of a particular word ***in the footnotes***, be sure to click "**Find in**" and reset the search location to "**Main Document**," and then click "**Find Next**" to resume searching the document text.

As you probably know, Word has the ability to search for formatted text. If you click the "**Format**" **button**, then click "**Font**," you can check one or more of the font attribute boxes so that Word searches for a word or phrase in italics, small caps, and so forth. You can also tell Word to search for highlighting. After you run a search for formatted text, be sure to clear the search criteria by clicking the "**No Formatting**" button at the bottom of the Find dialog. If you don't clear the criteria, Word will continue looking for formatted text, and you might not realize that's why it doesn't find your search term.

You also probably know that you can use the "**Format**" and "**Special**" options to search for specific styles, field codes, paragraph symbols, section breaks, footnote marks, highlighting, paragraph formatting such as line spacing and before and after spacing, and much more. For an extensive article that explains each of these options, see "Find and replace text or other items" (be sure to click "Show All" to display all of the content), located here: http://office.microsoft.com/en-us/word/HA012303921033.aspx

Another very useful option in the Find dialog is the one to "**Find all word forms**." I used it just now to search through the book manuscript for all forms of the word "find" (without quotation marks). It turned up "find," "finding," and "found." **TIP/CAUTION**: You can perform a Find and Replace operation using "Find all word forms," but it's advisable to review each instance of the word or phrase rather than using "Replace All," since Word, while smart enough to ***find*** all of the forms of a particular word, isn't smart enough to ***replace*** with the correct word form.

As with most advanced find options, just remember to clear the "Find all word forms" checkbox when you have finished with the search. Note that you might have to run another (quick) search with the box unchecked in order to make sure Word doesn't turn the option back on when you close the Find dialog. This choice seems to be particularly "sticky."

Bullets and Numbering

Creating Bulleted Lists

You can create a bulleted list in Word 2007 by inserting a bullet first or by typing text first and then applying bullets to the text.

Perhaps the easiest way is simply to click the **Bullets button** in the **Paragraph group** on the **Home tab** and then type some text. When you press the **Enter key**, Word inserts another bullet of the same type and with the same indentation so that you can type another bulleted paragraph. To end the bulleted list, click the **Bullets button** again.

Alternatively, you can type some text first and then click the **Bullets button**. To apply bullets to several consecutive paragraphs, **select the paragraphs** and then click the **Bullets button**.

If you wish, you can insert bullets in a couple of other ways:

- By pressing **Ctrl Shift L**; or
- If Automatic Bulleted Lists has been enabled, by **typing an asterisk** and pressing either the **Spacebar** ***or*** the **Tab key**

To enable or disable Automatic Bulleted Lists, click the **Office button**, **Word Options**, **Proofing**, **AutoCorrect Options**, and click the **AutoFormat As You Type** tab.

Creating a Multilevel Bulleted List

After you have inserted a bullet and typed some text (or applied a bullet to existing text), you can change the level of the bulleted paragraph by doing any of the following:

- pressing **Alt Shift →** (to "demote" the list level of the paragraph)[1]; or
- **right-clicking** within the paragraph, clicking **Numbering**, **Change List Level**, and clicking on one of the **list level icons**; or
- opening the **Bullets drop-down**, choosing **Change List Level**, and clicking on one of the **list level icons**.

Changing the Indentation of the Bulleted List

By default, the first level of Word's built-in bulleted lists indents the bullet by .25" and begins the text at .5". You can change the indentation of any list level by **right-clicking** somewhere within a paragraph, choosing **Adjust List Indents**, changing the indentation of the

---

[1]For any level of the list other than the first one, you can press **Alt Shift ←** to "promote" the paragraph to a higher level. Note that if "**Set left- and first-indent with tabs and backspaces**" is enabled, you can use the **Tab key** to demote a level and **Shift Tab** to promote a level. To check or change this setting, click the **Office button**, **Word Options**, **Proofing**, **AutoCorrect Options**, **AutoFormat As You Type** tab.

bullet and/or the text, then clicking **OK**. Note that doing so will change the indentation of all paragraphs in the current list that are at that level, but will not affect other bulleted lists in your document.

One way to change the indentation of those lists is to use the **Format Painter** (the **paintbrush icon** in the **Clipboard group** on the **Home tab**). With your cursor somewhere within one of the paragraphs whose indentation you wish to copy, **double-click the Format Painter**, then click on **every bulleted paragraph** that you want to adopt the indentation of the "model" paragraph. Be sure to click the Format Painter again to turn it off.

Changing the Bullet Size

It can be somewhat tricky to change the bullet size without also changing the size of the text in a bulleted paragraph.

The trick is to turn on **Show Nonprinting Characters** (by clicking the **paragraph symbol**/pilcrow [¶] in the **Paragraph group** or by pressing **Ctrl Shift** * (asterisk—the asterisk is above the number 8 at the top of the keyboard), then **select the paragraph symbol** at the end of the paragraph and use any method you like to decrease or increase the font size. (You might find it helpful to insert a space between the last character in the paragraph and the paragraph symbol at the end.) **NOTE**: ***Changing the size of the paragraph symbol changes the size of the bullet but not the size of the text***.

After you change the size of the bullet in one paragraph, you should be able to copy the formatting by using the Format Painter. However, in my tests I was unable to get that to work. What ***did*** work was **copying the paragraph symbol** from a "successful" paragraph and **pasting it** at the end of a paragraph whose formatting I wanted to change.

Changing the Bullet Character

To change the appearance of a bullet, insert the cursor into a paragraph whose bullet you wish to modify, then open the **Bullets drop-down** and select a bullet from the gallery.

If none of the existing choices appeals to you, click **Define New Bullet**. The **Define New Bullet dialog** will allow you to browse through various font sets to locate another symbol or to browse through a picture gallery and find an image that you can use for your bullet.

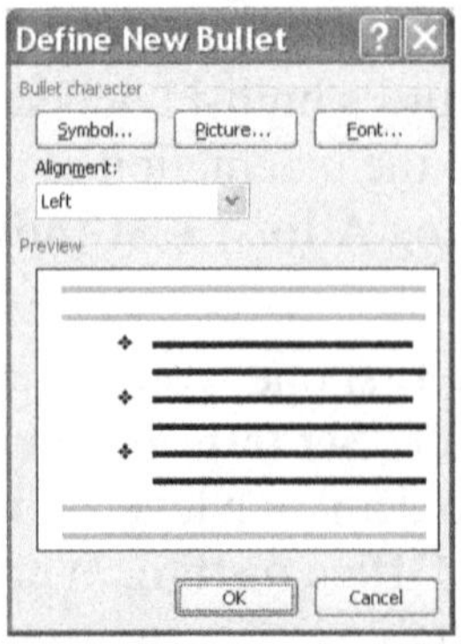

Multiple Bulleted Lists and Nested Lists

Word allows you to insert different bulleted lists in different parts of your document ***and/or*** to nest various types of lists (up to nine separate lists) inside one another.

Probably the easiest way to create nested lists is to type the text, select one section at a time, and then apply bullet and/or numbering formatting to that section. You can then format the remaining sections of the nested list in similar fashion.

WHERE DID IT GO? Watermark

The Watermark feature is now found on the **Page Layout tab** in the **Page Background group**. When you click the drop-down, you have the option of using one of the built-in watermarks available in the gallery (be sure to scroll down to see all of them) or creating your own customized watermark.

If you choose to create a custom watermark, a dialog opens that allows you to insert text or a picture. The Text watermark drop-down is pre-populated with some slogans you can use, but you can type your own words (as I've done in the example below). You can set the font, size, color, and layout (diagonal or horizontal) from the dialog.

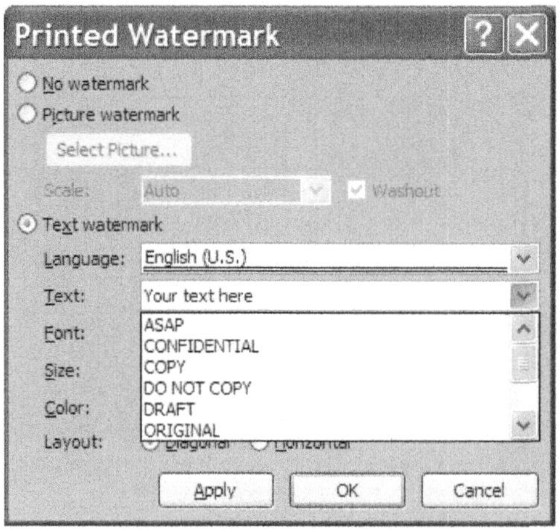

Note that the Watermark drop-down features a "Remove Watermark" option. It also has an option to save your custom watermark to the gallery.

Inserting Automatic Paragraph Numbers
With the Numbering Button

When you use the Numbering button in Word 2007 (found on the **Home tab**, in the **Paragraph group**), Word begins a ***single-level list.*** The program normally inserts the number code at the left margin and formats the text as a ***hanging indent***, like so:

1. This is the default formatting of numbered lists inserted via the Numbering button in Word. Word indents the first line of the paragraph (i.e., starts the number) at .25" and indents the remainder of the paragraph at .5".

Obviously, this isn't the right format for numbering in a complaint or cross-complaint, or even in a standard agreement.

There are a few workarounds for this problem. All involve tinkering with the formatting so that the number you insert with the Numbering button is indented half an inch (the standard indention for pleadings and most legal documents) and the text wraps around to the left margin.

Method 1:

This method is probably the best one to use, because it will retain your modified formatting even if you end your numbered list and then restart numbering later in the document.

1. **Right-click** somewhere near or within the paragraph number. (Right-clicking is one of the best ways to modify numbered lists in Word 2007; you can't modify a list directly from the list gallery). When the shortcut menu appears, click **Adjust List Indents**. The **Adjust List Indents dialog** will open.

2. If you want to use standard numbering for complaints and such, set the **Number position** at .5" and the **Text indent** at 0 (zero)—so that the text will wrap to the left margin. You don't need to check the "Add tab stop at:" box.

3. Click **OK** (or press **Enter**) to confirm your settings.

4. Type enough text to make sure the second line of the paragraph wraps to the left margin, and then press the **Enter key**. Word should insert another numbered paragraph with the same settings.[1]

5. In order to save this modified list style so that you can use it in future documents, ***right***-click near or within the number. When the shortcut menu appears, click **Styles**, **Save Selection as a New Quick Style…**

Type a name here

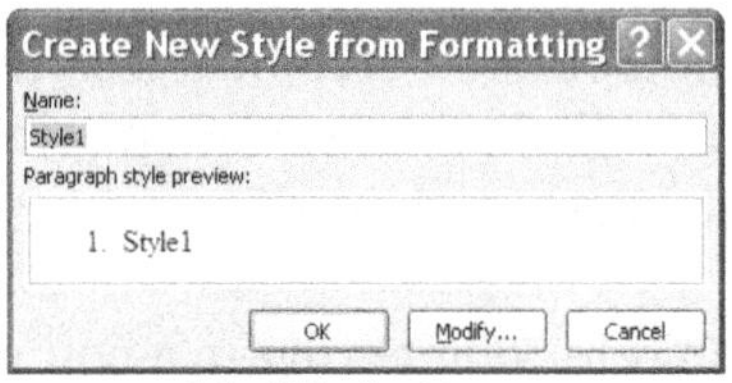

Modify button

6. When the condensed **Create New Style from Formatting** box appears, type a short descriptive **name** for the style (such as Numbered Paragraph).

7. ***Before OK-ing out of the dialog***, click the **Modify** button, which will open the full **Create New Style from Formatting dialog**. The reason for doing so is to allow you to save the new numbering style to the underlying template so that it is available in future documents. If you don't specify otherwise, the numbering style (with your modified indents) will be available only in the current document.

8. When the expanded **Create New Style from Formatting dialog** appears, make any further changes you want to the list style, then navigate to the bottom of the dialog and click to mark the "**New documents based on this template**" **radio button**. (See the screenshot on the next page.) **NOTE**: This is a critical step!

9. Click **OK** to save your changes.

---

[1] **NOTE**: When you use the Numbering button, Word inserts a number code both when you first press the button and when you press Enter after typing a numbered paragraph. To *turn off numbering*, click the Numbering button again. Alternatively, you can press the Enter key a second time, but doing so also will bump the next paragraph down a line, which may or may not be your intention. (If you wish to retain numbering but also want a blank line between numbered paragraphs, either (1) press **Shift Enter** rather than Enter, which inserts a **Line Break** ***or*** (2) open the Paragraph dialog and navigate to the **Spacing After** box, type **12** [to insert 12 points of blank space after each numbered paragraph], then click **OK**.)

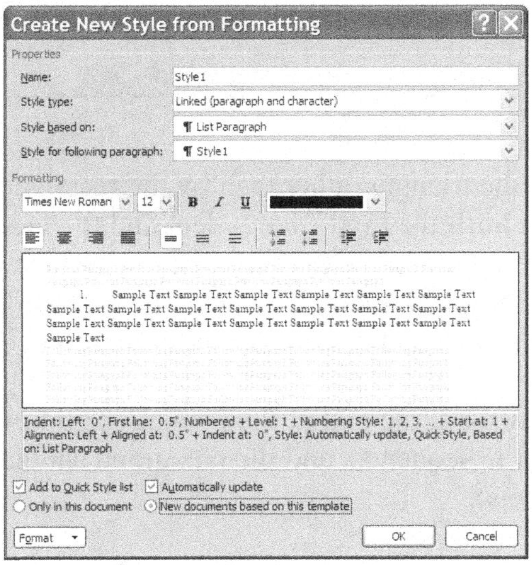

You'll need to click the "New documents based on the template" radio button

Create New Style from Formatting dialog

10. The new list style should now appear in the Quick Styles gallery on the Home tab as well as in the Styles pane.[2]

<u>Method 2</u>:

This method works, but if you have to restart numbering later in the document, the formatting (i.e., the indents) reverts to Word's defaults, which can be frustrating. You can, however, save the modified list as a Quick Style by following steps 5-9 above. That way, you'll be able to apply the style to a new list in any document by clicking within the first paragraph and then clicking the style name in the gallery or in the Style pane.

1. **Click the Numbering button** and type some text.

2. With the cursor somewhere within the paragraph, **drag the First Line Indent marker on the Ruler** (the downward-pointing triangle) so that the number is indented ½ inch.[3]

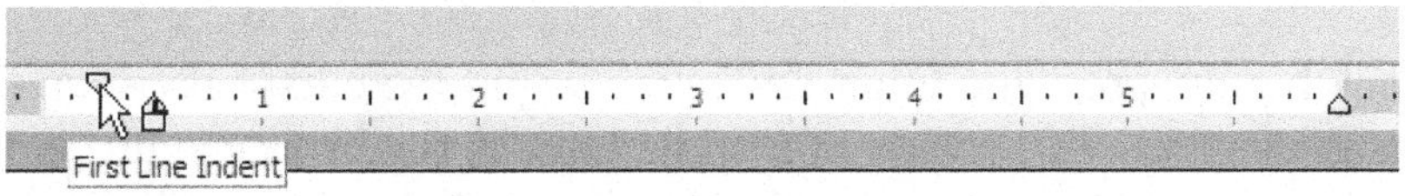

3. Next, **drag the Left Indent marker** (the upward-pointing triangle labeled Hanging Indent in the screenshot on the next page) to the left so that all subsequent lines of the paragraph will wrap to the left margin.

---

[2] **NOTE**: In case you have difficulty creating—and saving to your NORMAL template—a style that retains the indents you specify, I've provided a workaround in the Sidebar immediately following this section.

[3] If the Ruler is not visible, click the **View tab**, **Show/Hide group** and check the **Ruler box**.

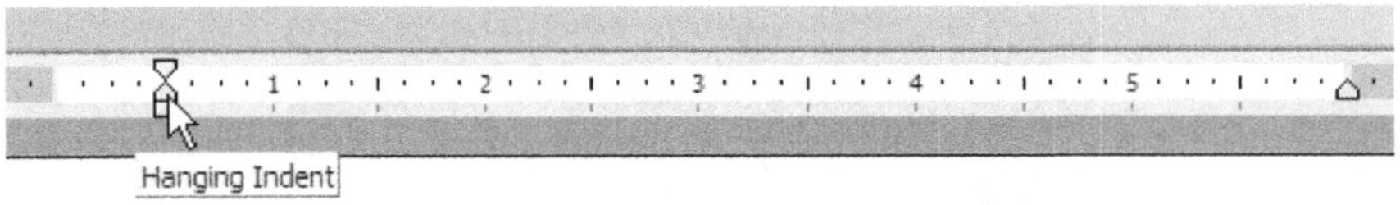

Be careful to drag by the triangle rather than by the rectangle. If you drag by the rectangle, you'll reset **both** the First Line Indent and the indentation of subsequent lines. (You might have to delete the "L," which is a left tab marker, in order to drag the Left Indent marker. To delete the "L," simply drag it down into the document editing screen and release the mouse button.)

4. Position the cursor at the end of the paragraph and **press the Enter key**. Word should insert the next number in sequence, and the paragraph should retain the formatting you just configured (i.e., the indents).

Method 3:

You can tell Word to indent the first line of every paragraph .5", but you have to do this ***after*** you click the Numbering button and start typing the numbered paragraph. (If you try to set up a first line indent beforehand, Word will undo the indentation as soon as you click the Numbering button.) Note that this method is subject to the same problem as Method 2—i.e., if you restart numbering, you might lose your formatting.

1. To indent the first line, ***either*** (a) make sure the insertion point (cursor) is somewhere within the paragraph ***or*** (b) select (block, highlight) the paragraph.

2. Next, click the **Paragraph dialog launcher**. When the dialog opens, navigate to **Special**, and choose **First Line Indent**. Make sure the indent is set for .5". Also make sure that the Left Indent is set to 0 (zero) (so that the text wraps to the left margin). Click **OK**.

3. When you finish typing the first numbered paragraph and press Enter, Word should retain the first-line indent. Again, unless you save this modified list as a style that is available for future documents, it will be available only in the current document.

To Stop/Skip or Restart Numbering:

To stop numbering, press the Enter key twice ***or*** put the cursor between the number and the text and press Backspace. (To remove the indent, press Backspace again.) Of course you also can stop numbering simply by clicking the numbering button again, but keep in mind that when you click the button to restart numbering, Word typically reverts to the original indentation (i.e., a hanging indent, with the number at .25 rather than at .5).

To skip numbering one or more paragraphs, press **Shift Enter** (to insert a manual **line break**) rather than Enter. The next number in sequence will be inserted when you press Enter again. **CAUTION**: Because a manual line break retains the formatting of the previous paragraph (other than the number), this method isn't always appropriate.

<u>To Resume Numbering in Sequence</u>:

There are several different ways to resume numbering:

1. Simply click within the first paragraph where you want the numbering to resume (continue from the previous list) and click the **Numbering button**.

2. Right-click within a numbered paragraph and select "**Continue Numbering**." **WATCH OUT**: Doing so might cause the indents to revert to Word's defaults.

3. Click the drop-down next to the numbering button, click "**Set numbering value**," make sure "**Continue from previous list**" has been marked, change the value as you wish, then click **OK**. **CAUTION**: This method sometimes causes Word to use the original (problematic) indentation.

If the paragraph number doesn't change appropriately, you might have to reopen the **Set Numbering Value** box and, in addition to clicking "**Continue from previous list**," click "**Advance value**" and manually set the number value for the paragraph before clicking **OK** (see screenshot).

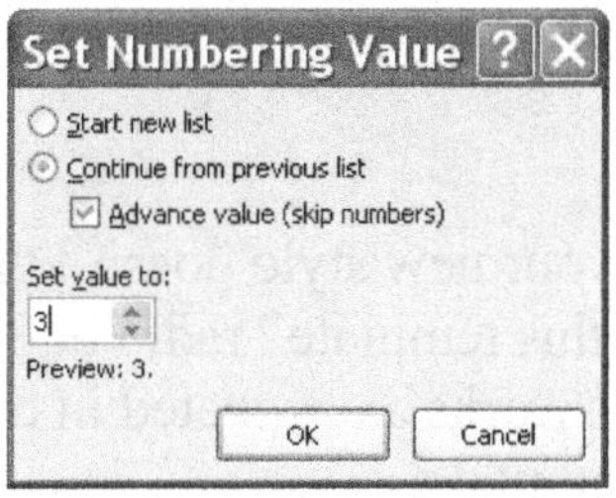

4. **TIP:** Perhaps the ***easiest way*** to resume numbering is simply to copy the paragraph symbol from the end of the previous numbered paragraph and paste it where you want to begin numbering again. The advantage of this method is that Word will restart numbering consecutively ***and*** will retain the indentation of the previous numbered paragraph, as well.

To copy the paragraph symbol, turn on Show Non-Printing Characters by clicking the paragraph symbol (pilcrow = ¶) in the Paragraph group, select the symbol, copy it, and paste it ***at the very end*** of the paragraph whose formatting you want to conform to the "good" paragraphs.

Note that copying and pasting the paragraph symbol also works well to insert a new paragraph 1 at the beginning of your list. Just insert the cursor ***ahead of*** any text in the first numbered paragraph before pasting the paragraph symbol.

SIDEBAR: Troubleshooting a Single-Level List Style

Creating a "global" style for a single-level list—i.e., one that is saved in the NORMAL template so that you can use it in all future documents—can be tricky. Sometimes it works fine, but other times you might attempt to apply the style in a new document, only to find that your indent settings have changed.

Without fully understanding the reasons why settings in list styles don't always stick, or why the fixes outlined below seem to work, I offer a few troubleshooting tips (based on my extended experiments with this feature) that should help you resolve the problem.

First, you are likely to have better luck if you base your new list style on the **Normal** style, on one of the **List Number** styles, or on "**(no style)**," rather than on the List Paragraph style. In my various tests, the List Paragraph style appeared to be somewhat quirky and unreliable. Avoid it.

Secondly, make sure you configure the indents for your list (the first-line indent and the text indent) via the **Adjust List Indents dialog** rather than the Paragraph dialog. The settings in the former seem to be "stickier" than the ones in the latter, at least when it comes to numbered lists.[1]

Thirdly, you might find that your new style doesn't "take" even though you are careful to click the "New documents based on this template" radio button in the Create New Style from Formatting dialog. In other words, it works as expected in the current document but apparently isn't being saved to the NORMAL template.

To correct that situation, position your cursor in a paragraph to which the style has been applied, ***right*-click** one of the numbers, click **Adjust List Indents**, make your changes to the **Number position** and the **Text indent**, and **OK** out. Then, use the **Style Organizer** to copy the style from the current document into the NORMAL template (normal.dotm). (For help using the Organizer, see page 118 and following.) For unknown reasons, that procedure sometimes works better than saving the list style to the template from within the Create New Style...dialog.

---

[1] **NOTE**: You can set up a keyboard shortcut to open the Adjust List Indents dialog. Just follow the instructions that start on page 35, making sure that "All Commands" is showing in the Categories list, and then scrolling down to AdjustListIndents in the Commands list.

Creating Multilevel Lists

In Word 2007, multilevel lists (formerly called outline numbered lists) work differently from the way they worked in previous versions. There are a few critical points to keep in mind as you are creating and applying multilevel lists in Word 2007:

1. You should avoid using the "Define New Multilevel List" option in the drop-down, because ***you can't edit lists that you create using that option***. Instead, use the "**Define New List Style**" option to create an editable list ***style***.

2. When you define a new list style, consider linking each level of the list with a heading style. You can set up a list without linking to heading styles, but if you use multilevel lists mainly in connection with headings, linking your list style to heading styles accomplishes two important tasks at once.

3. If you are going to create a list style and link it to heading styles, it helps to define the list style first, then modify the heading styles as necessary.

4. Unlike in prior versions of Word, you will ***not*** be able to tinker with the numbering in a heading style from within the Modify Style dialog; attempting to do so will lead to a dead end (a dialog that contains only single-level lists and doesn't let you format those lists). When you need to tweak the number formatting, you ***must*** do it from within the list style itself!

5. Be sure to save your new list style to the underlying template. Otherwise, it will be available only in the current document.

The Multilevel List Gallery

Microsoft has provided a number of "canned" multilevel lists, each with nine different "levels" of numbering. They are available via the **Multilevel List button** in the **Paragraph group** on the **Home tab** (top row, toward the center).

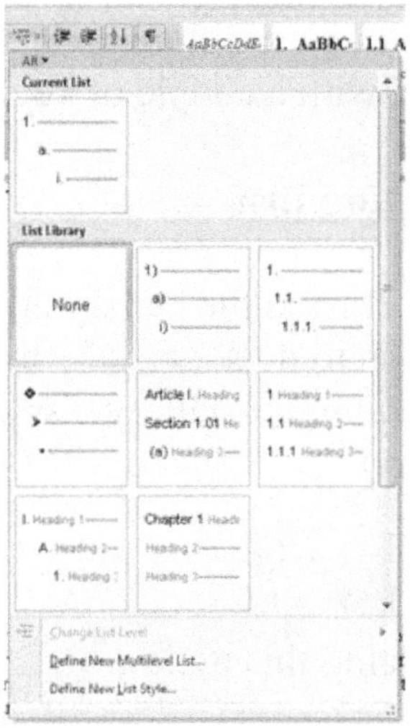

The Multilevel List gallery is divided into several parts: The top shows you the current list in effect in your document (if any); the second level shows you a "library" of built-in lists; the third level shows you the existing list styles (if any); and, if you have inserted several different lists in your document, the bottom level shows you those lists.

Unfortunately, there is no way to modify any of the pre-defined Multilevel lists from within the library, but not to worry. What you will do, instead, is ***create your own list styles*** for each type of numbered list you use (outlines, legal numbering, and the like) and perhaps link those list styles with heading styles. You can use an existing list as a model for your new style, or you can start from scratch.

When you set up a customized list style, you need to format each level of the list style. For each level, you will select the ***type*** (style) of number (Arabic, upper-case roman, lowercase roman, letters, etc.), any surrounding ***punctuation*** (periods or parentheses), how far the ***paragraph number*** is ***indented*** from the left margin, how far the ***text*** is indented from the left margin and whether the ***next line*** wraps to the margin or is set up as a ***hanging indent***, the ***font***, and several other attributes. If you like, you can add text (such as the word "Section") before a number code, as well.

Getting Started: Creating a New List Style

When you use the Multilevel list drop-down, you will see two options at the bottom:

1. Define New Multilevel List; and

2. Define New List Style.

Intuitively, you might think the best option is Define New Multilevel List. However, as mentioned previously, in Word 2007, you can't modify lists created with that option. If you try, what you'll end up doing is defining several new lists within the same document or template, which can lead to document corruption or other problems.

What you should do instead is use **Define New List Style**. That option allows you to set up and customize an editable multilevel list, save it as a **Quick Style Set** (and also save it to the NORMAL template) so that you can use it in future documents. You can even set up a keyboard shortcut so that you can apply the list with a couple of keystrokes.

Basing a New List Style on an Existing List

If you like, you can select a list from the gallery and use it as the basis for a new customized list style. Should you wish to do so, be sure to choose a list that already has heading styles associated with it (i.e., the image in the gallery displays text—Heading 1, Heading 2, Heading 3—next to the level numbers).[1]

[1] Thanks to Eva Eilenberg for suggesting this option.

Open the **Multilevel List drop-down**, navigate to the **List Library** section, and click one of the lists associated with heading styles. Word will insert a number. Ignore it.

Next, click the **MultiLevel List drop-down** again and click **Define New List Style**. The **Define New List Style dialog** will open.

Format button

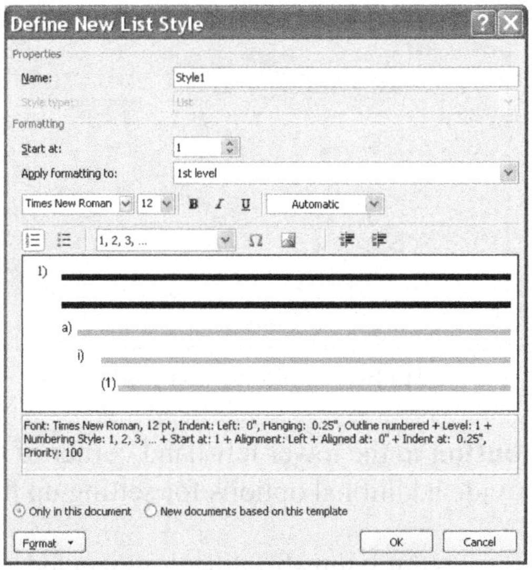

Define New List Style dialog

At this point, start creating your customized list style. I would suggest that you go through this process step by step, formatting each of the nine list levels from the same dialog. ***Do not click OK to save the style*** until ***after*** you have everything set up.

First, give the style a unique name, such as **Outline 1** or **Legal List 1**. Note that this name will apply to ***the entire multilevel list***, not merely to one of the levels within the list.

Second, navigate to the bottom of the dialog and click the "**New documents based on the template**" button so that when you save the list, you will be able to use it in future documents based on the template currently in use.

> **CAUTION**: Unless you take this step, your customized list will be saved ***only in the document in which you are creating it.*** (Technically, you'll be able to save the list as a Quick Style Set after you create it, but for a number of reasons it's better to get in the habit of saving new lists to the template as you create them.)

Third, ***do not click OK yet***. Instead, click "**Format**," then click "**Numbering**." You should see a **Modify Multilevel List dialog** similar to the one in the screenshot on the next page. Don't be concerned if yours differs in some respects from the screenshot.

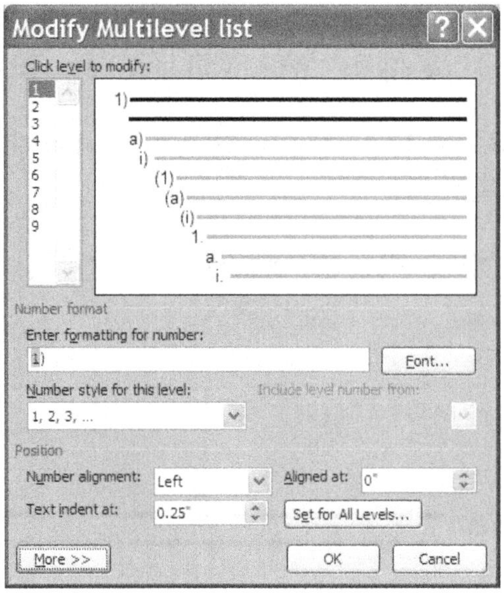

Modify Multilevel List Dialog

If you see a "**More**" **button** in the lower left-hand corner of the dialog, click it. The dialog should expand and provide additional options for setting up the list style.

Take a few minutes to acquaint yourself with the expanded dialog and its options.

Click level to modify

Enter formatting for number

Number style

Number alignment
Text indent

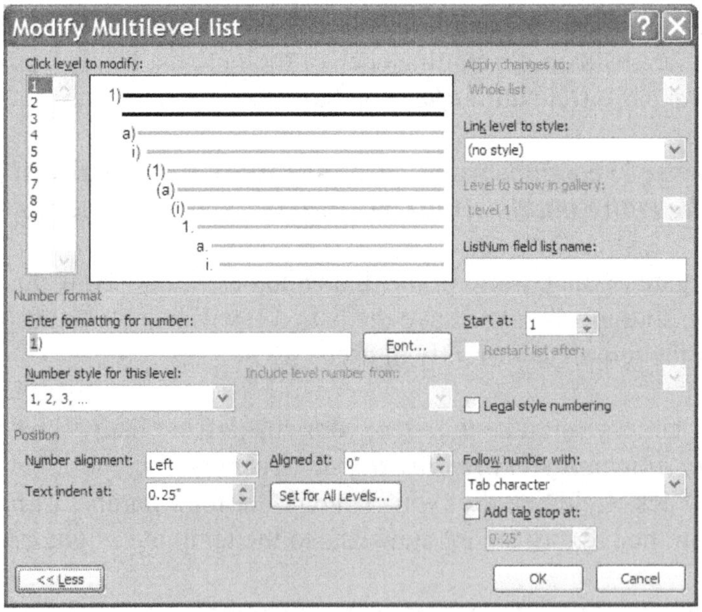

Link level to style

Follow number with:

Expanded Modify Multilevel List Dialog

The "**Click level to modify**" box on the left side of the dialog provides an easy way to modify each level of the list individually (simply click the level you wish to edit; the level number will be highlighted in blue).

TIP: Glance at it from time to time as you work to keep track of which level you're modifying (it's easy to get confused).

Note the "**Link level to style**" drop-down on the right. This option allows you to link each list level to a specific heading style (whether a built-in heading style or one that you have created), which is a good idea. I will walk you through this process, and after we set up the list style, we'll modify the heading styles as well.

Underneath the preview windows, you'll see a field labeled "**Enter formatting for number**." There should be a number in the field, highlighted in gray. The gray portion ***is a code*** and is based on the "**Number style for this level**" drop-down immediately below the field. If you wish to change the type of number or letter for a particular level, use the drop-down list. Then, ***being careful not to delete the gray number or letter code***, you can edit the characters or text before or after the number or letter. In the example above, there is an end parenthesis after the gray number 1. You can delete the end paren and replace it with a period if you like. Alternatively, you could add an open paren before the number code, or you could delete the end paren and add the word "Chapter" or "Section" and a space before the number code. It's up to you; just be careful not to delete the code itself.

Toward the bottom of the dialog, you can set the number and text positions. The **Number alignment** field is somewhat confusing. Essentially it determines whether numbers align on the first digit, even when the numbers increment above 9, or whether they align on any punctuation that follows (typically a period/decimal point or an end paren). The difference is exemplified by the following series, with the former pair of numbers left aligned and the latter pair right-aligned (aligned on the decimal point):

9.
10.

 9.
10.

Although right alignment seems preferable, it can result in heading numbers being outside the left margin, so you'll probably want left alignment. Remember that you can modify the list style later on if you decide you prefer to right-align the numbers.

"**Aligned at**" sets the left indent ***for the number itself***: i.e., how far over from the left margin the number starts. For instance, if you are creating a list level to be used in standard paragraphs in a Complaint, you'll probably use .5" for the "Aligned at" setting. Note that in Word 2007, you have the option of setting the indent for all levels at once, which can be very useful—particularly if your firm typically indents each outline level an additional .5" from the previous level.

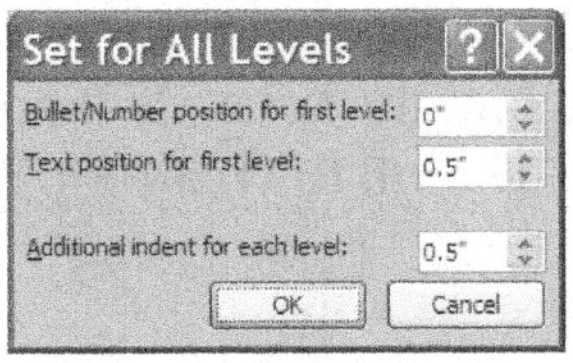

By contrast, "***Text indent at***" sets the left indent for every line of text following the number ***except*** for the first line. (The first-line indent is governed by the "Aligned at" setting.) So, again using the example of a numbered paragraph in a Complaint, you would set the text indent at 0"—because you want the text of the paragraph to wrap to the left margin.

Note that Word provides an option to follow the paragraph number with a Tab (the default setting), a space, or nothing (the "nothing" option is useful when you want a centered number with text centered **below** the number). It also allows you to add an extra tab stop, which can come in handy in certain situations.

When you start formatting a level other than level 1, you'll see an additional button: "**Restart list after [current level number]**." Ordinarily you will leave this option, which is the default, checked. When it is checked, each sublevel starts numbering anew (beginning with "1" or "a" as appropriate), rather than continuing the numbering from the previous level. That is desirable in most circumstances, because otherwise you could end up with a situation where you want the first sublevel after paragraph 6 to appear as 6.1 but, because the last subparagraph in the previous section was 5.6, it appears as 6.7 instead.

Once you are familiar with the various options, go ahead and ***set up each of the nine levels of the list*** (or fewer, if you're absolutely certain you won't use all nine levels). Click the representation of the level you want to format (modify) in either the narrow list of levels at the top of the dialog or the full preview window. Start with level 1. Just keep track of which level you're modifying by glancing periodically at the highlighted level on the left as you are working.

Checklist for Formatting Each Level of the List Style

For each level, do the following:

✓ Choose a number style from the drop-down.

✓ Format the number (delete and/or add punctuation, such as an open paren, a close paren, and/or a period).

✓ Decide on a number alignment (you can leave it set at Left, which is the default, or experiment with Right or Centered).

✓ Set the "Aligned at" (if you want level 1 to be aligned at the left margin, leave it set to zero; if you want it aligned at the first tab stop, set it to .5"—it's up to you).

✓ Set the "Text indent at" and, if you want all levels indented by the same amount, click the "Set for All Levels…" button (you won't need to do the latter after you create the first level of the list style).

✓ Assuming you want to link the list style with heading styles, click the **Link level to style drop-down** and scroll to **Heading 1**. Click to select it.

This is an important step. If you are associating the list style with heading styles, you need to make sure that ***each list level*** is linked to ***a corresponding heading style level***, as shown in the screenshot below.

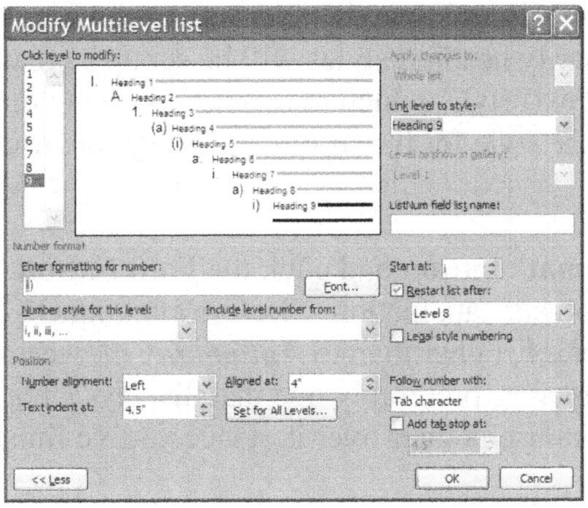

After you have set up each of the nine levels, click **OK**, then click **OK** again.

Modifying the Built-In Heading Styles

The next step, if you are linking the list style to heading styles, is to edit each of the nine heading styles to ensure that they use the font face, font size, and font color you want and that the paragraph formatting (indents, line spacing, and so forth) is set up to your liking.[2]

You can edit a heading style from the **Styles Pane** or from the **Quick Styles Gallery**. Because it's slightly less error-prone, let's use the Styles Pane. Either click the **dialog launcher** in the **Styles group** on the **Home tab** or press **Ctrl Alt Shift S**. Then scroll down to the Heading 1 style, ***right***-click it, and click **Modify**.

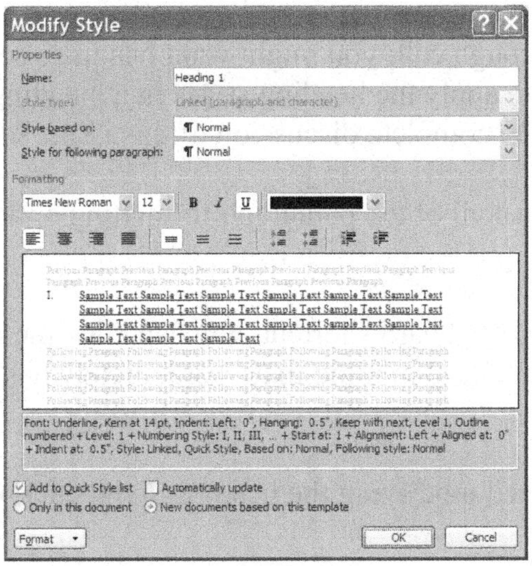

[2] If you plan to set up other list styles and associate them with heading styles, you should create additional heading styles and give them new names—such as Legal Heading 1 (through Legal Heading 9) or Outline Heading 1 (through Outline Heading 9).

When the **Modify Style dialog** opens, immediately click the "**New documents based on this template**" radio button.

Before doing anything else, look at the "**Style for following paragraph**" option toward the top of the dialog. Ordinarily heading styles will be set up so that a heading is followed by the Normal style (or the Body Text) style, which makes sense when you think about it. If for some reason you want to change the style for the following paragraph, use the drop-down list to select the style you want to use.

Next, click the "**Format**" **button** and click the **Font button**. Make sure the font face, font style, and size are set to your satisfaction.[3] Before clicking OK, also check to make sure that the font color is set to ***black***, rather than to ***Automatic***. If necessary, click the drop-down and click one of the black squares, preferably one that displays a pop-up that says "Black, Text 1" when you hold the mouse pointer over it. Once you've finished, click **OK—*but only once***.

Click the **Format button** again, and this time click the **Paragraph button**. When the **Paragraph dialog** opens, check the following settings to make sure they conform to your specifications:

- Indentation
- Special (first-line indent or hanging indent)
- Before spacing
- After spacing
- Line spacing

The indents should be set up correctly, assuming you were successful in setting the indents from the **Modify Multilevel List dialog**, but it's a good idea to check them to make sure.

The line spacing is a tough call; you might want headings set double-spaced or single-spaced, but if you are going to apply the heading styles in a pleading, you might need to apply "Exactly" spacing. For a more complete discussion of this issue, see pages 6, 66, and 161.

Take care to ensure that all of the paragraph formatting options are set the way you want, then click **OK**.

If you want to create a keyboard shortcut, you can click the **Format button** again and then click **Shortcut key…**, but keep in mind that Word already has built-in shortcuts for the first three heading level styles.

When you have finished modifying the heading style, click **OK** to close the **Modify Style dialog**.

---

[3] You also have the option of choosing to apply font formatting such as underlining and all caps to the heading text, although sometimes Word gets confused and continues to apply all caps or other font attributes to the text of the paragraph that follows.

Repeat the above steps for each of the nine paragraph levels.

Double-Checking to Make Sure Everything Works

To double-check to make sure the list style is set up correctly, open the **Multilevel List drop-down** and scroll down to the **List Styles** section. Take a look at your list style to see if the levels are linked to heading styles. If they're not, ***right***-click the style, check the "**New documents based on this template**" radio button, click **Format**, click **Numbering**, and for each level of the list that isn't associated with a heading style, link it to the appropriate style and then OK out.

Applying Your List Style

Once you have set up a list style, you can apply it two different ways: (1) by applying a heading level style to text (from either the Styles Pane or the Quick Styles Gallery) or (2) by applying the style from the Multilevel List gallery.

You can change levels of an existing list paragraph by clicking the Increase Indent (Demote) button or Decrease Indent (Promote) button in the Paragraph group on the Home tab or by pressing Alt Shift → (right arrow) or Alt Shift ← (left arrow). If you have "Set left- and first-indent with tabs and backspaces" enabled in Word Options (Proofing, AutoCorrect Options, Format as You Go tab), you can use Tab (Demote) and Shift Tab (Promote), too.

To save your list style as a Style Set, go to the **Styles group** in the **Home tab** and click **Change Styles**, **Style Set**, **Save as a New Quick Style Set**. When the **Save Quick Style Set dialog** opens, type a **descriptive name** (such as Legal Numbering or Outline Numbering) and click **Save**. The list style will appear in, and can be applied from, the Style Set menu.

Miscellaneous Tips

To modify the ***numeric*** formatting of any level of your multilevel list, do the following: Open a document containing the list, position the cursor ***within a Level 1 paragraph***, click the **Multilevel List drop-down**, locate the image of the list in the **List Styles** section, ***right***-click it, and click **Modify**. (The best way to ensure the integrity of multilevel lists in Word when making formatting changes is to begin the process from within a Level 1 paragraph.) Make sure to click the "**New documents based on this template**" radio button—every single time you modify the style—before proceeding.

To modify ***paragraph formatting*** (indents, etc.) of one or more levels of the list, either modify the underlying paragraph style (such as a Heading style) linked to that level ***or*** use **right-clicking** to open the context-sensitive menu discussed on page 131, in the section about the numbering button. Remember to place the cursor in or near the number code before right-clicking. Note that in this instance, the cursor should be within a paragraph of the level you want to modify, not necessarily a Level 1 paragraph. The **Adjust List Indents** option is particularly useful and, as noted in the sidebar about troubleshooting single-level lists, the settings in that dialog tend to be "stickier" than the indents configured via the Paragraph dialog.

QUICK TIP: Using the ListNum Field

A lesser-known form of automatic numbering in Word, the ListNum field actually can be very useful.

There are three main numbering schemes available with the ListNum field, each of which has nine levels: LegalDefault, NumberDefault, and OutlineDefault. The schemes work pretty much they way their names suggest. The Legal scheme uses typical legal-style numbering; the Outline scheme uses typical outline numbering; and the Number scheme uses the following number and letter formats for its nine levels: 1), a), i), (1), (a), (i), 1., a., i.

One of the advantages of using the ListNum field is that—as in WordPerfect—the list levels are not tied to tab stops, so you can insert a number code for any level at any cursor position. (However, if you insert several ListNum codes ***in the same line***, the level of each subsequent code will increment.) People often use ListNum codes to insert subparagraph numbers like (a) and (b) within the text of a numbered paragraph. And as with SEQ codes, you can have more than one type of ListNum code in the same document.

To insert a ListNum field code, click the **Insert tab**, **Quick Parts**, **Field** or press **Alt I**, **F**, then press the letter "L" a few times until the cursor lands on the ListNum field. Click to select one of the three numbering schemes. If you like, you can click to check one or both of the checkboxes to the right to select a particular level in the list and/or a default start-at value (the default level and start-at value are both 1).

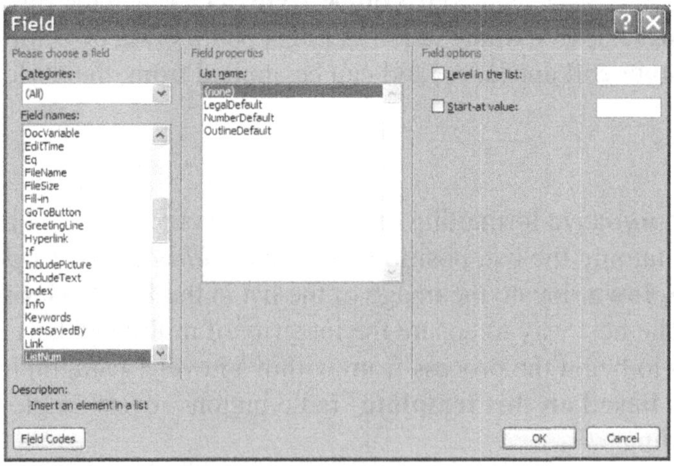

Level in the list
Start-at value

After you have inserted a ListNum code into your document, you can change the level or the start value by pressing **Alt F9** to display the code itself (rather than the code results) and then inserting the appropriate "switch." The switch for the list level is \l, so to change to a level 4 paragraph you would type "\l 4" (without quotation marks) within the French braces after the LISTNUM designation. The switch for the start-at value is \s, so to change to start at 3, you would insert "\s 3" (without quotation marks). Press Alt F9 again to switch back to the code results.

Outlining

Getting Started

To start an outline from scratch or apply an outline to an existing document in Word 2007, you need to switch to **Outline view**. You can do so either from the **View tab** or from the **View buttons** toward the right side of the Status Bar. Once you switch to Outline view, the **Outlining tab** becomes visible, allowing you to apply the Outline Tools as you work.

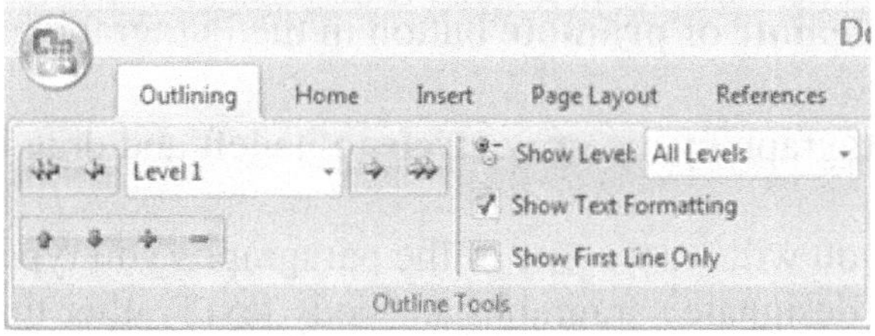

In Outline view, all paragraphs are assigned an outline level. There are nine levels, plus "body text" (for simple text that is not intended to be part of a heading). First-level paragraphs appear at the left margin, and each lower or subordinate level is indented one additional tab stop.

Gray circles appear next to each paragraph you type, including body text. If you like, you can move a paragraph up or down in the outline by dragging the gray circle, or you can use normal cut-and-paste operations.

Word's Heading Styles

When you start typing an outline from scratch, Word automatically applies a Heading 1 style to the text. Unless you have customized the heading styles to conform to your firm's standards, Word uses built-in heading styles based on its default "Theme." There are nine built-in heading levels in all.

Because the built-in styles aren't terribly useful as Microsoft has formatted them, you can —and probably should—modify them. (As noted throughout the book, you must take special steps to ensure that the changes you make to styles of any kind are available for all future documents, and not merely in the document that is on your screen when you modify the styles. By default, changes to styles are saved ***only*** in the document where you make the changes.) You can modify them before you begin working on an outline or at a later time. (To modify a style, see the instructions starting on page 118.)

Changing the Heading Levels

When you finish typing one paragraph and press the Enter key to begin another one, the following paragraph inherits the heading level of the previous one. To change the heading level, you can do any of the following:

- Press the **Tab key** to "demote" a paragraph (i.e., make it a lower or subordinate level) or press **Shift Tab** to "promote" a paragraph (make it a higher level)[1]

- Press **Alt Shift** → to demote a paragraph or **Alt Shift** ← to promote a paragraph

- Press the green "**demote**" or "**promote**" button in the Outline Tools group

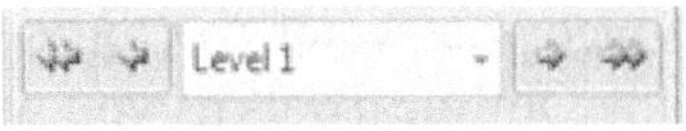

- Press the **demote** or **promote** button in the Paragraph group 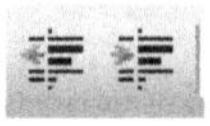

- Grab a paragraph by the **gray circle** to its left and drag it to the left or right

Needless to say, you will want some of the paragraphs you type to appear as simple text rather than headings. To designate paragraphs as "body text" rather than as headings, just click the right-pointing **double green arrow** at the top of the Outline tools ("Demote to body text") ***or***, with your cursor somewhere within the paragraph, use the drop-down and select "**Body Text**."

Showing Levels

On the right side of the Outline Tools group, there is a drop-down list that allows you to show only certain levels of the outline (i.e., collapse the outline) or show all levels (expand the outline). If your outline consists of, say, seven levels but you wish to display only the first three levels, select Level 3 in the drop-down.

Relationships Among Outline Level Paragraphs; Collapsing and Expanding Selected Paragraph Groups Within the Outline

A plus in the gray circle next to a paragraph in an outline indicates that it has sub-paragraphs. The sub-paragraphs can consist of lower-level outline paragraphs or of body text.

A minus in the gray circle next to a paragraph in an outline indicates that it does not have any sub-paragraphs. In other words, it stands alone.

In the section immediately preceding this one, you learned how to display only certain outline level paragraphs, such as the first three levels. You also have the option of collapsing or expanding only certain paragraph groups within the outline. For example, let's say one section of your outline contains a level 3 paragraph followed by four level 4 paragraphs, and you want to

[1] Note that the Tab key and Shift Tab work in Outline view to demote and promote paragraphs, even if you have not enabled the "set left- and first-indent with tabs and backspaces" function under Office button, Word Options, Proofing, AutoCorrect Options, AutoFormat as You Type. Note also that if you wish to insert an actual Tab while in Outline view, you need to use ***Ctrl Tab*** (the key combination in Word for a "hard tab").

see only the level 3 paragraph in particular section. To collapse that group (sometimes called an "outline family") so that you see only the level 3 paragraph, click the gray circle to the left of the level 3 paragraph, then click the minus sign in the Outline Tools group. That section should collapse so that only the higher-level paragraph is displayed. To expand a group or family of paragraphs again, click the plus sign in the Outline Tools group.

The plus and minus signs expand or collapse paragraph groups ("families")

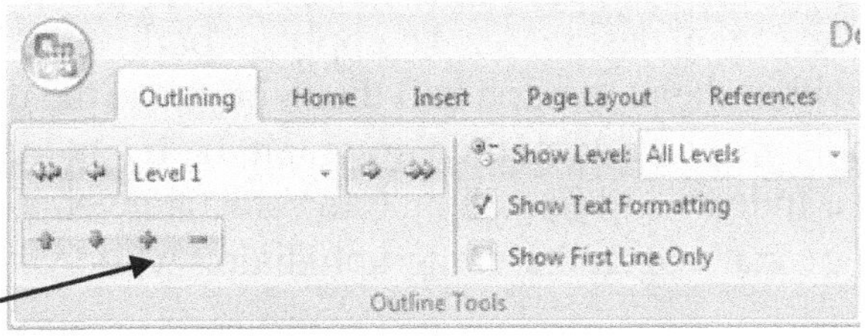

Show First Line Only

This option is similar to the option to collapse the outline (or to collapse certain paragraph groups or families within the outline), except that it displays only the first ***line*** of each paragraph in the outline, as opposed to only certain paragraphs.

Show Text Formatting

If this option is checked—which it is by default—Word will show the formatting that has been applied to the paragraphs (font face, font size, bolding, underlining, etc.). If you want to see plain text only, uncheck that option. **CAUTION**: With the option unchecked, you might not realize that incorrect formatting has been applied to one or more headings in your document.

Applying a Multilevel List to an Outline

Should you wish to apply a multilevel list to an outline, rather than using numbering linked to headings, just select the entire outline, then switch to the **Home tab**, click the **Multilevel list button**, and click the image of a list in the library that contains the number scheme you want to use.

A Few Tips About Outlines

- There is a relatively easy way to display the paragraph styles while in Outline view. Click the **Office button**, **Word Options**, then click **Advanced**. Scroll down about halfway to **Display**, and look for "**Style area pane width in Draft and Outline views**." Type a number in the box that is **at least 1"**, then **OK** out of the Word Options dialog.

- Word has a glitch that makes it impossible to print a condensed outline. If you try to do so, Word will print the outline in its expanded form. The only workaround is to generate a Table of Contents that includes all of the headings (and any non-heading paragraphs that you have marked as an outline level) and then print the TOC. To generate a TOC, position the cursor where you want it to appear, click the **References tab**, click the **TOC icon**, and click **Insert Table of Contents**. When the dialog box appears, ***un***check "**Show page numbers**," then click OK.

- You can apply an outline level to ***any*** paragraph, whether the paragraph consists of plain text or has had a style (other than one of the nine heading styles) applied to it. Doing so will ensure that the paragraph appears in the Table of Contents at the outline level you designate. To apply an outline level, insert your cursor anywhere within the paragraph and then either use the drop-down list from the Outline Tools group ***or*** open the Paragraph dialog and use the Outline level drop-down on the Indents and Spacing tab to select a level. OK out of the dialog. (NOTE: You can't open the Paragraph dialog while you are in Outline view.)

The Document Map

On the **View Tab**, in the **Show/Hide group**, there is a checkbox for **Document Map**. When you enable the Document Map, Word displays a pane at the left side of the screen showing an outline of your document (assuming that you have applied headings or outline levels to any paragraphs in the document). This feature can be useful in any document that uses heading styles, not merely in outlines.

Clicking a particular heading in the Document Map moves the cursor to that heading.

To close the Document Map, just click the "X" in the upper right-hand corner of the map.

<u>Using the "SEQ" Field for Automatic Numbering in Headings for Interrogatories, Rog Responses, etc.</u>

The "SEQ" or sequence field is extremely useful. What makes it particularly well-suited for legal documents is that it allows you to apply automatic numbering to different types of discovery headings in the same document (such as Interrogatories and Interrogatory Responses) and have each type of heading increment properly. Essentially the way it works is that it uses a different identifier for each list—for example, one identifier for the Interrogatories and another one for the Responses to Interrogatories.[1]

In this section, you'll learn how to use the SEQ field to set up headings for Interrogatories and Rog Responses, and then how to create a Quick Part so you can insert the headings with just a few keystrokes.

1. Let's start with the Interrogatories. Begin typing the heading as you normally would. For example, for an Interrogatory, you would turn on underlining (and perhaps also bold) and CAPS Lock, and type **<u>INTERROGATORY NO.</u>**

2. Press the Spacebar and then click the **Insert tab**, **Quick Parts**, **Field...** ***or*** press **Alt I, F**. When the Field dialog opens, locate the Field Names box and scroll down until you find "Seq" ***or*** (this method is faster) simply press the "S" key until "Seq" appears in the list of field codes. You should also see "SEQ" in the "Field codes" box under "Advanced field properties" (toward the right side of the screen).

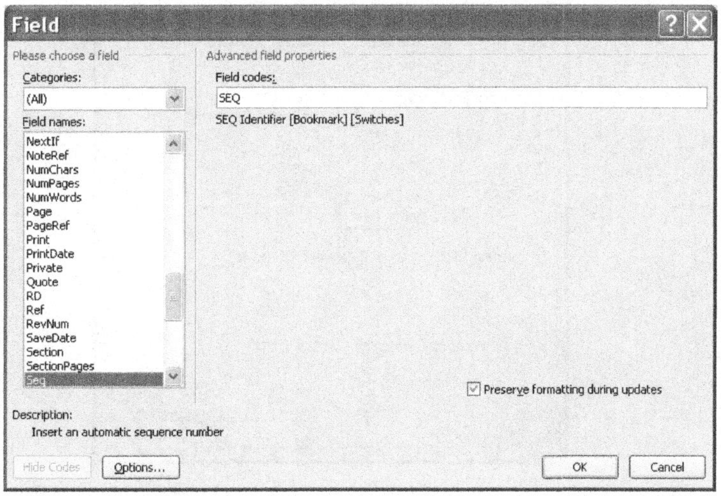

[1] It's similar to the Counters feature in WordPerfect.

3. You're not done yet! The SEQ code requires an "**identifier**." If you click OK before typing an identifier, you'll see the following message: "**ERROR! No sequence specified**."[2] To avoid that problem, position the cursor after "SEQ" in the Field codes box, and type a unique word such as "Rog," or "Int," or "Interrogatory"—some label that will tell Word, and you, exactly what this SEQ code does.

   The identifier can be up to 40 characters long, though shorter is generally better. Note that you should have a unique identifier for each type of SEQ code you use in your document; i.e., if you have a document that contains both Interrogatories and Interrogatory Responses (which you will from time to time), you ***must*** create one distinctive identifier for the SEQ codes you use in the Interrogatories and a different identifier for the SEQ codes you use in the Rog Responses.

4. You might notice that there is an Options **button** at the bottom left side of the Field dialog box. If you click the Options button, another dialog opens. In the "**Formatting**" **box** on the "**General Switches**" **tab** of the dialog there are several different types of numbering and lettering you can use with SEQ fields. The default is Arabic numerals, so you don't need to do anything special to format the numbering in your discovery headings. However, if you ever need to use SEQ fields for other types of automatic numbering or lettering—for example, to insert Exhibit letters (as in the section on Cross-Referencing that follows this section)—you would **click that format in the list**, then click the **Add to Field button**, then click **OK** to add a "switch" for the "ALPHABETIC" letter format to the SEQ code before proceeding.

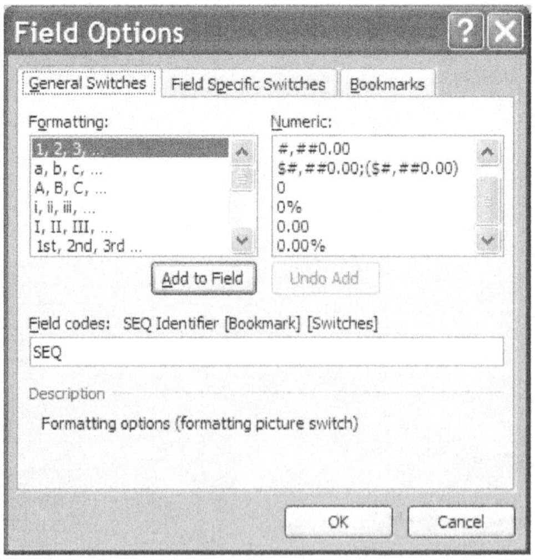

[2] If you accidentally click "OK" before typing an identifier, you can fix the problem without deleting the error message and starting over. All you need to do is press Alt F9 to display the code itself (as in paragraph 6 on the next page), then type an identifier after the word SEQ. Press Alt F9 to display the results of the code. If you still get an error message, make sure your cursor is somewhere within the error message and press F9 to update the code.

5. When you have created an identifier, click OK. You should see something like this:

INTERROGATORY NO. 1

6. If instead you see something like the following, simply press Alt F9 (the keystroke to toggle between displaying the field codes themselves and the field code results).

INTERROGATORY NO. {SEQ Rog * MERGEFORMAT }

Either way, continue to format your heading.

7. When you have finished, you can set up the heading as a "Quick Part" (formerly known as AutoText) so that you can insert it into ***any document*** you create or work on in the future (and have it automatically number correctly) with just a couple of keystrokes.[3] Select the heading (***be sure to include the paragraph symbol at the end of the heading*** so that Word inserts a new blank line underneath the heading when you expand the Quick Part) and then click **Insert tab**, **Text group**, **Quick Parts**, **Save Selection to Quick Part Gallery**. (Alternatively, after you select the heading, press **Alt F3**.) Next, type an abbreviation for the heading (such as "Int" or "Rog"), type a description if you like (optional), and click **OK**.

8. Now, when you want to insert a heading, just type the abbreviation you assigned to it (or the first few letters of the abbreviation, as long as they are unique and you don't have any other Quick Parts that start with those letters) and **press F3** to expand the abbreviation. **NOTE**: Word 2007 no longer includes an "AutoComplete" feature, so you can't simply type the first four characters and press Enter to insert a Quick Part.)

9. Remember that the heading contains an automatic numbering code. If you need to delete or move a heading (for example, if you need to move a series of interrogatories within the document, and move the headings with them), you don't have to do anything to change the numbering sequence. If the numbers don't automatically change when you move the text, just select the document by pressing **Ctrl A** and then press **F9** to "update" the codes.

10. To create headings for the Rog Responses, repeat the above steps, but be sure to use a different identifier—perhaps something like RogResp.

Once you have set up both types of headings using SEQ codes, you'll find that the numbering for the two separate types of headings remains distinct and increments

---

[3] Quick Parts are stored in a file called "Building Blocks.dotx," as mentioned elsewhere in the book.

appropriately, even when you alternate Interrogatories and Interrogatory Responses.

11. It is possible (and relatively simple) to insert a code that starts numbering with a number other than 1. To do so, press **Alt F9** to display the field codes. Position the cursor in the heading where you want to start renumbering, immediately following the backslash after your identifier. Then type the letter "r" (without quotation marks) followed by a space and the number you want to start with. Then type a space followed by another backslash. So, for example, if you want to start with the number 20, you'll insert "r 20 \" and the heading with the edited code will look something like the following:

INTERROGATORY NO. {SEQ Rog \r 20 * MERGEFORMAT }

12. Press Alt F9 again to display the field code results. If for some reason you get an error message, insert your cursor within the code (or press Ctrl A to select the entire document) and press F9 to update the code(s). The code results should display properly, and the Interrogatory number should be 20.

Cross-Referencing Exhibit Letters (or Numbers) and Automatic Paragraph Numbers

Word's Cross-Reference feature can be very useful in formatting legal documents. Many people use the feature to refer back to specific exhibits in a pleading or a contract. It also comes in handy when you need to refer to a particular numbered paragraph. I'll provide instructions for both types of cross-referencing below.

Cross-Referencing Document Exhibits and Similar Items[1]

1. **Select** the item to be cross-referenced, in this case an exhibit letter or number. (Note that you can select just the letter or number ***or*** the entire Exhibit title, such as Exhibit A or Exhibit 1. Whichever you choose to do, just be consistent throughout your document.)

2. Next, you need to create a bookmark. (You will create a unique bookmark for each exhibit to the document.) To do so, click the **Insert tab**, **Bookmark** (in the **Links group**).

3. **Type a name** for the bookmark you are creating. **NOTE**: The name cannot contain spaces, cannot begin with a number, and cannot contain non-alphanumeric characters (other than an underscore character at the beginning of the name, which will turn the bookmark into a hidden bookmark). The name should be descriptive, so that you remember what it does. A good name might be ExhibitA or ExhibitB, if you are identifying exhibits with letters, or Exhibit1 or Exhibit2, if you are identifying exhibits with numbers.

4. Click **Add**.

5. Next, position the cursor at the point in the document where you want to refer to the bookmarked item, and locate and click **Cross-Reference** (also on the **Insert tab**, in the **Links group)**[2]. The Cross-Reference dialog will open.

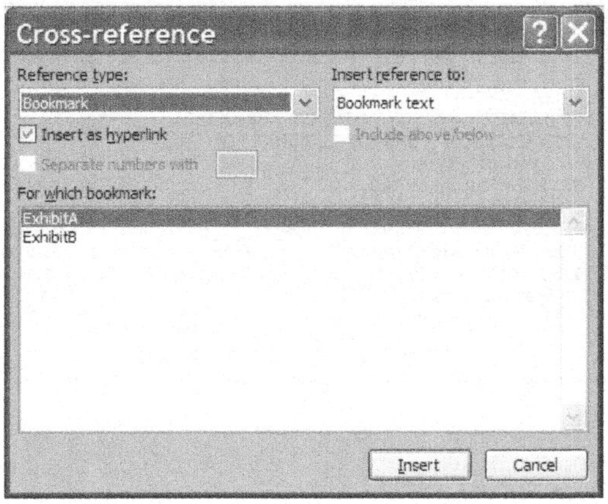

---

[1] Note that this feature works whether you create the exhibit letter manually or with SEQ codes, as in the previous section.

[2] There is also a Cross-Reference button in the **Captions** group on the **References tab**.

6. From the **Reference type** drop-down list on the left-side of the dialog, select **Bookmark**.[3] Make sure that the **Insert reference to:** drop-down is pointing to **Bookmark text**.

7. Click the appropriate bookmark name in the list, click the **Insert** button, then click the **Close** button.

8. Continue setting up Bookmarks and Cross-References for each exhibit (or other item) you wish to refer back to.

9. **NOTE**: If, later on, you add an exhibit to your document in a way that causes the existing exhibit numbers or letters to change, select the entire document (by clicking **Ctrl A**) and then press **F9** to update the bookmark and cross-reference codes.

<u>Cross-Referencing Numbered Paragraphs</u>

You can use the Cross-Reference feature to refer to any numbered paragraphs in your document. Assuming you are using automatic paragraph numbering, you don't need to create bookmarks for the numbered paragraphs; Word recognizes the number codes.

1. Simply position the cursor where you want to insert a cross-reference (for instance, "as mentioned in paragraph XX above," but without the XX placeholder), and click the **References tab, Cross-Reference**.

2. From the **Reference type:** drop-down list on the left-side of the dialog, click to select **Numbered item**.

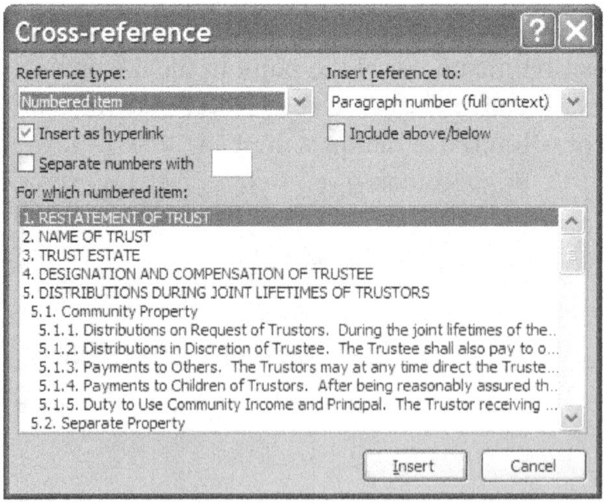

---

[3] The other available reference types include numbered item, heading, footnote, endnote, equation, figure, and table.

3. Click the **Insert reference to:** drop-down and point to **Paragraph number**, **Paragraph number (full context),** or **Paragraph number (no context)**.[4]

> **NOTE**: The different options for displaying a paragraph number are available only when a subparagraph is on a separate line from the "parent" paragraph.
>
> In that event, the "Paragraph" option uses a partial number for a subparagraph if you're referring to it from within the parent paragraph (because the full paragraph number is obvious from the context), whereas it uses a full number if you're referring to it from elsewhere in the document; the "Full Context" option uses the complete number (parent and child paragraphs); and the "No Context" option uses only the level of the selected paragraph.

4. Navigate to the "**For which numbered item**" section of the dialog and scroll down to locate the paragraph in question. Click to select it, then click the **Insert button**.

5. Finally, click **Close**. (The label on the Cancel button changes to "Close" when you click the Insert button.)

Caveats About the Cross-Reference Feature

It is very easy to "break" cross-references because they make use of a hidden "target" code that can be deleted, moved, or otherwise changed accidentally (and without your knowledge). Thus, you need to be extra-careful when ***deleting***, ***cutting and pasting***, or ***copying and pasting*** text and when ***attempting to insert additional text between existing paragraphs*** after you've inserted bookmarks or cross-references within that text.[5]

In particular, never start a new paragraph by pressing the Enter key from within a paragraph that contains a cross-reference (and especially not when the cursor is between the paragraph number and the text). If you need to insert a new paragraph, make sure your cursor is ***at the end of the paragraph ahead of where you want the new paragraph to go*** before you press the Enter key.

In addition, be careful not to paste text at the beginning of a paragraph that contains a cross-reference. Instead, paste into an "empty" paragraph.

---

[4] The other available "Insert reference to:" objects include Page number and Above/below (the latter inserts the word "above" or the word "below" instead of a specific page number reference).

[5] I am indebted to Linda Hopkins and Eva Eilenberg for these tips about methods for avoiding broken cross-references.

Also note that there is a bug in Word 2007 whereby if you update a cross-reference, it might not print correctly. For a description of the problem and a fix (which involves editing the Registry—something that should not be attempted by novices, and not without first backing up the Registry in case of a problem), see Microsoft Knowledge Base Article No. 954541:

"The Ref field is updated incorrectly when you print a Word 2007 document"
http://support.microsoft.com/kb/954541

Formatting Legal Documents

Aligning Text With Pleading Line Numbers

One of the most common problems people in the legal profession encounter with pleadings created in or converted to MS Word is that the text doesn't align with the pleading line numbers. This problem arises most frequently with documents originally created in WordPerfect (or some other word processing program) ***and*** documents originally created in an earlier version of Word.

The discrepancy usually results from an error in the configuration settings described below—and can be fixed by adjusting one or more of those settings. Note, however, that there can be other, less obvious, factors that affect the alignment of text. If the "typical" fixes don't work, try the workarounds suggested toward the end of this section.

The Usual Suspects

1. Line Spacing.

The line spacing of the text might be different from the line spacing of the pleading line numbers. If that's the case, you can change the line spacing of the text to match that of the pleading line numbers. To determine the line spacing of the numbers, click the **Insert tab**, **Header**, **Edit Header** and click somewhere within the line numbers at the left side of the header; then press **Alt O**, **P** to open the **Paragraph dialog** and note the setting in the **Line spacing** box. Close the Paragraph dialog box, close out of the Header editing screen, and check the line spacing of one or more "double-spaced" paragraphs. If in fact there is a disparity, **select** the relevant portions of the text, press **Alt O**, **P** (or click the Paragraph dialog launcher), configure the **Line spacing** to match (using **Exactly**—e.g., Exactly 22.75 pt, or whatever matches the pleading line numbers), and **OK** out of the dialog. **NOTE**: You will have to change the spacing of all single-spaced portions of text to be half that of the double-spaced portions (e.g., Exactly 11.375 pt, if the pleading line number spacing is set at 22.75 pt).

2. "Before" or "After" Spacing.

If any paragraphs have been configured to use "Before" or "After" spacing (for example, 6 pt before the paragraph or 3 pt after the paragraph), that could throw off the alignment of the text. Select some paragraphs randomly and check for "Before" and/or "After" spacing (launch the **Paragraph dialog box** and look at the **Spacing** section of the dialog box, about halfway down the Indents and Spacing tab). (It's especially important to check paragraphs to which a style has been applied.) If necessary, reset those boxes to zero (0) and OK out of the dialog. ***NOTE: In some situations, adding space before or after can help.*** In one sample pleading, going into the Header editing screen and adding 10 points before the first pleading line number (via the **Paragraph dialog**, Spacing Before) actually fixed the problem.

3. <u>Different Fonts That Handle "Leading" Differently</u>.

If the document uses one font for the pleading line numbers and a different font for the text, that can cause problems if the two fonts handle "leading" differently. ("Leading" has to do with the amount of white space inserted between lines of text). Sometimes you can fix things simply by changing either the font of the pleading line numbers ***or*** the font used in the document. (To change the font, select the text (you can use **Ctrl A** to select the entire document) and use the **Font dialog launcher** in the **Font group** on the **Home tab** ***or*** click **Ctrl D** to open the font dialog. To change the font used for the pleading line numbers, click the **Insert tab**, **Header**, **Edit Header**, and click within the numbers, press **Ctrl A**, use the **Font dialog launcher** ***or*** press **Ctrl D**, make any changes, **OK** out, and close the Header editing screen.)

4. <u>Unexpected or Seemingly Random Font Size Changes</u>.

Check the document for unexpected font size changes, especially with respect to blank lines between paragraphs. To do so, turn on Show Non-Printing Characters (click the paragraph icon in the **Paragraph group** of the **Home tab** ***or*** press **Ctrl Shift * [asterisk]**). Look for any paragraph symbols that seem larger than the rest. If you find any, select the paragraph symbol itself and change the font size via the font dialog box.

5. <u>Section Breaks</u>.

If the document contains section breaks, it's possible the sections are formatted differently. Take a look and make any necessary changes. (You can tell which section the cursor is in by looking at the left-hand side of the Status Bar, assuming you have enabled Display Section by right-clicking the Status Bar and checking Section.)

6. <u>Widows and Orphans</u>.

Sometimes having Widow/Orphan control enabled can cause problems with text alignment. This feature ordinarily shouldn't be enabled in pleadings because in general you want text going all the way to the bottom of the page, even if it means one line dangling by itself at the top or bottom of a page. However, ***it is enabled by default***, and because many people aren't aware of that fact, they don't think to turn it off. (It's also difficult to turn off in an entire document, even when you select the document, then launch the **Paragraph dialog**, click the **Line and Page Breaks tab**, and ***uncheck*** **Widow/Orphan control.**)

7. <u>Footers, Footnotes, etc.</u>

It can be worthwhile to check existing footers and footnotes to see if line spacing, "Before" and/or "After" spacing, or other configuration settings for those specific features could be causing problems with the alignment of the text in the body of the document.

Also Notorious

If the factors mentioned above aren't at fault, here are some additional things to investigate:

8. Compatibility Settings.

These settings, found under the **Office Button**, **Word Options**, **Advanced** (scroll all the way down to the bottom of the screen and click the plus sign next to **Layout Options**), can have a significant impact on document formatting. It's not necessary to be familiar with all of the options; just be aware that there are several—including "**Don't add extra space for raised / lowered characters**," "**Don't add leading (extra space) between rows of text**," and "**Don't center 'exact line height' lines**"[1]—that can change the appearance of your document. Selecting Microsoft Office Word 2003 from the drop-down list (so that your files will be compatible with that version of Word) can help in certain instances, but you will have to experiment (using ***copies*** of your documents, not originals).

9. "At Least" vs. "Exactly" Line Spacing.

"At Least" line spacing can be useful in desktop publishing, where there might be dropped caps, graphics in line with text, and other special effects. The "At Least" option ensures a minimum height (point size) for text but allows text to expand to accommodate such special effects. Pleadings, however, often need to use "Exactly" line spacing. When the "At Least" option is used in pleadings, it can create havoc. For example, in a sample pleading with no section breaks, the text on most pages started at 1" from the top of the page, but started at 0.8" on a couple of pages. Eventually I determined that the line spacing for one or more paragraphs on the problematic pages had been set using the "At Least" option. As soon as I changed to "Exactly," the misbehaving pages adjusted and the text moved down to the 1" point.

When All Else Fails

10. Page Setup/Margins and Layout for Headers and Footers.

As a very last resort, you can try fiddling with the top margin of the document and/or the header and footer margins. Note that Word uses negative top and bottom margins in pleadings ***by design*** in order to prevent the header and footer area from expanding (which could cause the body text and the pleading line numbers to become misaligned). See, for example, MS Knowledge Base Article #211611 (found here: http://support.microsoft.com/kb/211611). You

[1] Recently I attempted to save as a .docx file a pleading template I originally created in .doc format. The text alignment changed unexpectedly, such that the first line of the text (which had been aligned perfectly in the .doc version) began slightly above the first line number. I investigated all of the usual suspects listed above, to no avail. Finally, I unchecked the "Don't center 'exact line height' lines" option under Compatibility Settings, which fixed the problem. As you can imagine, troubleshooting this type of problem can be very difficult unless you are aware of obscure settings such as the ones I've mentioned here.

might be able to adjust the margins—for instance, you could change the top margin and/or the header margin from -1.19" to -1"—but just be aware that doing so could make matters worse. Make a note of the existing margins before changing them, and be prepared to undo if necessary.

Miscellaneous Tips

Always try the least drastic—and most obvious—solutions first. (Sometimes simply bumping text down a "single-spaced" line—which might mean a line that is 11.375 points or some other odd fraction—will solve the problem.)

Remember that more than one setting might need to be adjusted.

Check the options in the Paragraph dialog (both tabs) early in the process. It's possible there's an easy fix (for instance, "Before" and/or "After" spacing is the culprit).

Never assume that fixing the formatting of one paragraph will fix the formatting of the other paragraphs in the document—or that selecting the entire document and then changing the paragraph formatting options will succeed. Word can be quirky, and sometimes you have to go back in and change the formatting of individual paragraphs. If necessary, check a few paragraphs at random to see if your new settings have, in fact, taken effect.

Working With Tables to Create Case Captions (Etc.)

SUPERIOR COURT OF THE STATE OF CALIFORNIA

FOR THE COUNTY OF LOS ANGELES

PAPA DOE, MAMA DOE, and BABY	)	CASE NO. LC 12345678	
DOE,	)		
	)	NOTICE OF MOTION AND MOTION TO	
Plaintiffs,	)	COMPEL DEPOSITION TESTIMONY;	
	)	MEMORANDUM OF POINTS AND	
vs.	)	AUTHORITIES IN SUPPORT THEREOF;	
	)	DECLARATION OF PAPA DOE	
DO RE MI , SO LA TI DO, and DOES 1	)		
to 20, inclusive,	)	Date:	March 9, 2009
	)	Time:	9:00 A.M.
Defendants.	)	Dept.:	"Z"
	)		
	)	Discovery Cutoff:	None
	)	Motion Cutoff:	None
	)	Trial Date:	None

If for some reason you need to set up your own case caption, or you have to set up a Separate Statement of Disputed and Undisputed Material Facts, use Tables rather than Columns. Word doesn't have a parallel columns feature, and in addition, if you use Columns, you can't set a middle column narrow enough for just one character, as you can in WordPerfect.

To set up a caption, use the **Insert tab** and click the **Table** drop-down in the **Tables group**. You can either drag the mouse over the table graphic to signify the number of rows and columns you want ***or*** click **Insert Table…** and, when the Insert Table dialog appears, type the number of rows and columns.

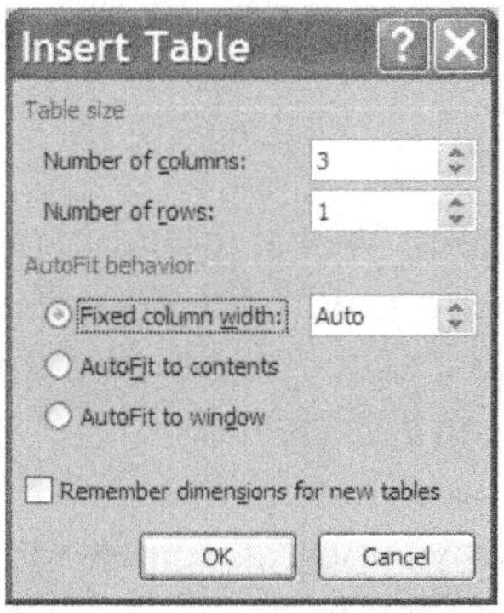

You'll likely want to create a table with three columns and one row (or four columns and one row, which allows you to use an "empty" column as a buffer between the end parentheses and the document title). For a Separate Statement, you can use two or three columns, or even four (two small columns for the numbers and one for the facts and supporting evidence).

One way to set the margins is to drag the column margin markers on the ruler—or the table margins themselves—until the columns are formatted to your liking. Of course, this method is best for people who are highly skilled at using the mouse. Alternatively, click within the table, then click the **Table Tools Layout tab**, and set the width of each column manually. In the screenshot below, the width appears in the second box from the top in the **Cell Size group** (where it displays 2.22").

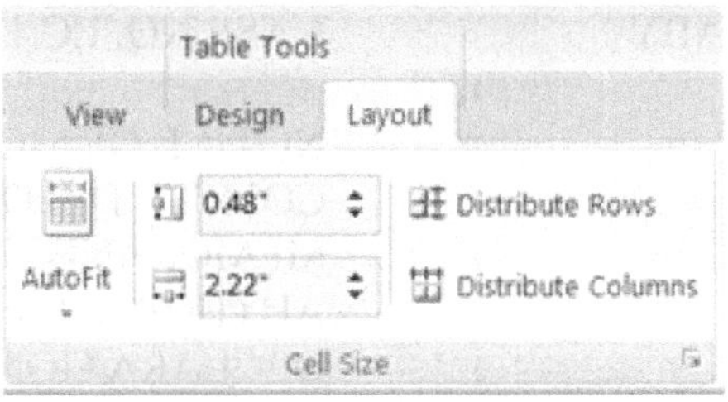

Or you can launch the **Table Properties** dialog box by clicking the arrow at the lower right-hand corner of the **Cell Size group**, click the **Column** tab, and set the column widths from there. (Note the "**Previous Column**" and "**Next Column**" buttons, which you can use to set the widths of the other columns.)

Table Borders and Gridlines

When you first insert a table in Word, the table ordinarily appears with borders around each cell. These borders normally print with the document. For purposes of a pleading caption, you will want to remove the borders, except for the bottom border of the left-hand column (i.e., the parties box portion of the caption).

There are a few different ways you can remove the table borders. Position your cursor within the table and do one of the following:

1. (a) With your cursor in the table, click the **Table Tools Design tab** and launch the **Borders and Shading** dialog by clicking the arrow in the lower right-hand corner of the **Draw Borders** group.

(b) Make sure that the **Apply to:** drop-down in the lower right-hand side of the Borders and Shading dialog displays "**Table**" (as opposed to "Cell" or "Paragraph"), and then click the "**None**" icon at the top of the left-hand column. Then **OK** out.

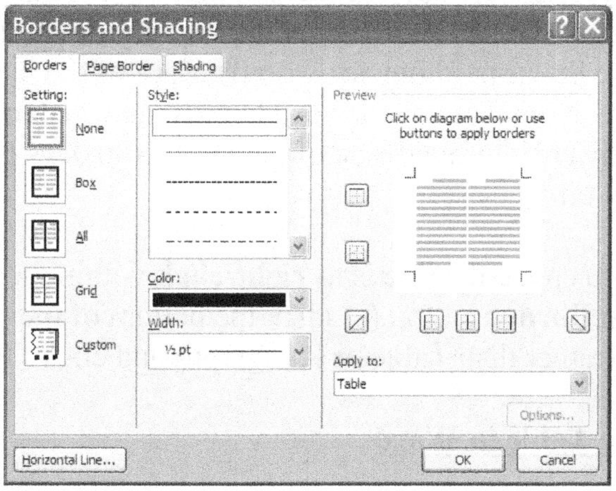

2. As an alternative, right-click somewhere within the table, then click the **Borders and Shading** command, and proceed as outlined in the paragraph immediately above; ***or***

3. Click the **Home tab**, **Paragraph group**, click the drop-down **Borders** icon, click the **Borders and Shading** command at the bottom of the list, and proceed as outlined in Paragraph 1(b) above.

Note that if you select "None" from the drop-down instead of the Borders and Shading command, Word will remove the borders ***only*** from the cell your cursor is in, not from the entire table.

When you remove the table borders, you may or may not see a pale blue or gray outline around the table and all table cells. This outline is called a "gridline." It is a non-printing border provided to help you navigate within the table. If you prefer not to see the gridlines, click inside the table, then click the **Table Tools Layout tab** and click **View Gridlines** (at the left side of the Ribbon). The View Gridlines button is a toggle; it alternates between turning gridlines on and off (depending on the state of the gridlines—i.e., whether they are visible or hidden—when you click the button).

Gridlines can be turned on or off, as well, from the **Borders** button on the **Table Tools Design tab**. That button opens a drop-down list; the second command from the bottom is **View Gridlines**.

Remember that gridlines do not print. If you ever create a table and you want the borders to print, you need to use one of the above methods to create or restore missing table borders.

CAUTION! In Word 2007, there is a "Gridlines" command on the View tab that has ***absolutely nothing to do with Table Gridlines***. Rather, it has to do with hidden ***drawing gridlines*** in the NORMAL template that comes with the program and that most users never see or need to see.

Creating the Line at the Bottom of Column 1

Once you have removed the table borders, you'll need to create a horizontal line at the bottom of the first column. There are several ways to accomplish this task. One particularly easy way is to click anywhere within the first column, then locate the **Borders** icon on the **Table Tools Design tab**, click the down-pointing arrow to the right of the icon, locate the icon with the bottom border, and click it. Note that you also can launch the **Borders and Shading** dialog by clicking the arrow in the lower right-hand side of the **Draw Borders** group, the right-most group in the **Table Tools Design tab**.

Another easy way to create the line is to **right-click** within the cell, click **Borders and Shading**, click the **Bottom Border** button (or click the bottom of the diagram), then make sure "**Apply to**" displays **Cell** (rather than Table or Paragraph) and click **OK**.

Moving Around Within a Table in Word

Start typing the text in column 1 normally. It will wrap around when it reaches the right-hand margin of the column. When you need to tab over within the cell to type the word "Plaintiffs," press **Ctrl Tab**. ***Pressing the Tab key by itself will move you to the next cell (column)***. (To move to the previous column, press **Shift Tab**.) Then create the middle and right columns the same way you create the middle and right columns in WordPerfect. (You don't have to turn off the columns when you're finished, but **don't press Tab when you reach the end of Column 3**, or you'll inadvertently create a new row! **Instead, use the down arrow to move the cursor out of the table.**)

Watch Out for Typing Replaces Selected Text

There is a configuration option in Word (under **Office Button**, **Word Options**, **Advanced**) called "Typing Replaces Selected Text" (formerly called "Typing Replaces Selection") that you should be aware of. If this option has been checked, when you press Tab to move to the next column, Word highlights the text in that column—and overwrites the text when you press any key to insert a letter or number. In other words, the highlighted text is deleted and replaced by whatever character(s) you type. (Pressing the cursor movement keys does not delete the highlighted text, but pressing the Spacebar does.)

If you accidentally delete highlighted text, press **Ctrl Z** or click the **Undo button** on the Quick Access Toolbar. If you like, you can turn off the "Typing Replaces Selected Text" option by clicking the **Office Button**, **Word Options**, **Advanced** and unchecking the box next to that option.

Some Additional Tips About Working With Tables

As in WordPerfect, you can add one or more rows easily by positioning the cursor in the last cell of the table and pressing the Tab key (keep pressing Tab to add more than one row).

If you are using a table that spans multiple pages (for instance, in a Separate Statement), you can create a header row that repeats at the top of each page. With the cursor in the row you wish to use as the header row, click the **Table Tools Layout tab**, **Table Properties**, click the **Row tab**, and check the "**Repeat as header row at the top of each page**" box.

CAUTION: There is a **Header Row** option in the **Table Tools Design tab**, **Table Style Options group** (the left-most group), and by default it is checked. This feature has to do with the design of tables that have alternating shaded rows; it determines whether the top row of the table is or is not shaded. Obviously, therefore, it has nothing to do with creating repetitive content at the top of each page of a table.

If you need to insert regular text in a row between rows that contain multiple columns, you can either merge the cells in one row or split the table. To merge cells, first select the cells, then click **Merge Cells** on the **Table Tools Layout tab**. To split a table, position the cursor in the row where you want to insert text and click **Split Table**, also found on the **Table Tools Layout tab**.

Note that you can choose to allow rows to split across pages or configure them not to do so. With your cursor in the row, click the **Table Tools Layout tab**, **Table Properties**, click the **Row tab**, and either check or uncheck the "**Allow row to break across pages**" box.

If your table appears to you to be off center, click the **Table Tools Layout tab**, **Table Properties**, click the **Table tab**, and make sure the alignment is set to Center.

One more quick tip: **Table Tools, Layout** (in the **Table group**, which is all the way to the left) has a **Select drop-down** that allows you to select an entire table, a row, a column, or a cell. Also, there is a keyboard shortcut for selecting an entire table: **Alt Num 5** (i.e., the number 5 on the Numeric Keypad). If you are working on a laptop, you might find that you need to press **Alt Fn 5** (where "Fn" is "Function" and the "5" is not the one on the row of numbers at the top but the one in a different color somewhere within the keyboard. On my main laptop, it is on the same key as the letter "I").

<u>WHERE DID IT GO?—Sort</u>

The **Sort command** is now available via a button in the **Paragraph group** on the **Home tab**. (It's located immediately to the left of the paragraph symbol or pilcrow.) The button looks like this:

There's another **Sort command** on the context-sensitive **Table Tools Layout tab** (in the **Data group**), which becomes available when your cursor is positioned within a table.

Basic Sorting: A Brief Review

If you wish to perform a simple sort and there's no other text on the page, you don't even have to select the text; just click the button and the **Sort Text dialog** will open. If there's any other text on the page, be sure to select the text first.

The default sort type is Paragraph. You can sort alphabetically by text (in either ascending or descending order) or, if the items to be sorted include numbers, you can sort numerically (in ascending or descending order).

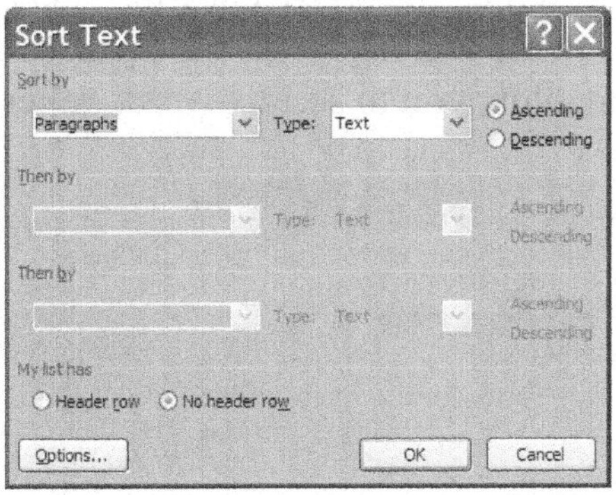

Depending on the items to be sorted, you might need to do some tweaking to the "Sort by" settings. If the information includes "fields" separated by tabs or commas, click the "Options" button and, if necessary, click to change the field separator type.

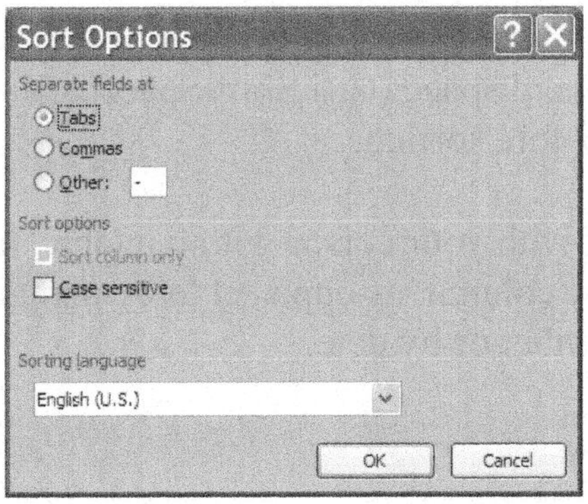

If you select Tabs or Commas, the "Sort by" options will change so that you can sort by field. For example, if Field 1 is the first name and Field 2 is the last name, you can sort by Field 2, then by Field1 (so that names are alphabetized first by last name, and then by last name, in case there are two or more people with the same last name).

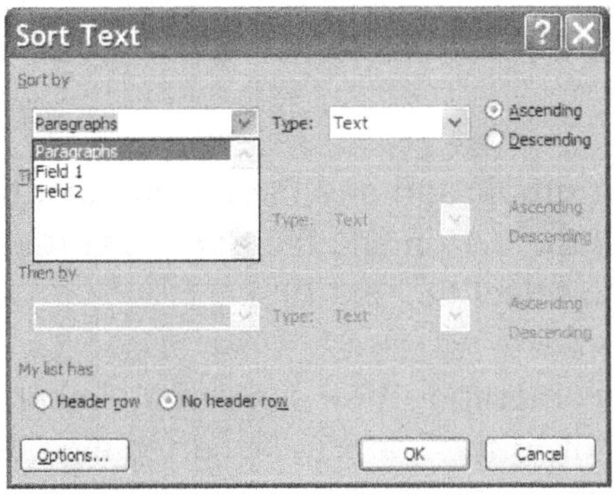

Note that you can sort by Word. To do so, click the "Other" option, then click in the box to the right, delete the character in the box and press the Spacebar instead, then click "OK." The "Sort by" drop-down changes to allow you to sort by word, rather than by field.

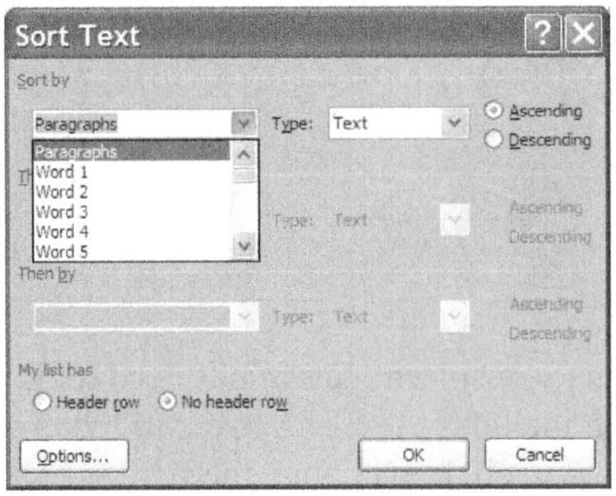

TIP: If you are sorting a list of names and some of the names have middle initials or compound first names, insert a hard space (Ctrl Shift Spacebar) between the first name and the middle initial or second name before sorting.

When you initiate a sort with your cursor within a table, the Sort dialog provides different options. It defaults to sorting by column, as opposed to by paragraph. You still have the option of sorting text, as well as by number or by date.

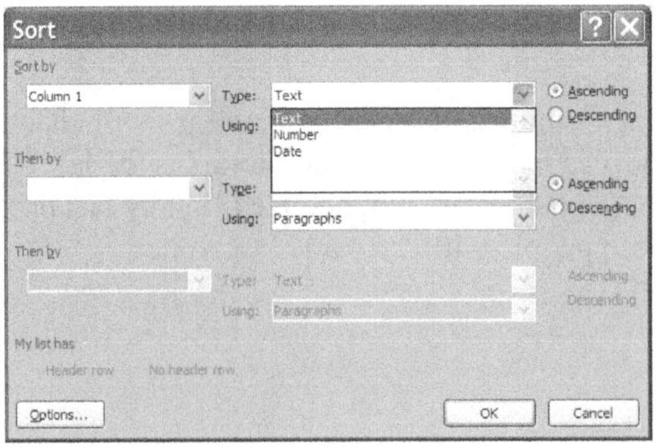

<u>Creating a California Rules of Court ("CRC")</u>
<u>Rule 2.110[1]-Compliant Footer</u>

1. With your pleading on the screen, click the **Insert** tab, then navigate to the **Header & Footer** group and click **Footer, Edit Footer**. Word puts you in a special footer editing screen.[2]

2. Once in the footer editing screen, press **Ctrl 1** to make sure the footer will be single-spaced.[3] If you forget to change the line spacing at this point, you can change it later on by selecting the entire footer (by pressing Ctrl A while in the footer editing screen) and then pressing Ctrl 1.

3. If you haven't already inserted page numbers in your document, position the cursor at the center of the footer (which is also the center of the page). There are two ways to do so:

   (a) by pressing **Ctrl E**; or

   (b) by clicking the **Home** tab, then clicking the **Center Justification** button in the **Paragraph** group.[4]

4. Next, insert a page number code by either (a) clicking the **Page Number** icon in the **Header & Footer group** on the **Header & Footer Tools Design tab**, **Current Position**, **Simple**[5] ***or*** (b) simply pressing **Alt Shift P**.

5. If you <u>have</u> already inserted page numbers in your document, press the **End** key to move the cursor to the end of the line.

---

[1] Formerly numbered 201(g).

[2] Note: To move between the footer editing screen and the header editing screen, you can either (a) click the **Go to Header button** on the **Design tab** (or the **Go to Footer button** if your cursor is in the header screen) or (b) press the **up or down arrow** as appropriate.

[3] If the your pleading text is based on "Exact" line spacing, it's preferable to use an "Exact" measure in the footer as well. To do so, open the **Paragraph dialog** by pressing **Alt O**, **P**, and under **Line spacing**, select **Exactly** from the drop-down, type 11.375 in the "**At**" **box**, and click **OK**.

[4]Pressing the **Tab key** once will move the cursor to the 3" mark, which isn't true center because our pleading uses margins of 1.5" on the left and .5" on the right. Note that although there is a ***center tab stop*** at 3" (which means any text you type will be centered around the 3" mark), this method does not use ***center justification***. In other words, when you press the Enter key to move the cursor to the next line, the cursor will go back to the left margin.

[5] **CAUTION**: If you use any of the other built-in options besides Current Position, Word will overwrite any text you've already inserted into your footer.

6. Next, press the **Enter** key to move the cursor to the next line so that you can insert a horizontal line below the page number. There are at least three ways to insert the horizontal line. The first one is particularly easy.

   (1) **Automatic Borders**. If you have automatic formatting of borders turned on, just type **three hyphens** and press the **Enter** key. (If that doesn't work, automatic formatting of borders is turned off. To turn it on, click the **Office button**, **Word Options**, **Proofing**, **AutoCorrect**, **AutoFormat As You Type**, click the **Border lines** checkbox, and click **OK**.) When you have finished, Word will automatically bump the cursor to the next line.

   (2) **The Border Button**. Using the up arrow key (not the Backspace key), move the cursor back up a line so that it is just past the number code and ahead of the paragraph symbol. Then locate the **Border button** on the **Home tab** (at the bottom right side of the **Paragraph group**), click the down-pointing triangle to the right of the button, and click the **Bottom Border icon**. Next, press the **down arrow key** to move the cursor to the next line.

   (3) **Shift + Underscore**. Alternatively, hold down the **Shift key** and press the **underscore key** (the key to the right of the zero/close parenthesis key) until the line stretches across the footer editing screen. (If you go too far, just press the Backspace key and delete any excess.) When you have finished, press the Enter key to move the cursor to the next line. **NOTE**: This is ***the least elegant method***, but it works.

7. For the short document title, you'll probably want to use a smaller font than what you're using in the body of the pleading. Remember that California Rules of Court mandates that pleadings for the Superior Court use a footer font no smaller than 10 points. To change to a smaller font, do one of the following:

   (a) Navigate to the **Home** tab, **Font** group, and make a selection from the drop-down font size list; ***or***

   (b) Open the Font dialog box (by pressing **Ctrl D**) and change the size from there; ***or***

   (c) Simply press **Ctrl [** (open bracket) once or twice. (Each time you press Ctrl [, the font size decreases by one point.)

8. To center the document title,[6] just start typing (assuming you turned center justification on in step 3).

---

[6] If you prefer (and if it is your firm's standard), you can right align the title. To do so, press Ctrl R and start typing. To indent the title from the left, press Ctrl M a few times and start

9. When you're finished, just click the **Close Header and Footer** button.

10. You may need to adjust the bottom margin of the pleading so that you're able to type on all 28 lines. To do so, click the **Page Layout** tab and launch the **Page Setup dialog** (or click **Alt P**, **M**, **A** or **Alt P**, **S**, **P**). Change the bottom margin setting as necessary. You might have to experiment with this setting.

11. If you want to "suppress" the page number on the caption page, you will have to divide the document into two ***sections*** (one consisting of the first page and the other consisting of the rest of the document); ***unlink*** the Section 2 footer from the Section 1 footer; then modify the footer in Section 1 by deleting the page number code.

    (a) To divide the document into sections:

        (1) First, switch to **Draft View** (use the icons at the right-side of the Status Bar or click the **View** tab, **Draft**) so you can see the section breaks and page breaks more easily.

        (2) Position the cursor at the bottom of the first page and click the **Page Layout** tab, **Page Setup** group, **Breaks**, **Next Page**.

        (3) The section break should replace the existing page break. If it doesn't, delete the page break.

    (b) To unlink the Section 2 footer from the Section 1 footer:

        (1) Change back to **Print Layout** view.

        (2) Click the **Insert** tab, **Footer**, **Edit Footer** and navigate to the Section 2 footer by clicking **Next Section**. Note the words "Same as Previous" at the right-hand side of the footer editing screen for Section 2.

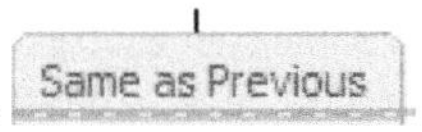

        (3) Locate and click the **Link to Previous button** (toward the center of the **Header & Footer Tools Design tab**) to turn it ***off***. The words "Same as Previous" should disappear.

---

typing. (To decrease the indent, either press Ctrl Shift M or click the Decrease Indent button on the formatting toolbar.)

(c) To modify the Section 1 footer:

(1) Now use the **Previous Section** button to move to the Section 1 footer editing screen.

(2) Select the page number code in the Section 1 footer—being careful not to select the paragraph symbol immediately to the right of the number code—and press **Delete** (or cut using Ctrl X or any method you prefer).

(3) Click **Close Header and Footer**. Scroll through the document to make sure the Section 1 and Section 2 footers are in fact different.

Creating a CRC Rule 2.110 Compliant Footer Using the "Different First Page" Option To "Suppress" the Page Number on the Caption Page

This section has been revised significantly to allow for "suppressing" the page number on the caption page of pleadings. In MS Word, when you want to have more than one header or footer—for example, a footer ***without*** a page number and a second footer ***with*** a page number—you must divide the document into different sections.

Word has a "Different First Page" option that lets you create a footer without a page number on the caption page, as well as footers on the remaining pages that have page number codes. But there is a very important "gotcha" to be aware of when you use the "Different First Page" option: Headers are linked to footers in Word, and the pleading paper is part of a header. As a result, when you first apply "Different First Page," ***the pleading paper will disappear!*** We can get it back, but we have to remember to follow all the steps outlined below.

1. With your pleading on the screen, click the **Insert tab**, **Header**, **Edit Header**. Word puts you in a special header editing screen. The first thing you need to do is press **Ctrl Shift * (asterisk)** (or click the paragraph symbol in the **Paragraph group** on the **Home tab**) to turn on Show Nonprinting Characters.

2. When Show Nonprinting Characters is turned on, you should see (among other things) paragraph symbols. Remember that the paragraph symbols contain formatting codes. The very first paragraph symbol at the top of the header editing screen contains codes that configure the pleading paper. We will need to reinsert this code in a few minutes, so **select (highlight) that paragraph symbol** and either press **Ctrl C** to copy or use any other method you prefer to copy selected characters.

3. Next, click the **Header and Footer Tools Design tab**, **Options group**, and check the "**Different First Page**" option.

4. The pleading paper disappears! Eek! But not to worry: Just press **Ctrl V** or use any other method you like to paste the paragraph symbol you copied in step 2 above in place of the paragraph symbol at the top of the header editing screen. The pleading paper should reappear.

5. With the pleading paper back, we will create a footer with no page number for the first page (caption page) of the pleading. To do so, you need to move the cursor to the footer editing screen by either (a) clicking the **Go to Footer** button ***or*** (b) pressing the **down arrow**.

6. Once in the footer editing screen, we need to make sure the footer will be single-spaced. Because of the way we generated our pleading, the numbered lines do not use standard double-spacing, so we will have to use "Exact" line spacing. First, select the entire footer by pressing **Ctrl A**. Then press **Alt O, P** to open the **Paragraph dialog**, and under **Line spacing**, select **Exactly** from the drop-down and type **11.375** (or whatever is exactly half the figure for double-spacing in your pleading), and click **OK**.

7. We are not going to insert a page number code in the first-page footer, but we want to leave a blank space—a sort of placeholder—where the page number ordinarily would go. Doing so ensures that the footers on the caption page and the succeeding pages all line up correctly.

8. Press the **Enter** key to move the cursor to the next line so that you can insert a horizontal line below the space where the page number ordinarily would go. There are at least three ways to insert the horizontal line. The first one is particularly easy.

   (1) **Automatic Borders**. If you have automatic formatting of borders turned on, just type **three hyphens** and press the **Enter** key. (If that doesn't work, automatic formatting of borders is turned off. To turn it on, click the **Office button**, **Word Options**, **Proofing**, **AutoCorrect**, **AutoFormat As You Type**, click the **Border lines** checkbox, and click **OK**.) When you have finished, Word will automatically bump the cursor to the next line.

   (2) **The Border Button**. Using the **up arrow key** (not the Backspace key), move the cursor back up a line so that it is just past the number code and ahead of the paragraph symbol. Then locate the **Border button** on the **Home tab** (at the bottom right side of the **Paragraph group**), click the down-pointing triangle to the right of the button, and click the **Bottom Border icon**. Next, press the **down arrow key** to move the cursor to the next line.

   (3) **Shift + Underscore**. Alternatively, hold down the **Shift key** and press the **underscore key** (the key to the right of the zero/close parenthesis key) until the line stretches across the footer editing screen. (If you go too far, just press the Backspace key and delete any excess.) When you have finished, press the Enter key to move the cursor to the next line. NOTE: This is ***the least elegant method***, but it works.

9. For the short document title, you'll probably want to use a smaller font than what you're using in the body of the pleading. Remember that California Rules of Court mandates that pleadings for the Superior Court use a footer font no smaller than10 points. To change to a smaller font, do one of the following:

(a) Navigate to the **Home tab**, **Font group**, and make a selection from the drop-down font size list; ***or***

(b) Open the **Font dialog box** (by pressing **Ctrl D**) and change the size from there; ***or***

(c) Simply press **Ctrl [** (open bracket) once or twice. (Each time you press Ctrl [, the font size decreases by one point.)

10. To center the document title,[1] turn on center justification by pressing **Ctrl E**, and then just start typing.[2]

11. Next, we will create a footer with a page number code. That footer will appear on every page of the pleading except the caption page. (Later on, we will need to insert section breaks so that we can change the page number to start at 1 on the first page of the Memorandum of Points and Authorities and to start at 1 and use small Roman numerals, rather than Arabic numerals, on the first page of the Table of Contents.) First, let's copy the existing footer by pressing **Ctrl A** (to select the entire footer), then pressing **Ctrl C** (or using any other method you prefer to copy selected text).

12. Then, let's move to the Section 2 footer editing screen by clicking the "**Next Section**" button on the **Header & Footer Tools Design tab**. (We automatically divided the document into two sections when we applied the "Different First Page" option.)

13. With your cursor in the Section 2 footer editing screen, press **Ctrl V** or use any other method you like to paste the Section 1 footer we copied in step 11 above. Once you've done so, position the cursor above the horizontal line, press **Ctrl E**, and insert a page number code by either (a) clicking the **Page Number** icon on the Design tab, **Current Position**, **Simple**[3] ***or*** (b) simply pressing **Alt Shift P**.

---

[1] If you prefer (and if it is your firm's standard), you can right align the title. To do so, press Ctrl R and start typing. To indent the title from the left, press Ctrl M a few times and start typing. (To decrease the indent, either press Ctrl Shift M or click the Decrease Indent button on the formatting toolbar.)

[2] Pressing the Tab key once will move the cursor to the 3" mark, which isn't true center because our pleading uses margins of 1.5" on the left and .5" on the right. Note that although there is a ***center tab stop*** at 3" (which means any text you type will be centered around the 3" mark), this method does not use ***center justification***. In other words, when you press the Enter key to move the cursor to the next line, the cursor will go back to the left margin.

[3] **CAUTION**: If you use any of the other built-in options besides Current Position, Word will overwrite any text you've already inserted into your footer.

14. When you're finished, just click the **Close Header and Footer** button. You may need to adjust the bottom margin of the pleading so that you're able to type on all 28 lines. To do so, click the **Page Layout** tab and launch the **Page Setup dialog** (or press **Alt P**, **M**, **A** ***or*** **Alt P**, **S**, **P**). Change the bottom margin setting as necessary. You might have to experiment with this setting.

Setting Up a Style (and Keyboard Shortcut) for Indented Quotes

1. Start typing the text for your indented quote.

2. With the cursor somewhere within the text, launch the **Paragraph dialog** by clicking the **dialog launcher** in the lower right-hand corner of the **Paragraph group** on the **Home tab** ***or*** by pressing **Alt O**, **P**.

3. Navigate to the **Indentation** box and set both the **Left indent** and the **Right indent** to 1". Make sure the **Special** box is set to **(none)**, unless you want the first line of the quote to be indented an additional half-inch, in which case click the drop down list in the **Special** box, select **First line** and set **By** to .5". Click **OK.**

4. With the cursor still within the text, launch the **Styles Pane** by clicking the dialog launcher in the lower right-hand corner of the **Styles group** on the **Home tab** ***or*** by pressing the key combination **Ctrl Alt Shift S**.

5. When the Style Pane opens, navigate to the very bottom and click the **New Style** button—the first one from the left. A **Create New Style from Formatting** dialog box appears. In the **Name** box at the top of the dialog, **type a name** for the style you are creating (for example, Double Indent, Indented Quote, or Block Quote).

6. In the box labeled **Style for following paragraph**, click the drop-down list and scroll until you find **Normal**. (**NOTE**: Setting the style for the following paragraph as Normal means that when you finish typing one paragraph of an indented quote and you press the Enter key, the cursor will go back to the left margin and you will be able to type a paragraph that has no special formatting. You might prefer to set up your new style so that when you press Enter, that style's formatting carries over to the next paragraph. If you do so, you can turn off the style at any point by pressing **Ctrl Shift N**, which applies the Normal paragraph style to the paragraph containing the cursor.)

7. Depending on how your firm formats indented quotes, you also might want to change the line spacing and/or the font in your style. To do so, click the **Format** button at the bottom of the dialog box, then click **Paragraph** (and/or **Font**), and change the settings to suit your preferences.

8. To set up a keyboard shortcut for your new style, click the **Format** button again, then click **Shortcut key**. Another dialog box appears with the cursor already in the **Press new shortcut key** box. Press the key combination you wish to assign to your style, such as Ctrl Shift F7 or Shift F4 (the WordPerfect keyboard shortcuts for Double Indent). If your preferred key combination already has been assigned to another feature, Word displays a message to that effect. If the key combination

is available or if you wish to override the existing assignment, click the **Assign** button to assign the keystrokes to your style, and click Close.

9. **IMPORTANT**: Before OK-ing out of the Create New Style from Formatting dialog box, be sure to click the **New documents based on this template** radio button at the bottom center. Otherwise, the style will be available ***only in the specific document in which you have created the style***. After you have clicked this radio button, click **OK** to save your new style and close the dialog box, and click the X in the upper right-hand corner of the Styles Pane to close it.

Type a **name** here

Set the style for the **following paragraph**

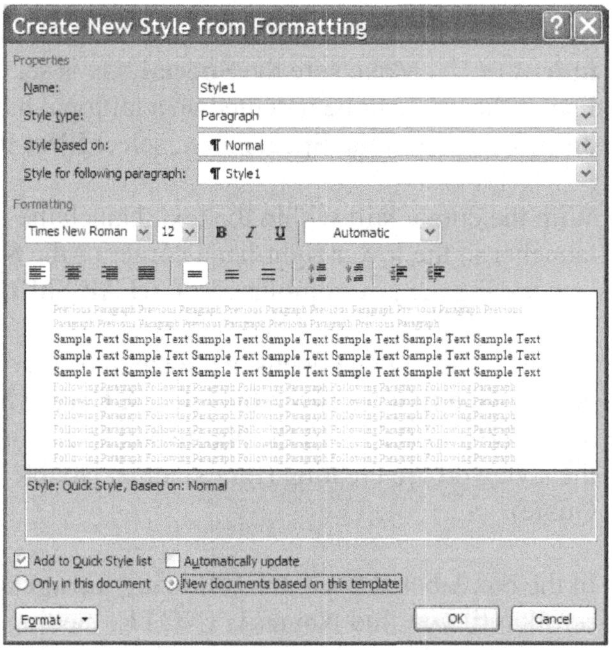

Format button—to set the font, indents, and so on

Be sure to click "**New documents based on this template**" to make the style available in all new documents

10. To use the style, just press the key combination you assigned and start typing. Alternatively, you can apply the style by using the keyboard shortcut after you have typed some text, so long as the cursor is somewhere within the paragraph or you have selected the text. Or you can click somewhere within the paragraph (or select some text), then press **Ctrl Shift S** to open the **Apply Styles** dialog, pull down the Style list, and click to apply a particular style.

Note that you can print a list of Styles (and/or a list of Key assignments) from the Print dialog box. When you invoke the Print dialog by pressing **Ctrl P** (or clicking the **Office button**, **Print**), you'll see a "**Print what**" drop-down on the lower left-hand side. That drop-down includes options to print Styles and Key assignments, among other things.

Creating and Generating a Table of Contents (TOC) and a Table of Authorities (TOA)

There are four basic steps involved in creating and generating a Table of Contents and a Table of Authorities in Word. These are:

- Changing the page numbers / inserting section breaks
- Marking the headings (TOC) and/or authorities (TOA)
- Generating the tables
- Editing the TOC/TOA.

Changing the Page Numbers / Inserting Section Breaks.

In my on-site training sessions, we typically use as a sample document a Notice of Motion and Motion for Summary Judgment that I provide. As you probably know, in a Motion, the Notice pages use Arabic numerals, starting with 1; the Motion itself (the Points and Authorities) uses Arabic numerals, starting with 1; and the TOC and TOA use small roman numerals, starting with i on the first page of the TOC and continuing consecutively through the last page of the TOA. (Do not start over with i on the first page of the TOA.)

To ensure that Word inserts the correct page numbers for all three parts of the document, we have to divide the document into three "***sections***." (Remember, to apply different page formatting options within a document in Word, you must divide the document into sections and format each section separately. For example, you must insert section breaks when you want to change the page numbering format, use multiple headers and footers, change page margins, switch from portrait to landscape orientation, or insert columns in the middle of a page that also contains regular text.) Our three sections will consist of the Notice pages (Section 1), the Motion (Points and Authorities) (Section 2), and the TOC / TOA (Section 3). In a hard copy of the document the TOC and TOA follow the Notice pages, but it's easiest to create them at the end of the Motion and then simply collate the pages by hand after printing.

Let's assume we've already inserted CRC Rule 2.110 compliant footers containing page numbers into our document.[1] Now we need to create section breaks. Because Word assumes that every new document already comprises one section, we'll actually insert only two section breaks: one between the Notice pages and the Motion and one at the end of the Motion, where we're going to insert our Table of Contents and Table of Authorities. We'll insert the section breaks first and then go back and format the page numbering in each section.

TIP: You might want to switch from Print Layout View to Draft View while working with section breaks, because it's easier to see the section breaks (and delete them if necessary) in Draft View. To do so, click the **View tab**, **Draft**, or click the **Draft View button** on the Status Bar.

---

[1] See pages 173 and 177.

First, we'll create a section break after the Notice of Motion.

(a) Put the cursor at the bottom of the second page of the Notice and click the **Page Layout tab**, **Page Setup group**, **Breaks**, **Section breaks**, **Next page**.

(b) If inserting the section break bumps the heading for the Memorandum of Points and Authorities down, simply press the Delete key to bring it back to the top of the page.

As mentioned above, the easiest way to set up a TOC and TOA in Word is to put it at the end of the document (and simply collate the pages after printing). So we'll create another section break at the end of the document, then set up a rudimentary TOC and TOA.

(a) Press **Ctrl End** to move the cursor to the very end of the document.

(b) Click **Page Layout tab**, **Page Setup group**, **Breaks**, **Section breaks**, **Next page**.

While we're here, let's create simple headings for the TOC and the TOA (unless the sample document already contains headings, in which case let's skip steps (a) through (e) below and move to the top of the next page). This exercise is for practice only. Don't worry about making the headings look perfect.

(a) At the top of the new page, press Ctrl E to center the cursor, press Ctrl U to turn on underlining, press Caps Lock, and type TABLE OF CONTENTS.

(b) Press Ctrl U to turn off underlining, press the Enter key twice, press Ctrl R to put the cursor at the right margin and turn on right alignment, press Ctrl U to turn underlining on again, and type PAGE.

(c) Press Ctrl U to turn off underlining, press the Enter key twice, and press Ctrl L to put the cursor at the left margin. Then press the Enter key and keep it depressed until you create a soft page break.

(d) Repeat steps (a) and (b) immediately above, except type TABLE OF AUTHORITIES instead of TABLE OF CONTENTS.

(e) Press Ctrl U to turn off underlining, press the Enter key twice, and press Ctrl L to put the cursor at the left margin. Then press the Enter key two or three times.

Now we've created two section breaks, which has divided the document into three sections. Section 1 is the Notice pages, Section 2 is the Motion (the Memorandum of Points and Authorities), and Section 3 is the Table of Contents and Table of Authorities. We've also created simple headings for the TOC and TOA.

Next, we need to format the page numbering in the two new sections.

(a) First, press Ctrl Home to move the cursor back to the very top of the document. Click the **Insert tab**, **Header & Footer**, **Footer**, and either click "**Blank**" or click "**Edit footer**." Word will put you in the footer editing screen for Section 1.

(b) Next, go to the footer editing screen ***for Section 2*** by clicking the **Next Section** button.

(c) At this point, click **Page Number**, **Format Page Numbers**. Make sure the Number format field is set for Arabic numerals (1, 2, 3) and that the "Start at" radio button is checked and the box shows the number 1. Click OK.

(d) When the footer for Section 2 is correct, press **Next Section** to move to the footer editing screen for Section 3. Click **Page Number, Format Page Numbers**, but this time change the Number format to small roman (i, ii, iii). Make sure that the "Start at" button is checked and the box shows the number i. Click OK.

(e) Click **Close Header and Footer** to close the Header and Footer editing screen.

1. Marking the Headings (TOC) and/or the Authorities (TOA).

Table of Contents

If you have used built-in or custom styles to create the headings, ***you don't have to do anything special (e.g., manually mark them) in order to have them appear in the TOC***. When you generate the TOC, Word automatically pulls headings created with styles into the TOC.

Prior to Word 2002, if you created the headings "manually" (i.e., simply typed the headings, without using ***styles***), you had to use the "Mark Table of Contents Entry" dialog box to mark them for inclusion in the TOC. Word 2002 introduced a somewhat simpler way of marking manually created headings in the TOC. I will provide the steps below, while still providing instructions on marking headings with the "Mark Table of Contents Entry dialog in case you ever need to use that method.

Marking "Manual" Headings by Applying Outline Levels

In Word 2007, you can mark a manually created heading simply by doing the following:

- Place the cursor within the heading.
- Click the **Paragraph dialog launcher** ***or*** press **Alt O**, **P**.

- Locate the Outline level drop-down toward the top of the dialog box.
- Select the appropriate heading level (from 1 to 9) and OK out.

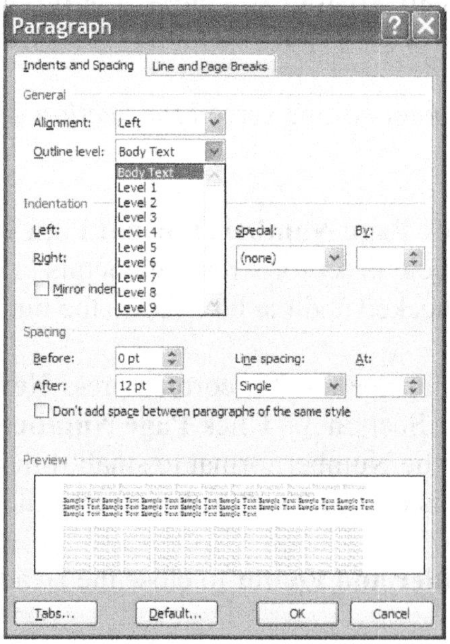

- Repeat for each manually created heading.

Here's an alternate way to do the same thing:

- Place the cursor within the heading and switch to Outline view.
- Use the drop-down to select a heading level (from 1 to 9).

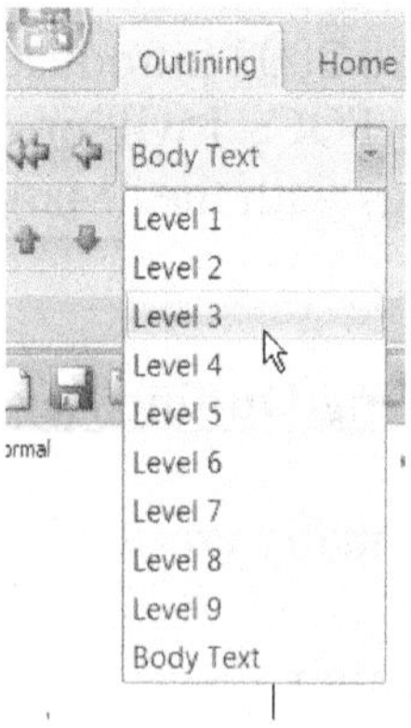

- Continue marking manually created headings in this fashion.
- After you have marked all the headings, change back to Print Layout view by clicking the View tab, Print Layout or pressing Alt V, P.

<u>Generating the TOC (See Also: Generating the Tables)</u>

When you have finished, position your cursor where you want the TOC to appear and click the **References tab**, **Table of Contents**.

At this point, you have the option of simply clicking one of the first two built-in "automatic" TOC schemes, which will generate the TOC and also inserts a heading at the top left margin of the page (either "Contents" or "Table of Contents"). In Word 2007, you have an additional new option: You can insert a "Manual Table," which simply sets up ***a TOC format*** with placeholders for text and page numbering that you need to type yourself. Note that this option ***does not allow for automatic updating of text or page numbers***; therefore, it is of somewhat limited utility. It is useful mainly for setting up a skeletal TOC ***format***, complete with dot leaders.

Rather than using any of the built-in schemes (automatic or manual), you might find it preferable to click "**Insert Table of Contents**" at the bottom of the TOC menu, which launches the TOC dialog box. This method gives you more control over the process by allowing you to check—and change—various settings before generating the TOC. **NOTE:** This method also is somewhat more reliable than using the built-in schemes.

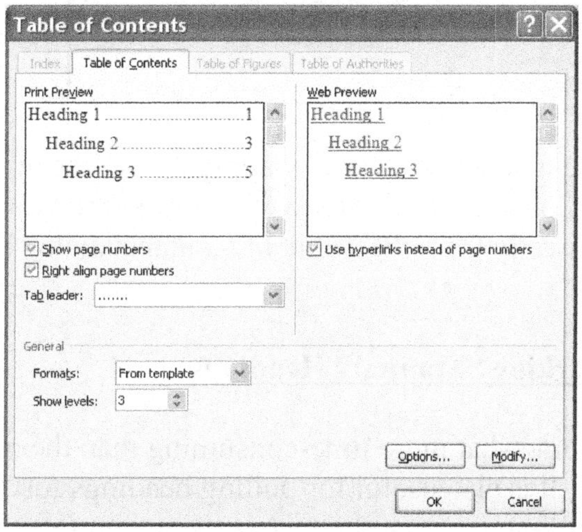

One of the settings you should examine is the "**Show levels**" field toward the bottom of the dialog box. Make sure that it is set to show as many heading levels as you wish to display in the TOC. In the screenshot above, the field shows the number 3, which means ***only the first three heading levels*** will appear in the generated TOC, regardless of the number of levels in the doc.

Also click the **Options button** so that you can review the checkboxes under "Build table of contents from" and make sure that the boxes for both "**Styles**" and "**Outline levels**" are checked, then click **OK**. (See the screenshot that follows.)

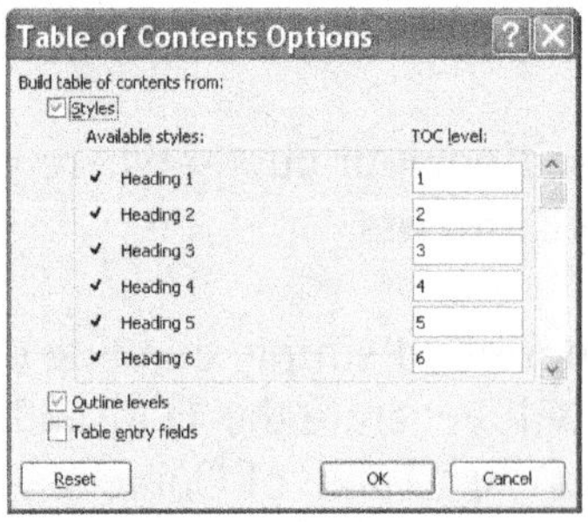

Once everything is set to your satisfaction, click OK to generate the TOC. Word will incorporate into the TOC the headings you have marked, and will apply the appropriate indentation for the outline level you selected. Note that generating the TOC from the dialog box rather than from one of the automatic TOC schemes in the drop-down will ***not*** insert a heading (i.e., a page title) at the top of the Table of Contents; you'll have to type that yourself.

After you generate the TOC, you can update it by **right-clicking** somewhere within the TOC, clicking **Update field**, clicking **Update entire table**, **OK**.

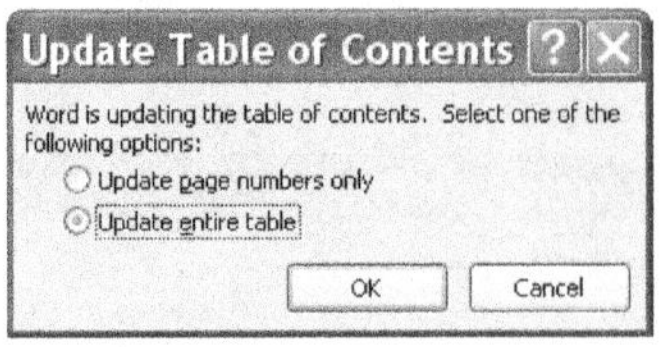

CAUTION: If you have marked headings by applying outline levels to them, right-clicking and using "Update Table of Contents" doesn't always work properly. You might find that you have to regenerate the TOC directly from the Table of Contents dialog box instead.

<u>The Old Method of Marking "Manual" Headings</u>

This method is somewhat more time-consuming than the method explained immediately above, but it still works. It is also useful for pulling headings for "run-in" style paragraphs into the TOC without also pulling in any of the text of the paragraph. For more information on "run-in" paragraphs, see the section on page 189 about using the Style Separator.)

To mark "manual" headings for inclusion in the TOC, do the following:

(a) **Select** (block, highlight) the heading.

(b) While text is selected, press **Alt Shift O**, which brings up the "Mark Table of Contents Entry" dialog box.

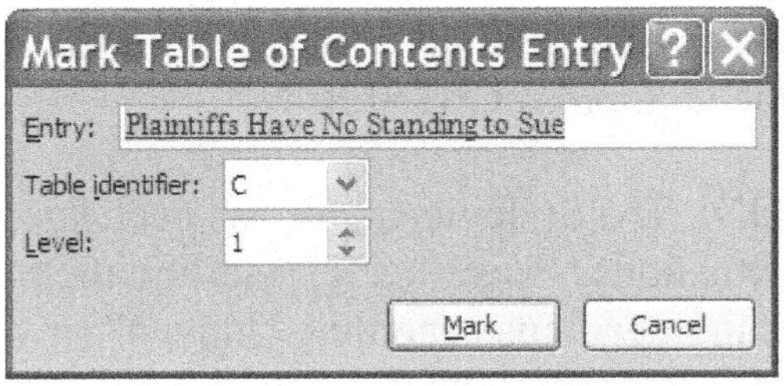

(c) For TOC entries, make sure the table identifier says "C" (for Table of Contents) and that the "level" field is set correctly (i.e., 1 for a level 1 heading, 2 for a level 2 heading, etc.) When everything looks okay, click "Mark."

NOTE: When Word marks the entries, it automatically switches to "Show Non-Printing Characters" mode. If you find this distracting, click the Paragraph symbol (¶) in the Paragraph group (on the Home tab) ***or*** just press Ctrl Shift * (asterisk) to turn "Show Non-Printing Characters" off.

Continue marking headings in this fashion.

Tip: Using the Style Separator in Word

Occasionally, you will work on a document in which the paragraph heading is in the same line as the text of the paragraph (a "run-in" paragraph). That can cause problems because when you apply a heading style, Word doesn't differentiate between the heading itself and the text of the paragraph. It pulls everything—text and all—into the TOC.

In order to prevent that from happening, you can insert a "Style Separator" between the heading and the text of the paragraph.[2] The easiest way to insert a Style Separator is by using a keyboard shortcut: **Ctrl Alt Enter**. Note that because the symbol for the Style Separator (a special paragraph symbol) is inserted as "hidden text," you should turn on Show Non-Printing Characters and reposition your cursor if necessary before inserting the Style Separator.

CAUTION: If you have already applied a style to the paragraph, make sure the Style Separator is positioned between the heading and the paragraph text. If necessary, you can cut and paste the Style Separator. After inserting the Style Separator, you might have to select the paragraph text and either apply the Normal paragraph style to it or apply some other style (such

[2] There is a feature in Word 2007 called "Linked Styles" that has been touted as a solution to the run-in paragraph problem. Linked styles are a sort of hybrid combination of a paragraph style and a character style. In theory, linked styles can be applied either to an entire paragraph or to selected text within a paragraph—such that you can apply one style to the heading and another style to the text that follows the heading. However, in my tests the results were quirky and somewhat frustrating (the paragraph text unexpectedly took on certain characteristics of the headings and had to be manually reformatted), and there are some reports on the web of problems with the linked styles feature. For now, it's probably better to disable linked styles by launching the Styles Pane and clicking the "Disable Linked Styles" checkbox at the bottom.

as Body Text) so that the text will not get pulled into the TOC. To apply the Normal paragraph style quickly after selecting the text, press **Ctrl Shift N**.

FURTHER CAUTION: The Style Separator has been known to cause problems with numbered headings in some situations. Specifically, inserting the Style Separator can result in paragraph numbers or even entire headings becoming "hidden" (invisible). This problem typically occurs in paragraphs where the numbered heading doesn't include any text or caption (for instance, it appears simply as "Section 1."—as opposed to "Section 1. Parties to the Agreement"). It is possible to work around this problem by using a TC code to mark the heading; you might also have to insert a second Style Separator to the right of the first one. Obviously, it's preferable to have text or a caption following a numbered heading, but if you ever need to insert numbered headings without any accompanying text, be on the alert for this issue.

Tip: Adding Text to the TOC

Word 2007 also makes it easy for you to mark a paragraph (or other unit of text in the document) for inclusion in the TOC without applying a style to the text. First, select the text or, if you want to include an entire paragraph, simply insert the cursor somewhere within the paragraph. Next, click the **References tab**, **Table of Contents**, **Add Text**. From the Add Text drop-down, mark the text as a Level 1, Level 2, or Level 3 paragraph, which automatically un-checks "Do not show in Table of Contents."

Conversely, you can use the drop-down to mark a paragraph so that it does ***not*** appear in the TOC; however, doing so can have unintended consequences (similar to the Style Separator issues mentioned above). Use with caution.

Table of Authorities

(a) Select (block, highlight) the citation.

(b) While text is selected, press **Alt Shift I**, which brings up the "**Mark Citation**" dialog box. (If you prefer, you can click the "**Mark Citation**" **button** in the **Table of Authorities group** on the **References tab**.)

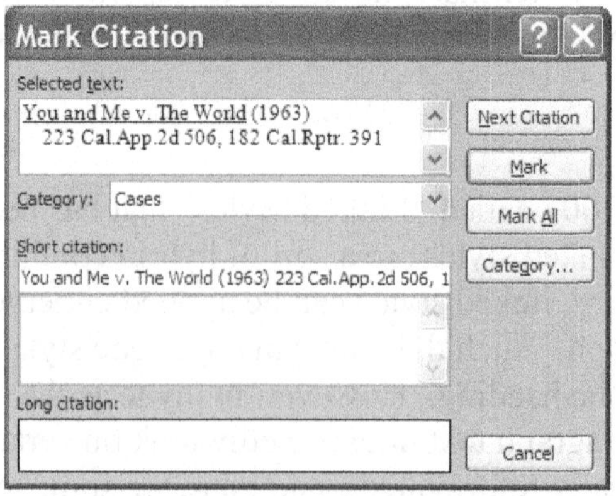

(c) In the "**Selected Text**" **box**, make sure the citation looks the way you want it to look in the Table of Authorities. (This step is comparable to editing the Full Form of the citation in WordPerfect.)

Next, make sure the box reflects **the correct category** for that citation—Cases, Statutes, Treatises, whatever.

NOTE: You can add a new category by **clicking on one of the numbers** in the Category field from 8 to 16, then **clicking on the Category button**, **typing a new name** in the "Replace with" box, and **clicking Replace**.

(d) Then **edit the Short Citation**. This is the "nickname" Word will use when it searches for this citation throughout the document. It's usually a good idea to ***use the most generic Short Citation possible*** because Word searches for the exact text string in this box. Thus, for example, if you use C.C.P. in your Short Citation, it won't find—or mark—any instances of the citation that use California Code of Civil Procedure (or vice versa). Nor will it find or mark the word "section" if the Short Citation uses the section sign (or vice versa). You might find it works best if you use just the code section number (and letters, if any), such as 127.5(a).

(e) When you have finished, click "**Mark All**" to mark all instances of the citation in the document.

Continue marking authorities in this fashion. (If you like, you can click the "Next Citation" button to move the cursor to the next citation, but this option is of somewhat limited utility, given that Word recognizes only a few of the "signals" commonly used in legal documents.)

2. **<u>Generating the Tables</u>**.

This step actually includes "defining" the tables, too.

NOTE: Be sure to ***turn off Show Non-Printing Characters*** before generating the tables. Otherwise, because the Non-Printing Characters take up quite a bit of space in the document (and actually can bump text down a page), the TOC and TOA might not reflect the correct page numbers for headings and citations!

NOTE FURTHER: In Word, unlike in WordPerfect, you generate the TOC and TOA separately. You can also generate individual sections of the TOA separately, which can be useful—or confusing!

Let's start with the **Table of Contents**.

(a) With the cursor at the exact spot where you want to generate the Table of Contents, click the **References tab**, **Table of Contents**, then click **Insert Table**

of Contents... to open the TOC dialog box. (NOTE: You can add a TOC button to the Quick Access Toolbar if you like.)

(b) Make sure you've selected the TOC format you want, and also that Show page numbers, Right align page numbers, Number of levels, and Tab leader are set the way you want. (The default settings are normally what you'll want, but check them anyway).

(c) The next step, which is ***critical***, is to click **Options**. You must check the Options tab because ***Word marks TOC entries differently depending on whether you've used styles to create the headings or you've just typed headings from scratch***. If the former, be sure the "**Styles**" box under "Build table of contents from" is checked. If the latter, be sure the "**Table entry fields**" box is checked. (You don't need to do so if you have applied Outline levels to the headings as per the discussion on pages 185 and 186.) If you've created headings using both methods, you must check both boxes.

(d) When everything is set right, click **OK**.

The process is basically the same for the **Table of Authorities**.

(a) With the cursor at the exact spot where you want to generate the TOA, click the **References tab**, **Insert Table of Authorities** (the button at the upper right side of the Ribbon).

(b) As with the TOC, make sure everything is formatted the way you want. ***The most important thing to check before generating the TOA is that the Categories field says "All." If it doesn't, only a portion of the TOA will generate***.

(c) When everything is set up right, click **OK**. The tables should generate properly, though you might need to do some "cleanup."

3. <u>Editing the TOC/TOA</u>.

If you need to edit a heading or citation that you have already marked, you need to edit the **code** for that heading or citation, as well as the heading or citation itself. Normally the codes are hidden text, so in order to edit them, you have to turn on Show Non-Printing Characters (see page 5). When the codes are visible, ***edit the text between the quotation marks***. (You can, if necessary, edit the heading level within the code, too.) Then regenerate the tables (quick method: right-click in the tables and click Update Field ***or*** select the entire document by pressing Ctrl A and then update all fields in the doc by pressing F9), and your changes will show up in the newly generated tables.

You might also want to modify the TOC and/or TOA style(s), although doing so can be somewhat complicated. For more detailed instructions, see the section entitled "Modifying TOC and/or TOA Styles in MS Word."

Modifying TOC and/or TOA Styles

After you have generated a Table of Contents and/or a Table of Authorities, you might notice that your tabs aren't exactly where you want them to be, that the table uses the wrong font, or that the headings don't look quite right. These elements of the TOC and TOA are determined by TOC and TOA ***styles*** that are pre-set in Word. You can, however, modify these styles and save your modifications--either in the particular document on your screen or, better yet, in the template on which your document is based. If you save the style changes to the template, all documents you create in the future that are based on that template will reflect those changes.

As you know by now, by default, Word saves your style changes **ONLY** in the specific document on your screen. To save those changes to the underlying template, you ***must*** click the "**New documents based on this template**" radio button on the Modify Style dialog box before clicking OK. If you forget to perform this step, you can do so at a later time—but you must have that particular document on your screen, or you'll have to modify the styles again from scratch.

There are two ways to modify the TOC heading styles, the TOA heading style, or the Table of Authorities (i.e., TOA text) style. The first way is to use the Styles Pane, as follows:

1. Insert the cursor into a heading or text whose style you wish to modify.

2. Launch the Styles Pane (using the dialog launcher or Ctrl Alt Shift S) and ***right-click*** the style name, then click **Modify**.

3. Click the **Format** button and then click the Font, Paragraph, or Tab button (etc.), and make all desired changes.

4. Remember to click (check) the **New documents based on this template** radio button if you want your changes saved to the template (for use in other documents), as opposed to saving them just in the current document. (You may or may not want to click the **Automatically update** box; because doing so can cause problems, it's probably best not to.) Once you've clicked the **New documents** radio button, click **OK**.

5. If you have checked the Automatically update box, all instances of that style in your document should change to reflect the modifications you have made. If the style doesn't update, you can click **Ctrl Shift S** to open the **Apply Styles** box and click **Reapply**. Word should offer you two choices: (1) Update the style to reflect recent changes and (2) Reapply the formatting of the style to the selection. To ensure that the document reflects the modifications you've made, choose (2). (Otherwise, the style will be modified to reflect the formatting of the text your paragraph is in.)

The second method is to click the **References tab**, and then:

1. To change a TOC style, click **Table of Contents**, **Insert Table of Contents**, **Modify**. **Select** the TOC style you wish to change and click **Modify** again. Then follow steps 3 through 5, above.

2. To change a TOA style, click the **Table of Authorities** button (at the upper right side of the Ribbon), click **Modify**, and follow steps 3 through 5 above.

Tracking Changes[1]

Many attorneys like to keep track of edits they make while drafting their documents, a process sometimes referred to as "redlining" (and occasionally as "blacklining").

There actually are two different ways you can "track changes" in your documents in Word. One involves turning on the "**Track Changes**" feature (called "Revisions" in early versions of Word), which highlights any text you add to and/or delete from your document, as well as certain formatting changes, ***as you type***. The other method, "**Compare Documents**," allows you to compare **two different drafts** of a document and produce a third, printable document that clearly displays all text that has been inserted into, deleted from, or moved in the more recent draft. The latter is the feature that is more commonly called "redlining."

In both cases, when you are ready to finalize your document, you can go through it line by line and accept or reject individual changes (either your own or those made by another reviewer). This section of the book explains how to use the Track Changes feature; the following section discusses the Compare Documents feature.

When Track Changes is enabled, Word marks—with distinctive font colors, underlining, strikeout marks, and other formatting attributes—text that you insert, delete, and/or move from place to place within a document.

To start tracking changes, you can do any of the following:

1. Press **Ctrl Shift E**; ***or***

2. Navigate to the **Review tab**, **Tracking group**, click the **Track Changes button**, and then click **Track Changes**; ***or***

3. If you have added the "**Track Changes**" **indicator** to the **Status Bar**, click it once to turn Track Changes on. When you're ready to turn Track Changes off, click it again (it's a toggle). **NOTE**: In Word 2007, unlike in previous versions, the Track Changes indicator is not displayed on the Status Bar unless you specifically add it. To do so, right-click the Status Bar and then click to put a check next to "Track Changes." (It's a good idea to put the indicator on the Status Bar because it can be difficult to tell if the feature is on or off otherwise.)

---

[1] **CAUTION**: Because Track Changes introduces a significant amount of "metadata" into your document, you need to be very careful to eliminate such hidden / confidential information before sharing the document with someone outside the firm (or anyone to whom you'd rather not reveal the metadata). There are a number of steps you can take to remove metadata from your documents, a few of which I'll discuss here.

Track Changes Options

Word is pre-configured to use certain colors and formatting attributes to highlight your edits. However, you can change the appearance of inserted and deleted text by clicking the **Track Changes button** in the **Tracking Group**, then clicking **Change Tracking Options**. (See the screenshot below).

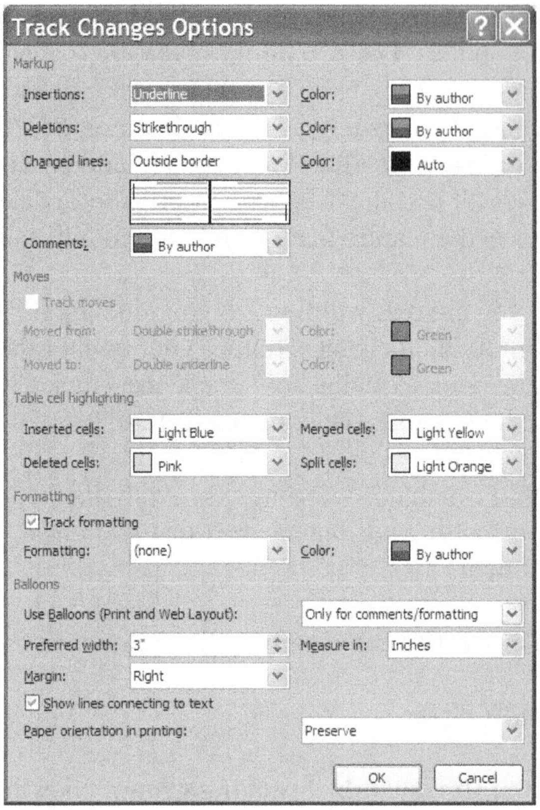

As you can see, there are several different options you can set.[2] You can change the formatting and color for any or all of the following:

- **Insertions** (by default set to use underlining)
- **Deletions** (by default set to use strikeout marks)
- The way that changes are flagged in the margins (labeled "**Changed lines**" in the dialog)
- **Comments**
- **Moves** (which includes marks indicating where text was moved ***from*** and marks indicating where text was moved ***to***)
- Changes to **table cells** (this option is new in Word 2007)

---

[2] **NOTE**: These settings are specific to each individual user (i.e., the person whose name and initials are shown on the "**Popular**" page of **Word Options**).

- **Formatting** (e.g., bolding, underlining, italics)

Note that the default color setting for Insertions, Deletions, and Comments is "**By author**." That setting means that if several different individuals are working on the document, Word will use different (unique) colors to indicate each person's changes.

Even if you do not use the "By author" setting, you can determine who inserted, deleted, and formatted text by placing the mouse pointer over a particular revision; when you do, a pop-up appears showing the initials of the author, the date and time of the modification, the nature of the change (insertion, deletion, formatting, or comment), and the content.

To change the various settings, just use the drop-downs. (For example, I typically use the color blue plus double underlining for inserted text and the color red plus strikeout for deleted text.) Once everything is configured to your liking, click **OK**.[3]

Balloons

Recent versions of Word allow you to display insertions, deletions, formatting changes, and comments in "**balloons**" in the document margins.

CAUTION: If this option is enabled, balloons not only appear in the document, but actually print with the document, which can be confusing, especially if you've never used this feature. Note that there is a drop-down list in the **Track Changes Options dialog** that allows you to limit the use of balloons (to comments and formatting only) or to turn them off altogether (the "Never" option).[4]

You can disable balloons from the Ribbon, as well (**Review tab**, **Tracking group**, **Balloons**). The Balloon options in the **Tracking group** are:

(1) Show Revisions in Balloons;
(2) Show All Revisions Inline; and
(3) Show Only Comments and Formatting in Balloons.

If you choose the first option, most of your changes—deletions, moves, formatting changes, comments, etc.—will appear in balloons in the margins. (Deletions will be indicated in the text by markers in the color you've selected for deletions.) Note that insertions will appear inline with the text, which makes perfect sense.[5]

---

[3] You can change these settings again at any time.

[4] The Balloons options are: Always, Never, and Only for comments/formatting.

[5] These generalizations assume you are using the **Final Showing Markup** option in the **Display for Review drop-down** in the **Tracking group** of the **Review tab**. If you are using the **Original Showing Markup** option, Insertions will appear in the margins and Deletions will appear inline.

If you choose the second option (Inline), your changes will be displayed in the body of the document only, without any balloons in the margins. (However, the vertical lines used to indicate which lines contain changes will continue to appear in the margins.)

If you choose the third option, only formatting changes and comments will show up in balloons.

Using the Feature

Once you've configured the options the way you want, turn on Track Changes (using any of the methods outlined above) and start typing. Word will keep track of your edits until you turn the feature off again.

Viewing Only Certain Types of Markup

If you don't wish to see revision marks for every type of edit, you can click the **Show Markup drop-down** in the **Tracking group** on the **Review tab** and turn off the display for one or more categories of "markup." These include: Comments, Ink (you can hand-write comments if you have a tablet PC), Insertions and Deletions, Formatting, Markup Area Highlight (i.e., the area where balloons display if you have balloons enabled), and Reviewers (if the document has been edited by more than one individual, you can selectively show or hide the markup by specific reviewers).

Previewing the "Final" Document / Viewing the "Original" (Unedited) Document

While you are revising a document, you can preview how the document would look if you accepted all the changes by navigating to the **Review tab** in the **Tracking group** and clicking the **Final** option on the **Display for Review drop-down** (the one at the top right of the group).

Alternatively, you can see how the document looked before you started making changes by clicking the **Original** display option. (Or you can see how the original and final drafts look with markings for insertions and deletions.)

Finalizing Your Edits / Removing Markup From a Document

TIP: You can't undo finalization of a document, so if there's any chance you'll want to re-create your edits at some later date, you should save a copy of the document before proceeding to this next step.

When you have finished making changes and you are ready to finalize the document, navigate to the **Review tab, Changes group**. If you are satisfied with all of your edits (whether insertions or deletions), click the **Accept drop-down**, then click **Accept All Changes in Document**. If, however, you aren't entirely certain you're happy with every revision, use the **Previous** and **Next** buttons to move to individual changes and click the **Reject drop-down**,

Reject Change to cancel the ones you don't want to retain, while clicking the **Accept drop-down**, **Accept Change** to confirm each of the others.

After accepting or rejecting all of the changes, be sure to save the finalized document.

NOTE: You can use this same process of going through the document and accepting or rejecting changes if you accidentally turn on Track Changes and can't figure out how to get rid of tracking marks you've inserted unintentionally.

CAUTION: Be aware that selecting Final from the **Show Markup drop-down** in the **Tracking group** on the **Review tab** ***merely alters the appearance of the document on your screen***. ***It does not remove the Track Changes marks***. That means that if you forward the document to someone else, ***they can view your edits simply by choosing a different option (such as Final Showing Markup) from the Display for Review drop-down***.

In order to remove the Track Changes marks from the document permanently—so that no one else is able to display them—you ***must*** accept or reject each individual change.

And, of course, be sure to turn Track Changes off before you send the document to anyone else.

SIDEBAR: What Does "Mark as Final" Do?

Word 2007 comes with a new feature called "**Mark as Final**." When Mark as Final is applied, no one can type in or otherwise change a document. Because of this fact, and because of the feature's name, it sounds as if it might be related to Track Changes.

Indeed, Microsoft intends for this command to be used when you are collaborating with others in the process of creating and reviewing documents. However, it is of somewhat limited utility, for the following reasons:

- It doesn't actually strip out revision marks, so it isn't a metadata removal tool and shouldn't be used as a substitute for accepting or rejecting all of the changes to a document.
- Although it makes the document read-only, anyone who receives the document can change the document status easily and make it editable again.
- And finally, if someone opens a "Marked as Final" document in an earlier version of Word, the read-only status is removed.

Still, you might find the feature useful as a reminder to others (or to yourself) that a document is a final draft and shouldn't be modified. To use it, click the **Office button**, **Prepare**, **Mark as Final**. A Mark as Final icon will appear in the Status Bar, and most icons in most tabs on the Ribbon will be grayed out, because you can't apply any formatting to the finalized document. To ***un***mark a finalized document, repeat the steps immediately above.

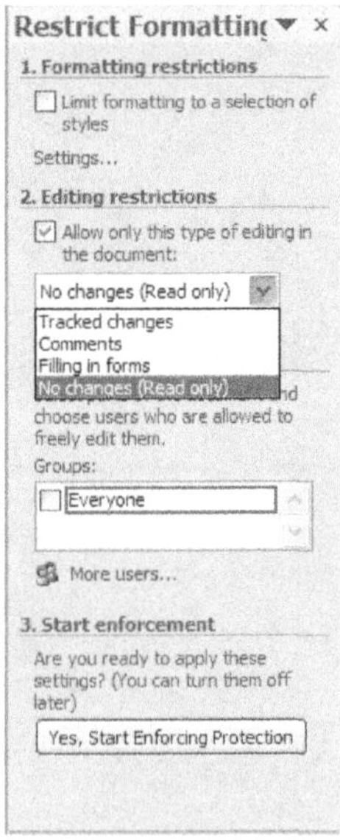

Should you wish to ***password protect*** a document, restrict the type of editing someone else can do, and/or restrict the styles someone else can apply, use **Protect Document** instead of Mark as Final. Protect Document is on the **Review tab**, all the way to the right under **Protect**. Click to open the **Restrict Formatting and Editing Pane**. The first option on the pane lets you limit the styles other people working on the document can use (you choose allowable styles from a list). There is also an option to permit only certain types of editing: Tracked changes, Comments, Filling in Forms, or No changes (Read only). You can specify exceptions—i.e., individuals who are allowed to edit all or a portion of the document.

Check one or both of those options, then click the "**Yes, Start Enforcing Protection**" **button**. When the dialog opens, type and confirm a password and click **OK**. **CAUTION**: Be sure to make note of the password and keep it in a safe, easy-to-remember location.

To disable protection, open the document, navigate to the **Protect group**, click **Protect Document**, then click "**Stop Protection**." You'll have to enter the correct password and then click OK in order to remove the password.

Comparing Documents (Redlining)

To compare two different drafts of a document, click the **Review tab**, **Compare group**, **Compare button**, and click **Compare....** A **Compare Documents dialog** opens.

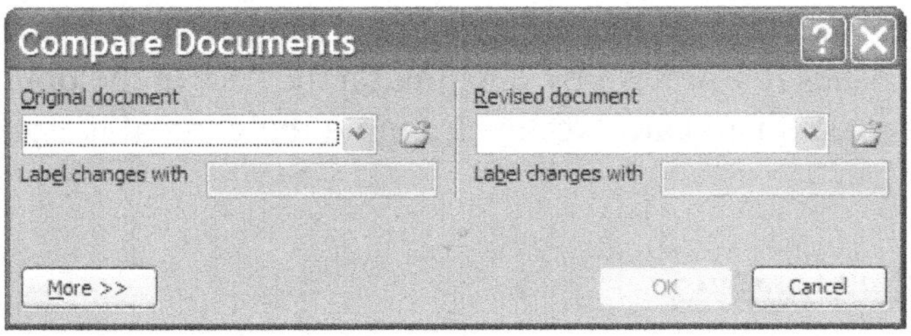

If you have used a previous version of Word, you'll notice that this dialog has been redesigned to make it easier to determine which document you should identify first. On the left side, there is a drop-down plus a browse button for the ***Original document*** (i.e., the older draft—which might or might not be the first draft), and on the right side, there is a drop-down plus a browse button for the ***Revised document*** (i.e., the later draft).

Clicking the "**More**" button displays a number of comparison settings you can adjust. You can choose to have the redlined document display—or not display—moves, comments, changes to formatting, case changes, white space, modifications to tables, headers and footers, footnotes and endnotes, text boxes, and/or fields.

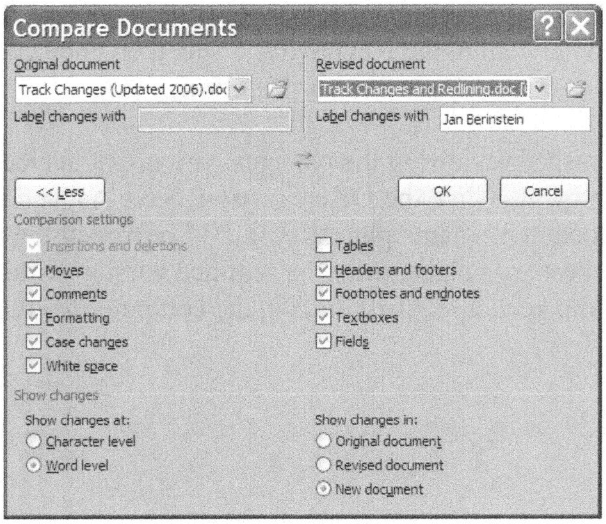

In addition, you can fine-tune the comparison to show changes at the character level (word level is the default). And, if you like, you can have Word show the changes directly in either the earlier (original) draft or the revised draft, although the default setting of "New document" has a compelling advantage: It prevents you from overwriting one of the existing drafts by accident.

Once you have verified that the comparison settings are to your liking, click **OK** to have Word compare the two drafts. The redlined document will appear on screen.

Unlike prior versions of the program, Word 2007 shows the results in a split screen similar to that of some popular third-party document comparison programs. The left "pane" summarizes the changes; the middle pane displays the document with redlining, strikeout, and other markup[1]; and the right side is divided into two panes: one containing the older draft and one containing the revised document.

This profusion of screens can be somewhat overwhelming. Not to worry; you can close any (or all) of the side panes if you wish by clicking on the "X" in the upper right-hand corner.[2] Alternatively, you can make them narrower by dragging the vertical margin(s) to one side of the screen.

Accepting and Rejecting Changes

As noted in the "Tracking Changes" section, after performing a comparison, you can choose to go through the redlined document and selectively accept or reject changes that you or other reviewers have made to the document—or accept or reject all of those changes at once.

To accept or reject changes, you can do any of the following:

1. Click the appropriate choice under **Accept** or **Reject** in the **Changes group** on the **Review tab**; ***or***

2. Right-click within the redlined text, then click **Accept Change** or **Reject Change**; ***or***

3. Right-click an item in the **Reviewing Pane**, then click **Accept Insertion** (or **Deletion**) or **Reject Insertion** (or **Deletion**).

Once you have finished reviewing the changes, you might decide to save the "redlined" version as a separate document. Click the **Office button**, **Save As**, and type a new name for the document (perhaps the document's name plus "Redline 1" or something similar to indicate that it's a redlined draft). You can, of course, print the redlined version without saving it, but attorneys frequently want to keep a redlined draft in the computer for future reference.

---

[1] The appearance and formatting of the markup—including whether or not any of it appears in "balloons" in the margin—depends on your settings under "**Change Tracking Options**" in the **Tracking group** on the **Review tab**.

[2] To re-display the left-hand pane, click **Reviewing Pane** in the **Tracking group**, and click **Reviewing Pane Vertical**. To re-display the right-hand panes, click "**Show Source Documents**" in the **Compare group**, then choose Show Original, Show Revised, or Show Both.

Comparing and Combining Documents (Formerly "Comparing and Merging")

Word actually offers two "comparison" options: (1) **Compare Documents** and (2) **Compare and Combine Documents**. The essential difference between the two is that option (1) typically is used for redlining sequential drafts of a document (ordinarily authored by a single individual) and option (2) typically is used for merging versions of a document worked on separately by different authors or reviewers in a collaborative environment.

The **Compare and Combine** process is very similar to that of comparing drafts of a document. One notable difference has to do with how revision marks inserted into the documents before the comparison (i.e., as a result of a document author using **Tracked Changes**) are treated. When you use the simple **Compare Documents** feature, any markup existing in either the earlier draft or the revised draft ***is blended into the redlined document as if you had clicked "Accept Change."*** Also, Word labels insertions and deletions (etc.) as if all changes were made by one author.

By contrast, when you use **Compare and Combine**, the redlined document shows ***all*** markup, including markup that existed in one (or both) of the documents prior to the comparison. It also attributes changes (insertions, deletions, formatting, moves, comments, etc.) to the specific people who made those changes.

NOTE: Remember that which revision marks are visible in the combined (redlined) document depends in part on settings in the **Display for Review** and **Show Markup** drop-downs in the **Tracking group** of the **Review tab**. If for some reason you are seeing fewer changes than you anticipated, check the settings on both of those drop-downs to make sure that they allow for the display of all markup.

General Troubleshooting Advice

Troubleshooting—Best Practices

Where (and How) to Start

As previously mentioned, when you're troubleshooting, it's always best to start with the simplest and most obvious solution and work your way toward more complex fixes. More often than not, whatever is causing the problem is something fairly straightforward.

Depending on the situation, you might try checking the settings in the **Paragraph dialog box** (and possibly the **Page Setup dialog box**) first. Review both tabs of the Paragraph dialog and both the Margins and Layout tabs of the Page setup dialog. Look for any setting that doesn't seem "normal." Is there a hanging indent where you intended a first-line indent or no indent at all? Does the Spacing After box show 3 points instead of 12? Is "Page Break Before" checked even though the paragraph ought to be on the same page as the previous paragraph? Is the header margin bigger (or smaller) than you meant it to be?

If nothing in those settings appears unusual or unexpected, display the **Non-Printing Characters** (**Ctrl Shift * [asterisk]**) and/or invoke **Reveal Formatting** (**Shift F1**). Again, look for anything out of the ordinary.

Line spacing and "Before" and "After" spacing can cause all kinds of havoc in your documents. Recently a client of mine had an issue with a table in which the text was squished up toward the top of the cells. Logic suggested to me that it might have been because of the text alignment in the cell (Table Tools, Layout, Alignment). I changed the text alignment so that it was centered, as opposed to being at the top of the cell. No difference. I checked the row height (Table Tools, Layout, Cell Size dialog or Table Tools, Layout, Properties, Row tab) to make sure there wasn't a setting that was limiting the height of the cell such that it was too narrow for the text. There wasn't.

Finally, with my cursor in one of the problematic cells, I launched the Paragraph dialog. And voilà! The line spacing was set to 6 points—half the height of a standard single-spaced line. As soon as I changed that to single spacing (or 12 points), the text appeared normal.

Next Stop: Word Options

If you have reviewed both the Paragraph dialog and the Page Setup dialog, displayed the Non-Printing Characters, and checked Reveal Formatting and you're still stumped, take a look at the Word Options (**Office button**, **Word Options**). Unfortunately, these settings can be somewhat difficult to explore, not only because they're significantly more scattered (and require more clicking and scrolling) than in previous versions of Word, but also because there are a number of obscure configuration options in the Advanced category.

Nevertheless, it's possible that some setting buried in the Word Options is the reason your document is misbehaving. Be sure to check the following (if they strike you as possible culprits):

AutoCorrect Options

AutoCorrect Options (under **Proofing)**—especially the **AutoFormat As You Type** tab. The settings for bulleted lists, numbered lists, border lines, and "**Set left- and first-indent with tabs and backspaces**" can cause unexpected behavior. In particular, if the latter option is enabled, pressing the Tab key will produce not a left tab, but a first-line indent (formatting that will carry over to the next paragraph automatically when you press Enter).

Set left- and first-indent with tabs and backspaces

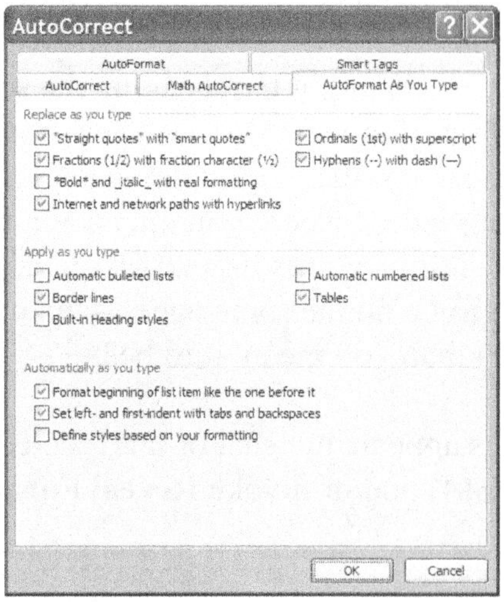

Display Options

There are a couple of Display options that could throw you off your stride. Many people don't realize that if any of the boxes under "**Always show these formatting marks on the screen**" is checked, those mark(s) will display in your document no matter whether you've manually toggled "Show Non-Printing Characters" on or off via the **paragraph symbol** in the **Paragraph group** (or by pressing **Ctrl Shift * [asterisk]**). In other words, the settings in Word Options take precedence over your manual settings.

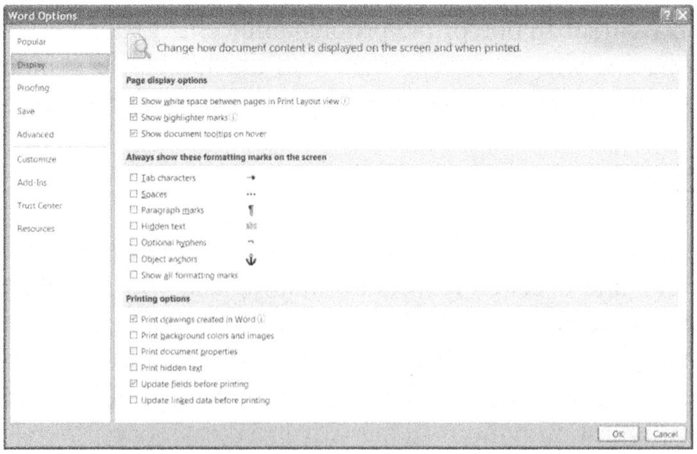

Also, if "**Update fields before printing**" is turned off for some reason, you might find that date codes, page numbering, headings that use SEQ codes, and similar items in your document don't look correct when you print your document because they're not updating.

Advanced Editing and Display Options

Under **Advanced**: Take a look at **Editing options** and, under the general heading of **Compatibility options**, **Layout Options**.

The main Editing option to watch out for is "**Typing replaces selected text**." If Typing replaces selected text is checked, you can delete text accidentally. For example, when you tab to the next column in a table, Word by default selects the text in the table cell to which you tab. If you then press a key (other than one of the arrow keys), Word will delete the selected text and replace it with whichever character is on the key you pressed.

Also under Editing, you'll find an option called "**Keep track of formatting**." This option isn't especially problematic, but it can be confusing. When Keep track of formatting is active, Word displays manually applied formatting (font attributes, paragraph formatting, and bullets and/or numbering) in the Styles Pane along with genuine styles. This option has its benefits: It makes it easy for you to select text with similar formatting and change the formatting all at once, an option that is available on the shortcut menu (under Styles) when you right-click text. Also, when you enable this option you can use the related option to "Mark formatting inconsistencies" (Word uses a blue squiggly line to flag such items), which can be valuable.

However, many people turn this setting off because they find it somewhat distracting. **NOTE**: If you disable this feature and Word still seems to be keeping track of manually applied formatting, open the **Styles Pane** (use the **Styles Pane launcher** or press **Ctrl Alt Shift S**), click "**Options**" in the lower right-hand corner, and when the Style Pane Options dialog opens, navigate to "**Select formatting to show as styles**" and ***uncheck*** all three boxes (Paragraph level formatting, Font formatting, and Bullet and numbering formatting). Then **OK** out of the dialog and close the Styles Pane. (Conversely, if you enable the feature and it doesn't seem to be working, take a look at the Style Pane Options and make sure the three boxes are checked.)

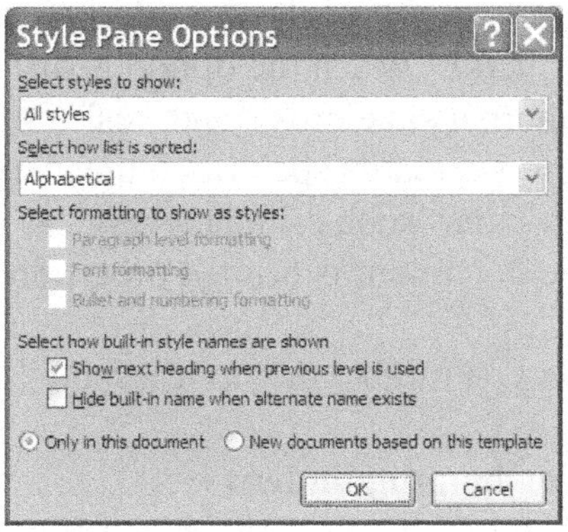

One Editing option you might want to enable—it is disabled by default in Word 2007—is "**Prompt to Update Style**." That option warns you when you reapply a style to text after changing the formatting of the text. It lets you choose between updating the style to reflect the modifications you've made—which may or may not be a good idea—and reapplying the formatting of the style to the selected text. Note that the message box also gives you the option of automatically updating the style when you make manual formatting changes, which ordinarily you ***won't*** want to do because of the havoc that option can wreak with your documents.

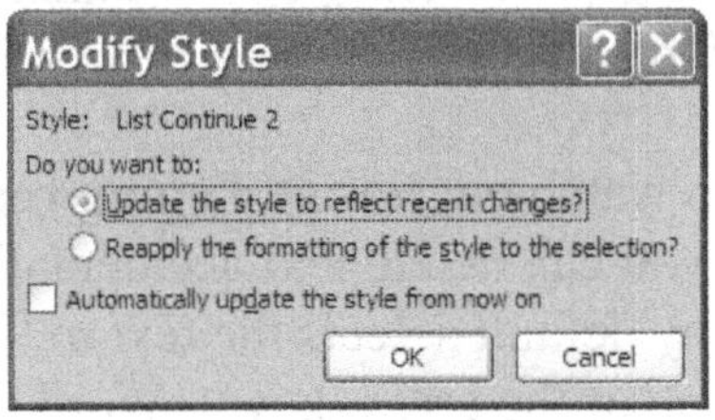

Layout Options

The **Layout Options**, which you'll find all the way at the end of the **Advanced tab**, are among the most complicated and inscrutable settings in Word. You might have to experiment to get these settings to work the way you want. If you get a chance, test some of them with a document that isn't critical (preferably, a copy of a document that contains complex formatting).

First, try changing the general **Compatibility** setting so that the document is laid out for **Word 2003** rather than Word 2007. Make note of what happens in the document, and make note of which specific Layout Options are checked or unchecked. Then change back to Word 2007 layout and observe what happens.

For a brief explanation of each of the layout options—at least, the ones available in Word 2003 (which are fairly similar to those in Word 2007)— see the following Microsoft Knowledge Base article:[1] http://support.microsoft.com/?kbid=288792

Perhaps the most important of these settings is the one labeled "**Use printer metrics to lay out document**." It's preferable to leave this option unchecked / disabled (which is the default) if you plan to print your document on multiple printers that aren't configured identically (for instance, if different people at your firm will be working on the document and sending it to printers that use different print drivers). When the option is disabled, Word lays out the document according to its own internal standards ("metrics"); when the option is enabled, Word lays out the document according to standards specific to the chosen printer and print driver. That means that the document—in particular, such critical aspects as the margins and page breaks—might not look the same when the document is printed on different printers.

Some other layout options you might want to test include the following:

Don't add automatic tab stop for hanging indent

By default, when you apply a hanging-indent format to a paragraph, Word inserts a tab stop at the position of the hanging indent. If the extra tab stop causes problems, you can disable (uncheck) this option.

---

[1] To the best of my knowledge, the article hasn't been updated for Word 2007 as of April, 2009.

Don't add extra space for raised / lowered characters

Worth testing if your text alignment seems off and none of the other potential solutions has helped.

Don't add leading (extra space) between rows of text

Worth testing if your text alignment seems off and none of the other potential solutions has helped.

Don't center "exact line height" lines

See the discussion about aligning text with pleading line numbers, starting on page 161. I have found that enabling this option sometimes resolves issues with text not aligning with the line numbers in pleadings that use "Exactly" line spacing. No guarantees, but it's worth a try.

Don't expand character spaces on a line that ends with SHIFT + RETURN

When you insert a line break (Shift Enter) in a justified paragraph, Word will add white space to stretch the line all the way across to the right margin unless this option is enabled. With the option enabled, the text acts more like left-aligned text (no extra white space in the line).

Split apart page break and paragraph mark

This option is important because when it is ***disabled***, page breaks in a document might behave differently depending on whether you open the document in Word 2007 or a previous version of Word. In previous versions, page breaks and paragraph marks could not occupy the same line. In Word 2007, that is no longer the case, so when you create a page break, it takes up less space than it would in an earlier version (the paragraph mark—representing one single-or double-spaced line, depending on your document—must be accommodated on the same page as the page break).

If you are experiencing problems with the way that page breaks in the same document work in Word 2007 and a previous version of Word (and it isn't because you are using different printers or printer drivers), make sure this setting is ***enabled*** (checked).

See the following Microsoft Knowledge Base Article:
http://support.microsoft.com/kb/923183

(But note that the article erroneously says to ***disable*** the option. The option should be ***enabled***.)

The **Suppress extra line spacing at bottom of page** and **Suppress extra line spacing at top of page** options are similar to what WordPerfect uses to ensure that there is no extraneous white space after (bottom of page) or before (top of page) text if the line spacing is set to a value higher than one. If they are not enabled and you are routinely having to delete extra space, particularly, at the top of a page, you might try testing to see if one or both of the options makes a difference.

File Conversion Issues

Opening Word 2007 Documents With Older Versions of MS Word

As you know, by default, Word 2007 saves documents in a new file format, ".docx," which is a form of Extensible Markup Language or XML. Microsoft chose that format in part to allow Word users to share documents with users of Open Office (another word processing program). Other reputed advantages of the .docx format are that it produces smaller files and supposedly is less prone to corruption than the standard file format used by earlier versions of MS Word (.doc).[1]

Unfortunately, the .docx format is not "backwards compatible" and won't open into any version of Word prior to Word 2007. That means you—and your clients and others with whom you share documents—won't be able to use Word 2003, Word 2002/XP, Word 2000, or Word 97 to open and read documents that were created in Word 2007 ***unless you download and install a special converter***.

The Word 2007 converter (also referred to as a "Compatibility Pack") is available online from Microsoft free of charge. According to Microsoft, you should install all of the latest ***Windows updates*** (i.e., patches for your operating system) prior to installing and using the converter.

For more information and a link to the converter, see the Knowledge Base article, "How to use earlier versions of Excel, PowerPoint, and Word to open and save files from 2007 Office programs," available here:

http://support.microsoft.com/kb/924074

Note that you can configure Word 2007 to save all new documents in the old ".doc" file format. To do so, click the **Office Button**, **Word Options**, **Save**. Under "**Save files in this format**," select **Word 97-2003 Document (.doc)** from the drop-down list and **OK** out. That effectively changes the default file format for all future documents (although you still have the option of saving an individual document in a different file format ***and*** you'll still be able to read .docx files that other people send you).

As mentioned elsewhere in the book, when you use the .doc file format, you will not have access to certain of the new features introduced in Word 2007, including Themes and Theme Fonts. And if you open a native Word 2007 file (.docx) in an earlier version of Word, some features will not work, or will work differently (many items that involve variables or placeholders in Word 2007, such as heading and body fonts and certain charts and diagrams, will become static text or images; text boxes that are positioned "relative to" an object and margins that change depending on which style is applied will take on an "absolute" position; text marked as "moved" in a document comparison will appear as an insertion or a deletion, since older versions did not have the ability to mark text as "moved").

---

[1] Or, at least, it reportedly does better at recovering and fixing corrupted files.

CAUTION: If a Word 2007 file is opened in Word 2000, you won't be able to open password-protected files, ***even if you know the password***. Also, you'll lose macros and macro signatures, as well as mail merge data. See this article for details:

http://office.microsoft.com/en-us/word/HA100444731033.aspx

WordPerfect to Word Conversions

Word 2007 can "read" native WordPerfect files.[1] However, some features of WordPerfect won't translate perfectly into Word. In general, the more complex the formatting of the original document, the less successfully it will convert. Word just doesn't "get" all of WordPerfect's codes. And, of course, macros, QuickWords, and similar automated features won't convert at all.

Opening a WordPerfect File into Word With "File > Open" or "Insert > File"

When converting pleadings, you might find that Word knocks out the pleading paper lines and/or loses one or more of the line numbers. Word typically inserts section breaks where there are changes in page formatting (particularly where the pagination changes, but sometimes also before and after the pleading caption, which many WordPerfect users create with parallel columns rather than with tables). It also might lose a portion of a generated Table of Contents and/or Table of Authorities. However, in my (somewhat limited) tests, Word actually inserted TOA codes for many of the citations and was able to regenerate part of the TOA correctly.

In the past, consultants commonly advised people to use Insert > File (in the case of Word 2007, **Insert tab**, **Text group**, **Object drop-down**, **Text from File**) instead of File > Open to pull a complex WordPerfect document into Word. When I tested opening a WordPerfect pleading into Word 2007, though, I found that File > Open (**Office button**, **Open**) actually produced better results. The document that I inserted by using the equivalent of Insert > File ended up with paragraphs with a **left margin** of .75" and a **first-line indent** of 1.25"; lost most of its **line numbering** (and what remained started about 2/5 down the page and appeared to be triple-spaced); and just generally looked like a big mess.

By contrast, the document that I opened "normally" kept all 28 line numbers (on all pages), properly spaced; used more or less normal paragraph indents, including a first-line tab that was not converted into a First-Line Indent (which you might or might not consider a plus, depending on how you feel about First-Line Indents); and generally had a cleaner appearance.

The **caption** in both documents converted nicely from columns into a table. **Automatic paragraph numbering** in both documents turned into ListNum fields in Word, which unfortunately used the wrong list level (so that Arabic numerals turned into small roman numerals to the left of an end paren). (The easiest way to fix the numbering turned out to be to select contiguous numbered paragraphs, right-click within one of the number codes, click Edit Field, and when the Field dialog appeared with ListNum selected, click "Outline" and make sure Level 3—corresponding to Arabic numerals in an Outline number style—was selected. I had to repeat this step several times to avoid applying numbering to unnumbered paragraphs.)

---

[1] Whether you use the File > Open method or the Insert > File method, you might find that only Word files are visible in the dialog box. In that case, take a look at the "**Files of Type**" field at the bottom of the dialog and, if necessary, use the drop-down to change to "**All Files**."

In both documents, the **pleading footers** came through reasonably well. The one in the Insert, File document looked a bit funky because of the incorrect left margins, but the page numbers came in as codes; the horizontal line was intact; and the font size was acceptable.

The **pleading lines** on the left and the right disappeared in both documents, and both documents inserted continuous section breaks in places where page formatting changed (as well as, mysteriously, in some places where page formatting ***didn't*** change).[2]

One rather noticeable issue affecting the "good" (File > Open) document was that Word applied **mirror margins** to the entire document. Thus, on even pages the line numbers appeared about .5" from the left margin and on odd pages the line numbers appeared in the correct position, about 1.5" from the left margin. I've also observed this issue when pleadings that originated in WordPerfect were opened into prior versions of Word.

In Word 2007, here's how to fix the problem: First, launch the **Page Setup dialog** (from the **Page Layout tab** or by pressing **Alt**, then **P, S, P**). **CAUTION**: Before proceeding, look at the very bottom of the dialog and make sure "**Apply to:**" is set to "**Whole document**." Next, locate the **Pages** section (about half-way down the Margins tab), change the **Multiple pages drop-down** from Mirror margins to **Normal**, and click **OK** to confirm your changes.

In short, although the documents weren't pretty, they came across reasonably well—especially the one I opened with the equivalent of File > Open. Both would require a certain amount of cleanup to make them presentable, but nothing terribly burdensome. With the File > Open document, the most time-consuming elements to fix were the mirror margins (relatively quick and easy) and the automatic numbering (more detective work and methodical tweaking involved).

<u>Saving the WordPerfect File in Word Format, Then Opening into Word</u>

Recent versions of WordPerfect allow you to save documents in "MS Word 97/2000/2002/2003 for Windows" format. You might consider asking people who send you WordPerfect files to save a copy as a Word doc and then, when you receive the .doc files, try opening them directly into Word. In my (limited) tests, a couple of WordPerfect pleadings saved as Word docs came through reasonably well. The caption looked fine, and both docs retained the line spacing and the automatic paragraph numbering. However, there were a few glitches:

- the pleading lines disappeared;
- the footer disappeared;
- paragraphs with automatic numbering didn't have a first-line indent; and
- for some reason, Word applied a different header and footer for odd and even pages.

It was relatively easy to fix those items.

[2] The section breaks didn't cause any problems, although a purist might want to delete them.

To add the pleading lines, I simply went into the header editing screen in a Word pleading—i.e., one that originated in Word—copied the first paragraph symbol in the header editing screen (which contains the formatting codes for the pleading lines), and pasted it into the header editing screen in the WP-to-Word doc. In one doc, I had to paste the paragraph symbol in the header into a second section, as well. (For a discussion about using this technique to reinsert disappearing pleading lines, see page 104.)

The line numbers came in single-spaced in one of the docs; from within the area of the header where the numbers are located, I had to "Select All" with Ctrl A and apply pleading double-spacing (in this case, 22.75 points) via the Paragraph dialog. (In the other doc, the line numbers came through double-spaced, which was the same spacing as that of the text in the pleading.)

In both docs, I also had to go into the Compatibility Options (Office button, Word Options, Advanced) and check "Don't center 'exact line height lines'" in order to move the attorney line down so that it aligned with the first line number. (For more about the ways in which the "Don't Center 'Exact Line Height' Lines" option can be helpful, see page 163.)

I had to manually re-create the footer, which took very little time.

I changed the indentation of the numbered paragraphs by right-clicking and using the Adjust Line Indent option. This procedure required some additional fiddling.

I unchecked the "Different Odd & Even Pages" option in the header editing screen.

Again, it wasn't a perfect conversion and it required some cleanup, but it wasn't overly burdensome or time-consuming. Knowing the trick about copying the paragraph symbol from the header of a good pleading and the trick about "Don't center 'exact line height lines'" helped.

Other Options

Sometimes WordPerfect documents just don't convert well. In those cases, the best solution might be to **copy the text** from the WordPerfect file and insert it into a blank Word document with **Paste Special, Unformatted Text**. Of course, that option transfers the text only, without any formatting. So you will need to go through the document and apply formatting line by line. It's a slow process, but at times you might find it preferable to struggling with the uncooperative codes that can result from a conversion.

Another possibility is to save the WordPerfect file as RTF (Rich Text Format), which is an "intermediate" format invented by Microsoft that both Word and WordPerfect can read, and then to open the file into Word. That didn't work very well with my WordPerfect pleading; when I opened the RTF into Word, the line numbering started with 2; the formatting of the caption and the footer went haywire; and there was an Error! code in the header. On the positive side, the left pleading line came through and the automatic paragraph numbers appeared correctly (as Arabic numerals), with the exception of the fact that both the first and the second paragraph were numbered "1."

But saving a WordPerfect file as RTF and then opening the RTF file into Word might be a good choice in certain circumstances. It's something to keep in mind when you need to convert files. (You might want to make a copy of the document before experimenting, even though you're not likely to overwrite the original file when you save it as an RTF. [3])

Third-Party Conversion Utilities

If you are migrating from WordPerfect to Word and you have a lot of files to convert, you might want to invest in a third-party conversion utility. There are a few available; I have limited first-hand knowledge of any of them, so I would suggest you do your due diligence before making a purchase decision. You might be able to obtain a trial version.

One of the best-known products is Levit & James's "CrossWords"; it has been around for more than a decade.

http://www.levitjames.com/crosswords/CrossWords.html

Another reputable third-party converter is "DocXchange" by Microsystems, available here:

http://www.microsystems.com/products/docxchange.php

---

[3] When you save a file in RTF format, it takes on the file extension .rtf, leaving the original file intact.

Word to WordPerfect Conversions

The first version of WordPerfect that is able to convert native Word 2007 files (i.e., files using the .docx format) directly is WordPerfect X4 (14). If you use WordPerfect X4, you should be able to open .docx files either through File > Open or through Insert > File.

If you have an earlier version, you will have to do one of the following:

1. Save your Word file as a .doc (a Word 97-2003 file);

2. Save your Word document in RTF format (which preserves much of the formatting) or as plain text (.txt) (which will strip out all the formatting), and then open the converted file into WordPerfect; or

3. Copy and paste text from the Word document into WordPerfect, which will wipe out all of the formatting. **CAUTION**: You might get an error message if you try to paste text from Word 2007 into a legacy version of WordPerfect. If so, use the **Paste Special** command (found on the **Edit menu** in WordPerfect) and then paste the text either as **Unformatted Text** or, if it possible, as **Rich Text Format**. I say "if possible" because that option, despite being available in the Paste Special dialog, doesn't work in some older versions of WordPerfect, and you'll get an error message if you attempt to use it.

NOTE: Although you will find several different variations on WordPerfect 5.X listed in the "Save as Type" box, Word 2007—unlike previous versions—actually ***doesn't allow you to save files in WordPerfect format***. If you attempt to do so, Word first warns you that you'll lose functionality because features in Word won't work properly in the WP files; if you click "Yes" to save the file in WP format anyway, Word then prompts you to install a converter. If you click "OK" to install the converter, Word appears to be proceeding with the installation, but the install aborts and Word displays an error message that says, in essence, that the converter can ***read*** WordPerfect 5.X files but in fact can't ***save*** files in that format.[1]

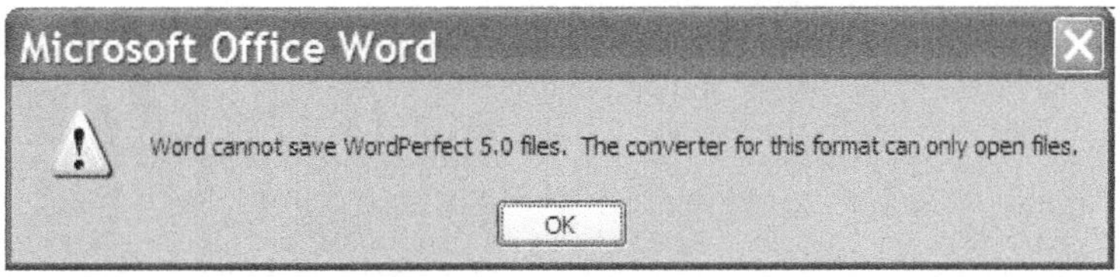

Typically, Word files (.docs) that are opened directly into WordPerfect bring a lot of extraneous codes with them, including First Ln Ind (First Line Indent) codes and Lft Mar Adj (Left Margin Adjustment) codes. If the profusion of codes is problematic, you can clean up the document with WordPerfect's Find and Replace feature, using either Match Codes… or Type >

[1] Or you might get the "cannot save" message without the intermediate message about installing a converter. Whether you get the message about installing the converter appears to depend, at least in part, on which of the WordPerfect 5.X formats you try to use.

Specific Codes…, and replace each instance of a particular code with <Nothing> (the "Replace All" option makes relatively short work of this process). Note that you might have to run through the document more than once.

As with WordPerfect-to-Word conversions, the translation often leaves something to be desired. Still, in some situations it might be preferable to the tedious alternative of copying and pasting unformatted text and then reapplying formatting to the document line by line.

Avoid Round-Tripping Your Documents

One of the most important bits of advice consultants commonly offer to people who work in both Word and WordPerfect is not to "round-trip" documents between the two formats. In other words, avoid bringing a WordPerfect file into Word, saving it as a Word doc, and then pulling it back into WordPerfect. Doing so is a well-known—and a leading—cause of file corruption. A one-way conversion isn't particularly risky, but going back and forth is just asking for trouble.

Converting Word 2007 Files to PDF

Microsoft has made available for downloading a nifty little add-in utility you can use to save Word 2007 files in Portable Document Format (PDF).[1] You can find that utility here: http://www.microsoft.com/downloads/details.aspx?FamilyId=4D951911-3E7E-4AE6-B059-A2E79ED87041&displaylang=en

It's a quick and easy download—assuming you have a reasonably fast Internet connection. Once you've downloaded the executable, double-click to install it. Afterwards, you will see a new item, "**PDF or XPS**," in the **Save As** portion of the **Office button** drop-down. (XPS, or XML Paper Specification, is another electronic file format. At this time, it is not widely used; most users are "techies." Note that you need a special "reader" to view XPS files.)

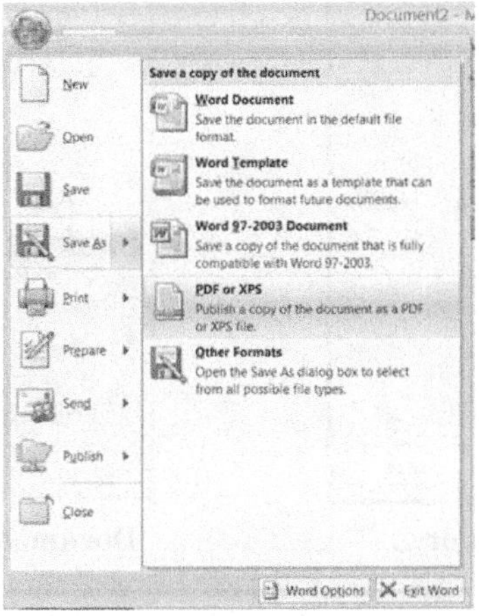

When you click that option, a **Publish as PDF or XPS dialog** will open. At this point, type a new file name if you like, select the "Save as" type, and choose among various other options displayed in the dialog. **NOTE**: It's a good idea to click the **Options button**, particularly if you plan to distribute the PDF file to others and you want to minimize the amount of metadata embedded in the file.

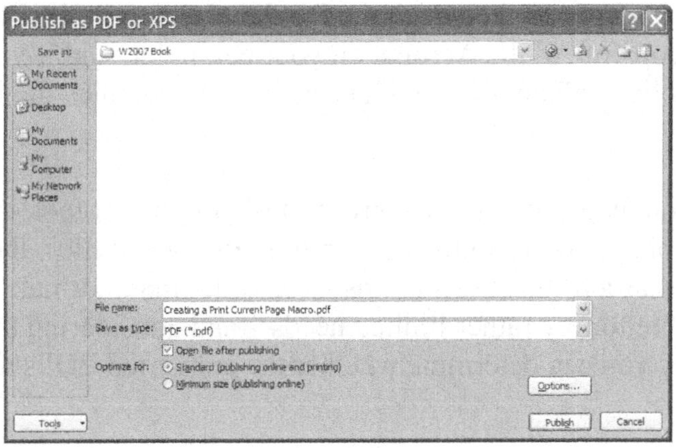

Options button

Publish button

---

[1] As we go to press, Microsoft is set to release Service Pack 2 for Word 2007, which incorporates the Publish to PDF utility. Future releases of the program will include the PDF feature.

The Options Dialog

Clicking the **Options button** opens an **Options dialog** with several additional options. Note especially the **Document properties** checkbox. If you want to exclude the document properties from the final PDF document, click to ***uncheck*** that box. Also, if the document contains markup, the "**Document showing markup**" radio button, which normally is grayed out, will be active. Unless you click the "**Document**" radio button instead, the PDF will display the markup in the document.

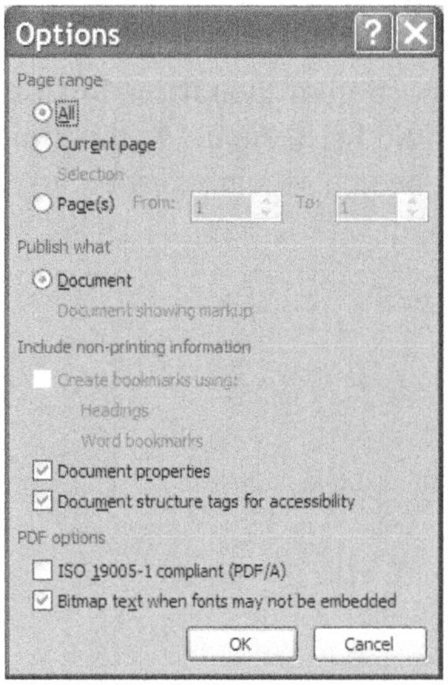

Publish Document or...

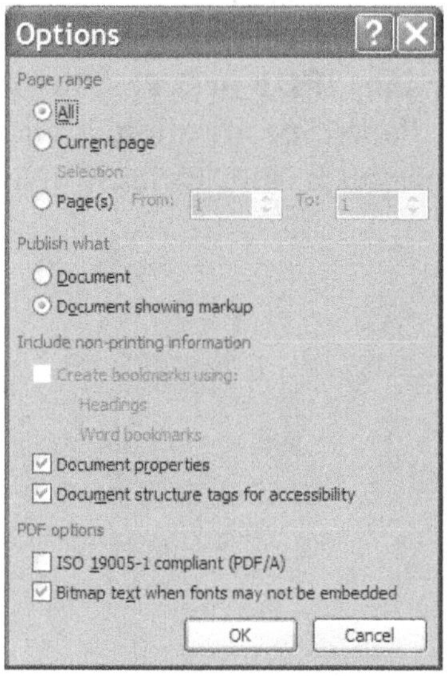

Document showing markup

You can convert the entire document, the page the cursor is on (Current page), or a range of pages. Also, if you so choose, you can create bookmarks in the PDF file using headings and/or Word bookmarks (this option, which you'll find toward the middle of the dialog box, is disabled by default.)

Once you have everything set up the way you want, click OK to confirm your choices and close the **Options dialog**, and then click the **Publish button** in the **Publish as PDF or XPS dialog**. If you have a copy of Adobe Acrobat on your computer, and if you have not unchecked the "Open file after publishing" option (which is enabled by default), the PDF version of the file will open in Acrobat.

It's important to recognize that the converted file might not look exactly the way it would if you used Adobe Acrobat to perform the conversion. In my test files, the fonts appeared to be condensed and (perhaps as a result) the margins were wider than normal. However, the results were perfectly acceptable for my rather limited needs—and considering that the converter is available for free. Only you can determine whether the converted PDFs adequately suit your purposes.

Printing to a PDF Printer

As an alternative to saving the file as a PDF as outlined above, you can simply print the document to a PDF printer. Just click the **Office button**, **Print** or press **Ctrl P**, choose the **Adobe PDF** printer from the **Printer Name drop-down**, and click **OK**.

CAUTION: If you use the print-to-PDF option instead of the Save As option, ***be sure to change back to your normal printer before attempting to print another document***.

Coping With Metadata

How Metadata Gets Embedded in Your Documents and What You Can Do to Get Rid of It

Metadata: Definition and Origins

Metadata refers in part to information embedded automatically in a document by software,[1] as well as document properties and other information that can be inserted deliberately by a human author.

This information, much or all of which is "hidden" under normal circumstances—such that the person writing the document might not realize it exists—can include the identity of the author(s) and any reviewer(s), the company where the document author works, the software used to create the document, the computer and the exact path where the document is stored, the date and time the document was created and/or modified, the title of the document and any keywords or summary used to identify it, the amount of time spent on editing the document, the template on which it was based, and so on. If a document was routed by e-mail to other people in your firm, detailed routing information could be hidden in the document.

In addition, and of greater concern to many lawyers, revisions—insertions, deletions, and comments—can be stored in a document. Even if you are not seeing such "markup" on your screen, it may be possible for others to change configuration settings so that they can view that markup unless you take definite steps to remove material that has been superseded by later edits.

According to Microsoft:

> "...hidden text, revised text, comments, or field codes can remain in a document even though you don't see such information or expect it to be in the final version. If you entered personal information, such as your name or e-mail address, when you registered your software, some Microsoft Office documents store that information as part of the document. Information contained in custom fields that you add to the document, such as an 'author' or 'owner' field, is not automatically removed. You must edit or remove the custom field to remove that information."

From "Remove personal or hidden information,"
http://office.microsoft.com/en-us/word/HP051901021033.aspx

Word 2007's Native Metadata Removal Tool: The Document Inspector

Word 2007 comes with a metadata removal tool called the Document Inspector. When you use this tool, it combs through the document, looking for comments, revisions, annotation, document properties, personal and company information, data in headers and footers (as well as watermarks), and hidden text. You can have the Inspector remove any or all of the items it finds.

---

[1] Some of this information is added/tracked by the operating system, as well as by the particular application used to create the document.

Before running the Document Inspector, ***make a copy of your document***. It's a good idea to create a backup (and possibly even search for and strip metadata from the copy) because once certain items are eliminated from the document, it can be difficult if not impossible to restore them without going through the laborious process of re-creating them manually. In other words, some metadata removal can't be "undone." That can be problematic, especially because:

(1) you can't see exactly which information the Document Inspector has identified before choosing to remove it;

(2) you don't have an opportunity to pick and choose which items in any given category to remove (it's an all-or-nothing proposition); and

(3) in an attempt to be meticulous, Word sometimes gets rid of innocuous information, such as entire headers and footers.

So try to get in the habit of copying your document prior to using the Document Inspector.

When you are ready to test the feature, click the **Office button**, **Prepare**, **Inspect Document**. You will see a dialog similar to the one below. It consists of checkboxes for various types of document content the Document Inspector can examine for metadata: Comments, Revisions, Versions, and Annotations; Document Properties and Personal Information; Custom XML Data; Headers, Footers and Watermarks; and Hidden Text.[2]

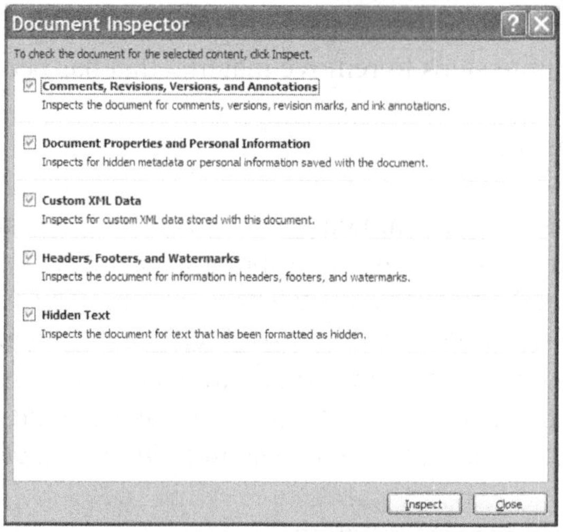

All of the boxes are checked by default, but you can uncheck any types of content that you don't want the Inspector to review.

After you click "Inspect," the Inspector will go through the document, searching for various types of metadata. If it finds any, it will alert you with an exclamation point next to the type of content it located. See, for example, the next screenshot.

---

[2] "Hidden Text" means text to which the "Hidden" property has been applied through the Font dialog. Note that the Document Inspector will ***not*** identify and remove text to which the color white has been applied (to make it invisible on a white background) or text that has been sized so small that it is not visible at normal screen magnifications.

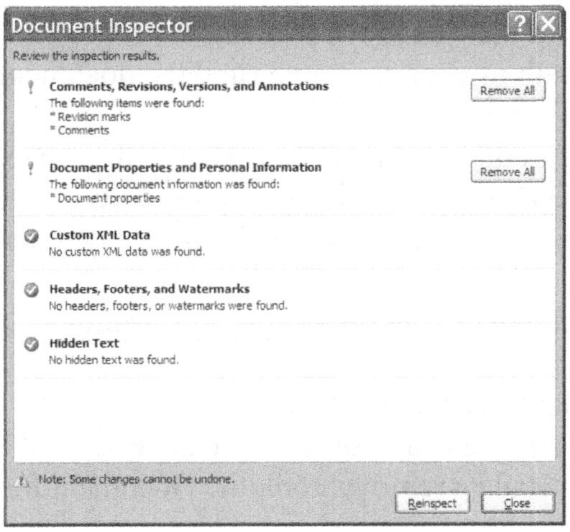

As mentioned above, the mere fact that the Document Inspector has found some "metadata" doesn't necessarily clue you in to what, exactly, that information includes. (In the screenshot, we see that Word found Revision marks, Comments, and Document properties, but we don't know the specifics.) If you click the "Remove All" button next to a category of data, the Inspector will remove everything in that category.

Note that you can click the "Reinspect" button to have the Inspector go through the document again.

After you click "Remove All," the Inspector does its thing and then shows you the results, which might look something like this:

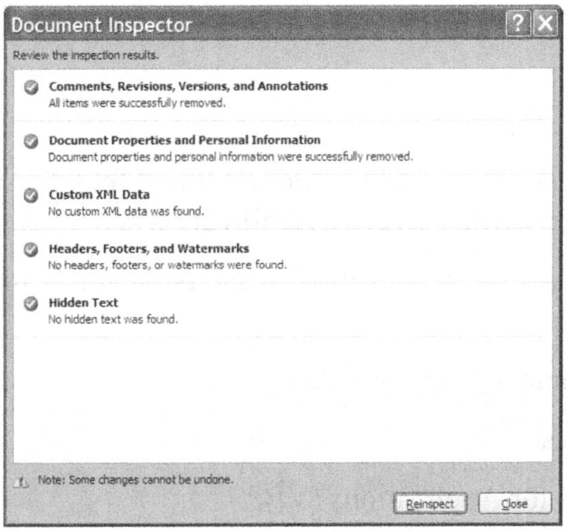

As you can see, the results appear to indicate that the items in question "were successfully removed" from the document.

Note that if you look at the Advanced Document Properties, you can still see the document location (i.e., its path in your computer) and the document type.[3]

CAUTION: If you run the Document Inspector and are happy with the results, be sure to SAVE the inspected document. This is a critical step because if you close it without saving, the metadata you thought had been removed will remain in the document!

Some Items That the Document Inspector Might Not Remove

Besides the above-mentioned items, there are other types of information or objects that can be embedded in your documents and potentially can be viewed by others. These additional items, which Word 2007's metadata removal tool, the Document Inspector, might not flag or remove, include:

- Bookmarks
- Creation date
- Document variables
- Field codes
- Hyperlinks
- Linked objects
- Modified date
- OLE graphics
- Print date
- Smart Tags
- Text that is hidden by applying a very small font size (so that it is invisible, or nearly so, at a normal screen magnification)
- Text that is hidden by coloring it white (so that it is invisible on a white background)
- Unlink document property fields
- Unused styles
- Visual Basic for Applications (VBA)

Some of these items might not be problematic, but it's worth investigating further before deciding whether to rely exclusively on the Document Inspector or to invest in a third-party program.

---

[3] In one of my tests, the Document Inspector removed information from Advanced Properties, Statistics, indicating that I had printed a draft of the doc; stripped out my name under "Last saved by"; changed the revision number from 5 to 1, and changed the total editing time to 0 (zero).

Third-Party Metadata Removal Programs

Because the Document Inspector doesn't eliminate all types of metadata from Word documents, you might want to consider purchasing a third-party metadata removal program and using it in conjunction with (or instead of) Word's built-in utility. There are several such programs available. I don't have enough personal experience with any of them to enable me to make a recommendation, but you can request evaluation copies (usually good for 30 days). That might be a good way to compare the various utilities.

Do ask about any possible incompatibilities with other software you have and make sure you can uninstall the trial versions easily. Also, you might want to install the trial versions on different computers, just in case they are incompatible with one another (and also to make it easier to differentiate among them).

There are a few articles on the web that discuss metadata in MS Office and the third-party metadata management utilities. See, for example:

H. Craig Hall, Jr., "Dealing with Metadata in the Non-Discovery Context"
(Utah State Bar Journal, March 31, 2008)
http://webster.utahbar.org/barjournal/2008/03/dealing_with_metadata_in_the_n.html

"The Meta Monster: Hidden data in e-documents trips up GCs"
(Inside Counsel, July 2006)
http://www.insidecounsel.com/Issues/2006/July%202006/Pages/The-Meta-Monster.aspx?page=3

Links to Metadata Removal Product Web Sites

I've listed a few of the better-known programs below—in ***alphabetical*** order. Most of them remove metadata in Microsoft Office documents and other types of files (including PDF), but you should double-check. **NOTE**: This list is not, and should not be construed as, an endorsement of any of the products.

iScrub (by Esquire Innovations)
www.esqinc.com

If you go to this page of the site, you can request an online demo or a 30-day evaluation copy: http://esqinc.com/section/howtobuy.html

MetaDact (by Softwise)
www.softwise.net

Previously called Out-of-Sight. You can request a 30-day evaluation copy.

Metadata Assistant (by Payne Consulting):
www.payneconsulting.com

Offers both a "retail" version and an "enterprise" version.

MetaReveal (by BEC Legal)
www.beclegal.com/products.aspx?id=64

Like the other companies, BEC Legal allows you to test-drive its product for 30 days and/or request a demo.

Workshare Protect (by Workshare Technology):
www.workshare.com

You can download a 30-day trial version from Workshare's site and/or request a demonstration.

Resources

Where Important Word 2007 Files Are Stored

It can be helpful to know where key files—such as the NORMAL template and the template where Building Blocks / QuickParts (formerly called AutoText)—are stored in the computer. Because some of these files contain your customizations, you might want to create backup copies from time to time (and perhaps save them to a CD, a USB drive, an external hard drive, or a different computer). That way, if something happens to your computer and one of the files is damaged or is inaccessible, you don't have to re-create all of your customizations from scratch.

What follows is a list of some of the most important files and their typical locations.

NORMAL Template (Normal.dotm)

The NORMAL template (normal.dotm) is the basis for all new documents in Word. Each user has one. Many customizations are stored in the user's NORMAL template, including his or her default Normal Paragraph style, other styles he or she has created or modified, AutoCorrect entries, and macros (but ***not*** the user's personalized Quick Access Toolbar or Quick Parts / Building Blocks, which are located in separate files).

Ordinarily you will find the NORMAL template in the following locations:

In Windows XP:
C:\Documents and Settings\<User Name>\Application Data\Microsoft\Templates

In Windows Vista and Windows 7:
C:\Users\<UserName>\AppData\Roaming\Microsoft\Templates

Custom Templates

Each user's customized templates typically are stored in the same place as the NORMAL template:

In Windows XP:
C:\Documents and Settings\<User Name>\Application Data\Microsoft\Templates

In Windows Vista and Windows 7:
C:\Users\<UserName>\AppData\Roaming\Microsoft\Templates

Building Blocks

The building blocks template is called **BuildingBlocks.dotx**. Word 2007 comes with two instances of the Building Blocks.dotx template. One is an original that should never be edited directly; the other is a working copy that contains your own custom Quick Parts / Building Blocks.

The original (generic) template is located here in Windows XP, Vista, and Windows 7:
C:\Program Files\Microsoft Office\Office12\Document Parts\1033

The user-specific copy is located here in Windows XP:
C:\Documents and Settings\<User Name>\Application Data\Microsoft\Document Building Blocks\1033

The user copy is located here in Windows Vista and Windows 7:
C:\Users\<UserName>\AppData\Roaming\Microsoft\Document Building Blocks\1033

If something happens and the user-customized file becomes corrupted, Word creates a new customizable file based on the original template. (You likely will lose your Quick Parts if that happens, which is why it makes sense to make a copy of the customized file every so often.)

List styles gallery

The **ListGal.dat** file contains the user's customized gallery of numbered lists (i.e., it includes the lists that came with the program as well as any list styles you've created).

In Windows XP:
C:Documents and Settings\<User Name>\Application Data\Microsoft \Word

In Windows Vista and Windows 7:
C:\Users\User Name\AppData\Roaming\Microsoft\Word

Heading styles

Heading styles ordinarily are stored either in the NORMAL template (**normal.dotm**) or in the ***document*** in which they were created, although you can copy styles to (or create them in) your own custom templates. In fact, most built-in styles typically are saved in normal.dotm.

Note that whenever you create a new style or modify a built-in style, the default setting in the Modify Style dialog is to store the style ***in the current document***. (WordPerfect works the same way). The only other choice available in the dialog box is to save to the NORMAL template, but you can use the Organizer to copy styles to other templates. (And you can copy styles between documents; see page 118 above.)

Quick Styles / Style Sets

Quick Styles and Style Sets are located in the following places:

In Windows XP:

The built-in QuickStyles and Style Sets are found here:
C:\Program Files\Microsoft Office\Office12\1033\QuickStyles

User-customized QuickStyles and Style Sets are located here:
C:Documents and Settings\<User Name>\Application Data\Microsoft\QuickStyles

In Windows Vista and Windows 7:
C:\ Users\<User Name>\AppData\Roaming\Microsoft\Quickstyles

Themes

Theme files have the extension **.thmx**.

Built-in themes are located here in Windows XP, Windows Vista, and Windows 7:
C:\Program Files\Microsoft Office\Document Themes 12

Custom themes (i.e., themes that you create) are located here in Windows XP:
C:\Documents and Settings\<User Name>\Application Data\Microsoft\Templates\Document Themes

Custom themes are located here in Windows Vista and Windows 7:
C:\Users\<User Name>\AppData\Roaming\Microsoft\Templates\Document Themes

AutoRecover files

Files that Word automatically recovers in the event of a "crash" or other serious problem have the extension .asd. Normally you don't have to look for them because Word opens them in a separate pane at the left side of the screen after a power outage or similar event. They can be found here:

In Windows XP:
C:\Documents and Settings\<User Name>\Application Data\Microsoft\Word

In Windows Vista and Windows 7:
C:\Users\<User Name>\AppData\Roaming\Microsoft\Word

QAT (Quick Access Toolbar)

The QAT file, called Word.qat, is stored in the following locations:

In Windows XP:
C:\Documents and Settings\<User Name>\Local Settings\Application Data\Microsoft\OFFICE\Word.qat

In Windows Vista and Windows 7:
C:\Users\<UserName>\AppData\Local\Microsoft\Office\Word.qat

Note that you can create a customized QAT for a particular document.[1] The settings for a document-specific QAT are stored in that document.

[1] When you customize the QAT, you'll see a drop-down on the upper right-hand side of the screen. By default it is set to save your customizations globally—i.e., to the Word.qat file (***not*** to the NORMAL template, despite the wording of the drop-down). If you like, can click the drop-down and change it to save settings in the current document.

Selected MS Word Resources on the Internet

The following are a few selected Word 2007 (or general MS Word) resources that you might find helpful. Please let me know if any of the links don't work or turn out to be obsolete.

Microsoft's Knowledge Base (MS Word, Excel, Access, Windows XP, etc.):
http://support.microsoft.com/support/search

On-line technical support for all Microsoft products. You can run searches (queries) using natural language or key words. (Note, for example, that searching for the word "pleading" returns several articles dealing with problems related to pleading paper.)

Microsoft's Word 2007 Training Courses
http://office.microsoft.com/en-us/training/CR100654561033.aspx

On-line tutorials categorized by topic. They include self-guided lessons, plus practice and easy "tests," on bulleted and numbered lists; header and footer basics; headers and footers for document sections; table of contents; and more. Microsoft estimates the length of the lessons at between 25 and 50 minutes.

Microsoft Interactive Word 2003 to Word 2007 Command Reference Guide
http://office.microsoft.com/en-us/word/HA100744321033.aspx

This tutorial is interactive in that you can point to a Word 2003 menu command to find out where the same command is in Word 2007. Clicking the command launches an animation that shows you the location of the command in the newer version.

List of Keyboard Shortcuts for Word 2002, 2003, and 2007
http://support.microsoft.com/kb/290938

These shortcuts work with the U.S. keyboard layout, but not necessarily with keyboard layouts for other countries/languages.

Word Viewer
http://www.microsoft.com/downloads/details.aspx?FamilyID=3657ce88-7cfa-457a-9aec-f4f827f20cac&displaylang=en

Downloadable Word Viewer available from Microsoft allows people who don't have Word to view Word files (including .docx format).

Microsoft Word MVP FAQ Site
http://word.mvps.org/FAQs/index.htm

Very helpful site. Lots of tips and workarounds, as well as explanations of how Word works. (Note that if you type "html" instead of "htm," you'll get a "404 Not Found" error.) The site was redesigned a couple of years ago and isn't as user-friendly as it once was, unfortunately, but it's still an excellent source of information.

Links to Web Sites of Various Word "MVPs":
http://www.mvps.org/links.html

Scroll down almost to the bottom for links to web sites run by Word gurus.

Word FAQs site (by Suzanne Barnhill, Word MVP):
http://sbarnhill.mvps.org/WordFAQs/

Barnhill is one of the best MVPs (and that's saying a lot). Her explanations tend to be unusually clear and readable.

Making the Most of Word (by Shauna Kelly, Word MVP):
http://www.shaunakelly.com/word/index.html

Lots of terrific tips here. Kelly's instructions for using automatic numbering are especially useful, though she hasn't updated them yet for Word 2007.

Windows Secrets (formerly Woody's Office Portal):
http://lounge.windowssecrets.com/ or www.wopr.com

Unofficial site started by Microsoft guru/gadfly Woody Leonhard. Offers hints & tips, downloads, bug alerts, a bulletin board, shareware/freeware, and links. The Word Processing section of the Lounge is a great place for posting questions about MS Word.

Woody's Office Watch:
http://office-watch.com

Another of Woody Leonhard's MS Office sites.

An Expert's Guide to Word 2007 Numbering
http://www.beclegal.com/hot_topics.aspx?id=2994

A white paper available as a downloadable PDF. From BEC Legal Systems (www.beclegal.com). Extremely thorough explanation of how multilevel lists work in Word 2007—and how to avoid possible glitches.

CompuSavvy's Word & WordPerfect Tips (blog)
http://compusavvy.wordpress.com

My new-ish blog. I try to add new posts at least once a week, sometimes in response to search terms people have used to try to find answers to their Word or WordPerfect questions. I also make an effort to write new material most of the time, rather than cribbing from existing handouts. Many of the posts go into considerable detail.

How to Import WordPerfect [for DOS] Files into Microsoft Word:
http://www.columbia.edu/~em36/wpdos/wptoword.html#2003word

From Edward Mendelson's wonderful web site about WordPerfect ***for DOS***. This particular page provides instructions for converting WordPerfect for DOS files to Word.

HotDocs Knowledge Base:
http://help.lexisnexis.com/tabula-rasa/hdknowledgebase/ home?lbu=US&locale =en_US&audience=all

For help with issues having to do with the interaction between Word and document assembly program HotDocs.

INDEX

DISCOUNT COUPON

This coupon entitles the bearer

to a ***$50.00 discount***

on an on-site software training session
lasting six (6) hours or more*‡

* May not be used in combination with any other discounts

‡ One coupon per organization (or individual trainee)

Made in the USA
Monee, IL
05 November 2026

67807089R00149